What Readers Are Saying About
The RSpec Book: Behaviour-Driven Development with RSpec, Cucumber, and Friends

The RSpec Book is a fantastic introduction to all things BDD. It goes much deeper than just testing to provide you with the right tools you need to fully embrace the ideas that the framework has baked in.

▶ **Aaron Bedra, principal, Relevance Inc.**

This book covers the territory of writing great software, and the authors are your experienced guides. If you follow the map that they have drawn, you'll learn to write only the code that you need, and you'll write it simply and clearly. You'll come home from this journey with some experiences that will have immediate and lasting effects on the code in your editor and the code yet to flow from your fingertips.

▶ **Craig Demyanovich, 8th Light, Inc.**

The RSpec Book teaches you much more than how to use RSpec's features; it teaches you how to write code the way the RSpec team does: patiently, and with great precision and clarity. There is something here for everyone: beginners are given plenty of gentle attention but there is some real meat for the more experienced reader to chew on, too.

▶ **Matt Wynne, independent programmer and coach**

The second generation of tools for the XP generation explained by their creators and maintainers. Awesome, a must read.

▶ **Marcus Ahvne, software developer, Valtech**

Some authors would be satisfied with just writing the definitive guide for a technology. These folks go a step further, and show you insider tips that will keep your tests clean and maintainable.

▶ **Ian Dees, Software Engineer**

The RSpec Book

Behaviour-Driven Development
with RSpec, Cucumber, and Friends

The RSpec Book

Behaviour-Driven Development
with RSpec, Cucumber, and Friends

David Chelimsky

with Dave Astels
Zach Dennis
Aslak Hellesøy
Bryan Helmkamp
Dan North

The Pragmatic Bookshelf
Raleigh, North Carolina   Dallas, Texas

Our Pragmatic courses, workshops, and other products can help you and your team create better software and have more fun. For more information, as well as the latest Pragmatic titles, please visit us at http://www.pragprog.com.

The team that produced this book includes:

Editor:	Jacquelyn Carter
Indexing:	Potomac Indexing, LLC
Copy edit:	Kim Wimpsett
Layout:	Steve Peter
Production:	Janet Furlow
Customer support:	Ellie Callahan
International:	Juliet Benda

Printed in the United States of America.

ISBN-10: 1-934356-37-9
ISBN-13: 978-1-934356-37-1
Printed on acid-free paper.
P1.0 printing, December 2010
Version: 2010-11-11

Contents

Foreword

Caution! You've fallen for a trap. You've picked up this book thinking it was about RSpec. Fortunately, you decided to read the foreword. Good! That gives me the opportunity to tell you about the mistake you just made and possibly save you from an unexpected fate.

You see, this book isn't about RSpec at all. Oh, RSpec is certainly mentioned. There are lots of examples of how to use it. There's even a very detailed reference manual in Part III. But that's all just part of an insidiously clever deception, because this book is not about RSpec.

Perhaps you thought you might read about Cucumber? After all, Part IV is named "Cucumber." Oh, these authors are clever; God they are! They've littered this book with examples and details that tell you all about Cucumber in all its intricacies and all its copious fiddledy-bits. There's even a section on using it with Rails and Webrat and all the other gory things that you'll need to become a Cucumber expert. But this book is *not* about Cucumber.

No. This book is not about RSpec. And this book is not about Cucumber. This book is about. . .

I'm not sure I should tell you. I mean, once the secret gets out, it's liable to cause mayhem. If it ever got out who the audience for this book *really* is, if the masses learned of the diabolical plan being executed in their midst, I'm not sure our civilization would survive.

You see. . . (come closer, and cover this part with your hand so nobody else can see it). . . you see, this book is not for. . . (covered?). . . it's not for *Ruby programmers*!

There, I've said it! Now don't panic, and don't drop the book—*whatever you do, don't drop the book*! Hold on tight, and keep it covered. Don't let anyone else see.

Yes, you see, this book is not about RSpec. It's not about Cucumber, It's not for Ruby programmers. This book is for. . . (covered again?). . . it's for *all programmers*!

Keep a good tight grip. I know it's hard. Don't look around suspiciously. Don't draw attention to yourself. Just try to stay calm, breathe normally, and keep reading.

Yes, all the code is in Ruby. Yes, all the examples use RSpec and Cucumber to one degree or another. Yes, if you read this book, you *will* learn RSpec, Cucumber, and things about Ruby and Rails and Webrat that you didn't know before. No doubt about it. Remember, the best lies are near-truths.

Here's the thing. While you read this book, you will *think* you are learning about all those cool tools. You will think "Oh, cool, I'm learning RSpec and Cucumber." But you will be learning something else at the same time! Something unexpected. Something unadvertised. Something, perhaps, unwelcome.

As you read these pages, a hidden meme will creep into your mind—a meme of such potency and power that it is likely to change *everything* about the way you program. And not just how you program in Ruby!

If you read this book, that meme will change the way you program in Java, C#, Python, or (oh, God, the thought) COBOL! This book will change the way you code—period!

Worse, you don't have to be a Ruby programmer to be infected by this meme. As I said, these authors are clever. Their unholy plan is to infect *all* programmers with this meme. You see, they've cleverly constructed the Ruby code in this book so that it can be understood by (gasp) *any programmer at all*! I mean, this is worse than Fluoridation!

Any programmer who picks up this book will be infected by the meme. And the meme is subtle. And the meme is persistent. And the meme will have its way. And when it does, our industry will never be the same again. Are you willing to risk that?

What is this meme? What name shall we give it? The meme is *legion*! It's not just Agile, though Agile is there. It's not just TDD and BDD, though both are there. It's not just Continuous Integration, Acceptance Test–Driven Development, Acceptance Test–Driven Planning, or even Extreme Programming, though all those things are present in the meme.

No, the meme is more than any one of those things. The meme is a synergistic witches brew of some of the most contagious and effective ideas of the past two decades. The meme is. . .

Dare I say it?

The meme is. . .

. . . Craftsmanship.

—*Robert C. Martin*

About the Authors

David Chelimsky is the lead developer/maintainer of RSpec, and has contributed to several other open source projects including Cucumber, Aruba, and Rails. He has been developing software for over a decade, including three years training and mentoring agile teams at Object Mentor. He is currently a Senior Software Engineer at DRW Trading Group in Chicago, IL. In his spare time, David likes to play guitar, travel, and speak something resembling Portuguese.

Dave Astels is the Director of Technology at ChannelFireball.com and has been involved with software and computing for over 25 years, recently having spent several years working exclusively with Ruby and Rails. Dave wrote the article that prompted Steven Baker to start the RSpec project.

Zach Dennis is a co-founder and fellow human at Mutually Human Software, an expert custom software strategy and design consultancy in Grand Rapids, Michigan. He has been enjoying Ruby for nearly eight years and has contributed to several projects such as Ruby's standard library documentation, Ruby on Rails, and RSpec. In his spare time, Zach loves spending time with his family, continuously learning, playing music, and running continuousthinking.com.

Aslak Hellesøy is a Senior Software Engineer at DRW Trading Group in London. While contributing to this book he was the Chief Scientist of BEKK Consulting in Oslo. In 2003, after seven years of professional Java programming, he fell in love with Ruby. He has contributed to dozens of open source projects and is the founder of the Cucumber project. Aslak likes to cook, ski, and travel.

Bryan Helmkamp maintains Webrat, a Ruby library to implement acceptance tests for web applications in an expressive and maintainable way, and is an active participant in the New York City Ruby community. Bryan is the CTO of Efficiency 2.0, a startup that helps people understand and reduce their energy use.

Dan North writes software and coaches teams and organizations in agile and lean methods. He believes that most problems that teams face are about communication and understanding, which is why he puts so much emphasis on "getting the words right." In 2003–4 this led him to develop the ideas that would become Behaviour-Driven Development. He is delighted by the community that has grown up around RSpec and Cucumber, and especially the enthusiasm and dedication of their core contributors. Dan is currently a Senior Software Engineer at DRW Trading Group in London, where he gets to actually code again!

Acknowledgments

This book is the product of a lengthy journey that started back in 2006 when Dave Astels' proposal was accepted by the Pragmatic Bookshelf. Dave, Aslak, and I (David) were working hard to push RSpec along, so Dave invited us to join him in writing the book.

It turns out that software maintainers writing about the software they maintain presents some interesting challenges. There were many times when we'd be writing about a particular aspect of RSpec and realize that there was a better way. Next thing you know, we're cracking open RSpec to make improvements and returning to the book to update all the newly obsolesced references. Add to that assorted personal and professional trials that have pulled us all in different directions, and it's a miracle that you're even reading this.

Big thanks to Dave, Aslak, Dan, Bryan, Zach, and Brian for the content they each contributed. The breadth of experience and knowledge each brought to the book are invaluable.

Thanks, also, to Dan for BDD, and to Dave for introducing me to BDD and the RSpec project.

Thanks to Steven Baker for creating RSpec.

Thanks to our technical reviewers: Marcus Ahvne, Aaron Bedra, Ian Dees, Craig Demyanovich, Corey Haines, Stuart Halloway, Sean Kellogg, Ben Mabey, Frederick Ros, Brett Schuchert, Dean Wampler, and Matt Wynne.

Thanks to all the beta readers who made suggestions and did a great job of pointing out inconsistencies in the code examples.

Thanks to Uncle Bob Martin for his inspired and inspiring foreword and for taking me under his wing at Object Mentor. It was Bob who first introduced me to FitNesse and the idea of customer-readable acceptance tests. And it was that experience that ignited my interest in RSpec and Dan's RBehave (Cucumber's predecessor).

Thanks to Jacquelyn Carter, our editor, for your endless patience. It was a long road, Jackie, but we actually made it.

Thanks to my longtime friend and colleague, Randy Stearns, for the cover art.

In addition to all the people who contributed directly to the book, I'm very lucky to be surrounded by friends who stood by me and held me up through all of the personal challenges I faced while this book was in process. To Randy Stearns and Stacey Bashara, I thank you for not only being great friends but for being the sort of employers who provide the perfect balance of room to work (and feel productive and valuable) and room to breathe in the face of personal challenges.

And lastly, to Flor Pinho, my partner in so many things, I thank you for seemingly endless love, support, and patience (we can finally stop saying "after the book!"). Thank you, thank you, and, again, thank you.

Preface

The RSpec Book is an exploration of Behaviour-Driven Development and tools that Ruby developers use when practicing BDD: RSpec, Cucumber, et al.[1]

All the tools and libraries used in this book are under regular development with contributions from vibrant communities. By the time you read this, there are very likely new releases of many, if not all of them. The examples in this book have all been run to ensure that they execute and are free of typos. To provide yourself the smoothest path through the lessons in this book, we strongly encourage you to use the same versions we used.

Ruby and Gem Versions

- ruby-1.8.7[1]

- rubygems-1.3.7

- rspec-2.0.0

- rspec-rails-2.0.0

- cucumber-0.9.2

- cucumber-rails-0.3.2

- database_cleaner-0.5.2

- webrat-0.7.2

- selenium-client-1.2.18

- rails-3.0.0

---

1. The examples should all work with ruby-1.9.2 as well as ruby-1.8.7, but the output will be different from time to time.

Downloading the Code Examples

Most of the code examples in this book are available for download from http://pragprog.com/titles/achbd/source_code. The files are generally grouped by chapter and are often in numbered directories that represent snapshots of the code as you progress through an exercise.

What's in This Book

We begin with a hands-on tutorial in Chapter 3, *Describing Features*, on page 19, in which we build a simple logic game that you can play on the command line. This will get you up and running quickly with RSpec and Cucumber and will provide a sense of the BDD technique practiced by RSpec's maintainers and contributors.

Beginning with Chapter 10, *The Case for BDD*, on page 109, the next part of the book provides background information intended to put these tools and practices into a greater context. In this part, you'll read about the initial motivations for BDD, its history in Extreme Programming (XP), and what we mean when we say that we find Test-Driven Development (TDD) to be as much a design and documentation practice as it is a testing practice.

Once you've been through the tutorial or if you already have a working knowledge of RSpec, you'll find a detailed exploration of RSpec beginning with Chapter 12, *Code Examples*, on page 137. Read this part to improve your understanding of the various facilities you get with RSpec, ranging from the simple expectations that are built in to the custom formatters for presenting output appropriate for various audiences.

You'll also find material on RSpec's evolving extension API, which supports IDE integration by making it easy to hook into RSpec's runner. It also supports framework-specific extensions (like rspec-rails), making it simple to extend example groups with custom expectations, and expressive macros that do a lot with little effort.

A similarly detailed study of Cucumber begins on Chapter 17, *Intro to Cucumber*, on page 243. Cucumber is Aslak Hellesøy's reimplementation of Dan North's RBehave framework, which is a BDD framework targeted at expressing application behavior in automated scenarios described from outside the application.

In this part of the book, you'll learn all about the BDD triad—*Given, When, and Then*—and various approaches to organizing automated scenarios to keep them expressive, lean, and maintainable.

RSpec certainly owes a debt of gratitude to Ruby on Rails for helping build and foster a community that cares about testing. Beginning with Chapter 19, *BDD in Rails*, on page 277, we'll introduce you to Rails-specific extensions to RSpec and Cucumber and help you develop a practical understanding of how to approach Rails development from the *outside in*.

Whether you are looking for tutorials, reference material, integration tips, extension tips, and so on, you've come to the right place.

Part I

Getting Started with RSpec and Cucumber

## Chapter 1

Introduction

Behaviour-Driven Development began its journey as an attempt to better understand and explain the process of Test-Driven Development. Dan North had observed that the developers he was coaching were having a tough time relating to TDD as a design tool and came to the conclusion that it had a lot to do with the word *test*.

Dave Astels took that to the next step in the seminal article "A New Look at Test-Driven Development,"[1] in which he suggested that even experienced TDDers were not getting all the benefit from TDD that they could be getting.

To put this into perspective, perhaps a brief exploration of Test-Driven Development is in order.

1.1 Test-Driven Development: Where It All Started

Test-Driven Development is a developer practice that involves writing tests before writing the code being tested. Begin by writing a very small test for code that does not yet exist. Run the test, and, naturally, it fails. Now write just enough code to make that test pass. No more.

Once the test passes, observe the resulting design, and refactor any duplication you see.[2] It is natural at this point to judge the design as too simple to handle all the responsibilities this code will have.

---

1. http://techblog.daveastels.com/2005/07/05/a-new-look-at-test-driven-development/
2. Refactoring: improving the design of code without changing its behavior. From Martin Fowler's *Refactoring* [FBB+99].

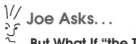

Joe Asks...

But What If "the Testers" Is Me?

Not all project teams have a separate tester role. On teams that don't, the notion of pushing off the responsibility of testing practices to other people doesn't really fly. In cases like this, it's still helpful to separate testing practices from TDD.

When you're "wearing your TDD hat," focus on red/green/refactor, design, and documentation. Don't think about testing. Once you've developed a body of code, put on your "tester hat," and think about all the things that could go wrong. This is where you add all the crazy edge cases, using exploratory testing to weed out the nasty bugs hiding in the cracks and documenting them as you discover them with more code examples.

Instead of adding more code, document the next responsibility in the form of the next test. Run it, watch it fail, write just enough code to get it to pass, review the design, and remove duplication. Now add the next test, watch it fail, get it to pass, refactor, fail, pass, refactor, fail, pass, refactor, and so on, and so on.

In many unit testing systems, when a test fails, we see the results printed in red. Then when it passes, the results are printed in green. Because of this, we often refer to this cycle as *red/green/refactor*.

Emergent Design

As a code base increases in size, we find that more attention is consumed by the refactoring step. The design is constantly evolving and under constant review, though it is not predetermined. This is *emergent design* at a granular level and is one of the most significant by-products of Test-Driven Development.

Rather than thinking of TDD as a testing practice, we see it as a technique used to deliver high-quality code to testers, who are responsible for formal testing practices (see the *Joe Asks...* on the current page).

And this is where the *Test* in TDD becomes a problem. Specifically, it is the idea of *unit testing* that often leads new TDDers to verify things such as making sure that a register() method stores a Registration in a Registry's registrations collection and that collection is specifically an Array.

This sort of detail in a test creates a dependency in the test on the internal structure of the object being tested. This dependency means that if other requirements guide us to change the Array to a Hash, this test will fail, even though the behavior of the object hasn't changed. This brittleness can make test suites much more expensive to maintain and is the primary reason for test suites to become ignored and, ultimately, discarded.

So if testing internals of an object is counterproductive in the long run, what should we focus on when we write these tests first?

1.2 Behaviour-Driven Development: The Next Step

The problem with testing an object's internal structure is that we're testing what an object *is* instead of what it *does*. What an object *does* is significantly more important.

The same is true at the application level. Stakeholders don't usually care that data is being persisted in an ANSI-compliant, relational database. They care that it's in "the database," but even then, they generally mean is that it's stored *somewhere* and they can get it back.

It's All Behavior

BDD puts the focus on behavior instead of structure, and it does so at every level of development. Whether we're talking about an object calculating the distance between two cities, another object delegating a search off to a third-party service, or a user-facing screen providing feedback when we provide invalid input, *it's all behavior*!

Once we acknowledge this, it changes the way we think about driving out code. We begin to think more about interactions between people and systems, or between objects, than we do about the structure of the objects.

Getting the Words Right

We believe that most of the problems that software development teams face are communication problems. BDD aims to help communication by simplifying the language we use to describe scenarios in which the software will be used: *Given* some context, *When* some event occurs, *Then* I expect some outcome.

Given, When, Then, the BDD triad, are simple words that we use whether we're talking about application behavior or object behavior. They are easily understood by business analysts, testers, and developers alike. As you'll see in Section 17.8, *Given/When/Then*, on page 253 and throughout the book, these words are embedded right in the language of Cucumber.

1.3 RSpec

RSpec was created by Steven Baker in 2005. Steven had heard about BDD from Aslak Hellesøy, who had been working on a project with Dan North when the idea first came to light. Steven was already interested in the idea when Dave Astels suggested that with languages like Smalltalk and Ruby, we could more freely explore new TDD frameworks that could encourage focus on behavior. And RSpec was born.

Although the syntactic details have evolved since Steven's original version of RSpec, the basic premise remains. We use RSpec to write executable examples of the expected behavior of a small bit of code in a controlled context. Here's how that might look:

```
describe MovieList do
  context "when first created" do
    it "is empty" do
      movie_list = MovieList.new
      movie_list.should be_empty
    end
  end
end
```

The it() method creates an *example* of the behavior of a MovieList, with the *context* being that the MovieList was just created. The expression movie_list.should be_empty is self-explanatory. Just read it out loud. You'll see how be_empty() interacts with movie_list in Section 13.3, *Predicate Matchers*, on page 167.

Running this code in a shell with the rspec command yields the following specification:

```
MovieList when first created
  is empty
```

Add some more contexts and examples, and the resulting output looks even more like a specification for a MovieList object.

```
MovieList when first created
  is empty

MovieList with 1 item
  is not empty
  includes that item
```

Of course, we're talking about the specification of an object, not a system. You *could* specify application behavior with RSpec. Many do. Ideally, however, for specifying application behavior, we want something that communicates in broader strokes. And for that, we use Cucumber.

1.4 Cucumber

As you'll read about in Chapter 11, *Writing Software That Matters*, on page 123, BDD is a full-stack agile methodology. It takes some of its cues from Extreme Programming, including a variation of Acceptance Test–Driven Development called Acceptance Test–Driven *Planning* (ATDP).

In ATDP, we use customer acceptance tests to drive the development of code. Ideally, these are the result of a collaborative effort between the customer and the delivery team. Sometimes they are written by the delivery team and then reviewed/approved by the customer. In either case, they are customer facing and must be expressed in a language and format that customers can relate to. Cucumber gives us that language and format.

Cucumber reads plain-text descriptions of application features with example scenarios and uses the scenario steps to automate interaction with the code being developed. Here's an example:

```
Line 1    Feature: pay bill on-line
  -
  -         In order to reduce the time I spend paying bills
  -         As a bank customer with a checking account
  5         I want to pay my bills on-line
  -
  -         Scenario: pay a bill
  -           Given checking account with $50
  -           And a payee named Acme
  10          And an Acme bill for $37
  -           When I pay the Acme bill
  -           Then I should have $13 remaining in my checking account
  -           And the payment of $37 to Acme should be listed in Recent Payments
```

> ### Cucumber Seeds
>
> Even before we started exploring structures and syntax for RSpec, Dan North had been exploring a completely different model for a BDD tool.
>
> He wanted to document and drive behavior in a simplified language that could be easily understood by customers, developers, testers, business analysts, and so on. The early result of that exploration was the JBehave library, which is still in active use and development.
>
> Dan ported JBehave to Ruby as RBehave, and we merged it into RSpec as the Story Runner. It only supported scenarios written in Ruby at first, but we later added support for plain text, opening up a whole new world of expressiveness and access. But as new possibilities were revealed, so were limitations.
>
> In the spring of 2008, Aslak Hellesøy set out to rewrite RSpec's Story Runner with a real grammar defined with Nathan Sobo's Treetop library. Aslak dubbed it Cucumber at the suggestion of his fiancée, Patricia Carrier, thinking it would be a short-lived working title until it was merged back into RSpec. Little did either of them know that Cucumber would develop a life of its own.

Everything up to and including the Scenario declaration on line 7 is treated as documentation (not executable). The subsequent lines are steps in the scenario.

In Chapter 4, *Automating Features with Cucumber*, on page 35, you'll be writing *step definitions* in Ruby. These step definitions interact with the code being developed and are invoked by Cucumber as it reads in the scenario.

Don't worry if that doesn't make perfect sense to you just yet. For now, it's only important to understand that both RSpec and Cucumber help us specify the behavior of code with examples that are programmatically tied to that code. The details will become clear as you read on.

We use Cucumber to describe the behavior of applications and use RSpec to describe the behavior of objects.[3] If you've ever done TDD before, you're probably familiar with the red/green/refactor cycle. With the addition of a higher-level tool like Cucumber, we'll actually have two concentric red/green/refactor cycles, as depicted in Figure 1.1, on the following page.

Both cycles involve taking small steps and listening to the feedback you get from the tools. We start with a failing step (red) in Cucumber (the outer cycle). To get that step to pass, we'll drop down to RSpec (the inner cycle) and drive out the underlying code at a granular level (red/green/refactor).

1.5 The BDD Cycle

At each green point in the RSpec cycle, we'll check the Cucumber cycle. If it is still red, the resulting feedback should guide us to the next action in the RSpec cycle. If it is green, we can jump out to Cucumber, refactor if appropriate, and then repeat the cycle by writing a new failing Cucumber step.

In the next chapter, we'll get you set up with Cucumber and RSpec and walk you through a simple example of each tool. In the tutorial that begins in Chapter 3, *Describing Features*, on page 19, we'll use a number of features in Cucumber and RSpec. In most cases, we'll only touch the surface of a feature, covering just enough to be able to use it as needed for this project, with references to other places in the book where you can go to learn more of the detail and philosophy behind each feature.

---

3. Although we use Cucumber to focus on high-level behavior and use RSpec to focus on more granular behavior, each can be used for either purpose.

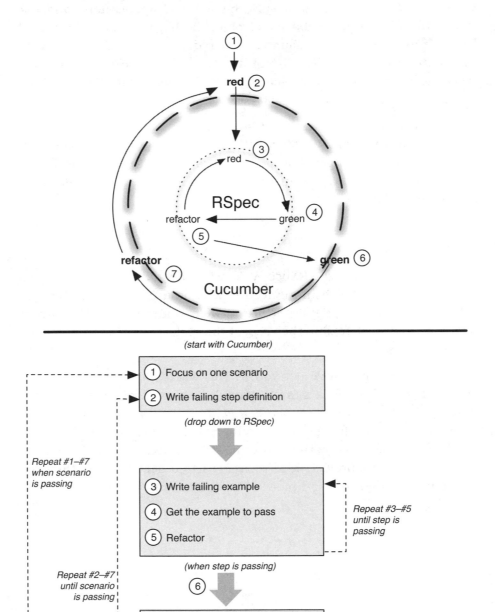

Figure 1.1: THE BDD CYCLE

Chapter 2

Hello

All good programming language books start with the obligatory *Hello World* example. Although RSpec is not an all-purpose programming language, it is sometimes described as a domain-specific language (DSL), for describing the behavior of objects. Similarly, Cucumber is a DSL for describing the behavior of applications.

To satisfy this requirement, we'll write *Hello* examples for both RSpec and Cucumber. But first things first, let's get the environment set up.

2.1 Installation

If you haven't done so already, the first thing you'll need to do is install the rspec and cucumber gems.[1] Open a shell, and type the following (you may need to prefix this with sudo on some systems):

```
gem install rspec --version 2.0.0
```

Now type rspec --help, and you should see output that starts like this:

```
Usage: rspec [options] [files or directories]
```

If you don't see that, or something close, then the installation failed for any number of reasons. If that happened, we recommend you email the rspec-users mailing list. All the authors of this book and many other knowledgeable members of the community are members and will be happy to help you sort it out.[2]

---

1. We assume that you already have a basic working knowledge of Ruby and Rubygems. If you don't, we can recommend *Programming Ruby: The Pragmatic Programmers' Guide* [TFH05] to learn about Ruby 1.8 and/or *Programming Ruby 1.9: The Pragmatic Programmers' Guide* [TFH08] if you want to learn about Ruby 1.9.
2. http://rubyforge.org/mailman/listinfo/rspec-users

Assuming all is well so far, the next thing to do is install Cucumber by typing this:

```
gem install cucumber --version 0.9.2
```

Again, you may need to prefix this command with sudo on some systems. Now type cucumber --help, and you should see output that starts something like this:

```
Usage: cucumber [options] [ [FILE|DIR|URL][:LINE[:LINE]*] ]+
```

In the unlikely event of a Cucumber installation failure, please consult the Cucumber Google group for assistance.[3]

Now that the tools are installed, it's time to *say hello!*

2.2 Hello RSpec

Create a file named greeter_spec.rb anywhere on your system, open it in your favorite text editor, and type the following code:

`hello/1/greeter_spec.rb`

```
Line 1  describe "RSpec Greeter" do
     2    it "should say 'Hello RSpec!' when it receives the greet() message" do
     3      greeter = RSpecGreeter.new
     4      greeting = greeter.greet
     5      greeting.should == "Hello RSpec!"
     6    end
     7  end
```

We'll get into all the details of this later in the book, but briefly here's an explanation.

We start by declaring an *example group* using the describe() method on line 1. On line 2, we declare an *example* using the it() method.

Within the example, we initialize a new RSpecGreeter on line 3. This is the *Given* in this example: the context that we set up and take for granted as a starting point.

On line 4, we assign the value returned by the greet() method to a greeting variable. This is the *When* in this example: the action that we're focused on.

---

3. http://groups.google.com/group/cukes

Lastly, on line 5, we set an expectation that the value of greeting should equal "Hello RSpec!" This is the *Then* of this example: the expected outcome.

As you'll see throughout this book, we use these three simple words—Given, When, and Then—because they are easily understood by both technical and nontechnical contributors to a project.

Now save the file, open a command shell, cd into the directory in which it is saved, and type this command:

```
rspec greeter_spec.rb
```

You should see output including this in the shell:

```
uninitialized constant RSpecGreeter
```

This is RSpec telling you that the example failed because there is no RSpecGreeter class defined yet. To keep things simple, let's just define it in the same file. Adding this definition, the entire file should look like this:

hello/2/greeter_spec.rb

```ruby
class RSpecGreeter
  def greet
    "Hello RSpec!"
  end
end

describe "RSpec Greeter" do
  it "should say 'Hello RSpec!' when it receives the greet() message" do
    greeter = RSpecGreeter.new
    greeting = greeter.greet
    greeting.should == "Hello RSpec!"
  end
end
```

Run the file again by typing rspec greeter_spec.rb, and the output should be something like this:

```
.

Finished in 0.00075 seconds
1 example, 0 failures
```

Success! The dot on the first line represents the one example that was run, and the summary on the last line reports that there was one example and zero failures.

This is a bit different from the *Hello World* examples we're used to seeing in programming language books because it doesn't actually print *Hello RSpec* to the command line. In this case, the feedback we get tells us the example ran and the code works as expected.

2.3 Hello Cucumber

For Cucumber, we're going to need a little bit more structure, so let's create a small project directory named hello. Inside the hello directory, add two directories named features and spec, and then move the greeter_spec.rb file from the RSpec example into the hello/spec directory. Now create a file greeter_says_hello.feature in the features directory, and enter the following text:

`hello/3/features/greeter_says_hello.feature`

```
Feature: greeter says hello

  In order to start learning RSpec and Cucumber
  As a reader of The RSpec Book
  I want a greeter to say Hello

  Scenario: greeter says hello
    Given a greeter
    When I send it the greet message
    Then I should see "Hello Cucumber!"
```

In the shell, cd to the project root, the hello directory, and type cucumber features. You should see output like this:

```
Feature: greeter says hello
  In order to start learning RSpec and Cucumber
  As a reader of The RSpec Book
  I want a greeter to say Hello

Scenario: greeter says hello                # features/greeter_says_hello.feature:7
  Given a greeter                           # features/greeter_says_hello.feature:8
  When I send it the greet message          # features/greeter_says_hello.feature:9
  Then I should see "Hello Cucumber!"       # features/greeter_says_hello.feature:10

1 scenario (1 undefined)
3 steps (3 undefined)
0m0.003s

You can implement step definitions for undefined steps with these snippets:

Given /^a greeter$/ do
  pending # express the regexp above with the code you wish you had
end
```

```
When /^I send it the greet message$/ do
  pending # express the regexp above with the code you wish you had
end

Then /^I should see "([^"]*)"$/ do |arg1|
  pending # express the regexp above with the code you wish you had
end
```

We'll go into the details of this output later, but the high points are that we see the feature and scenario text from the greeter_says_hello.feature file, a summary of everything that was run, and then some code snippets that we can use for our *step definitions*.

A step definition is a method that creates a step. In this example, we use the Given(), When(), and Then() methods to write step definitions, each of which takes a Regexp and a block. Cucumber will read the first step in the scenario, *Given a greeter*; look for a step definition whose regular expression matches that step; and then execute that step definition's block.

To get this scenario to pass, we need to store step definitions in a file that Cucumber can load. Go ahead and add a step_definitions directory inside hello/features, and add a file named greeter_steps.rb with the following code:

hello/4/features/step_definitions/greeter_steps.rb

```
Given /^a greeter$/ do
  @greeter = CucumberGreeter.new
end

When /^I send it the greet message$/ do
  @message = @greeter.greet
end

Then /^I should see "([^"]*)"$/ do |greeting|
  @message.should == greeting
end
```

This looks a lot like the code snippets that we got from running the cucumber command, but we've added some code in each step definition. Now run cucumber features again, and the output should look more like this:

```
Feature: greeter says hello
  In order to start learning RSpec and Cucumber
  As a reader of The RSpec Book
  I want a greeter to say Hello
```

```
Scenario: greeter says hello ↩
                              # features/greeter_says_hello.feature:7
  Given a greeter              ↩
                              # features/step_definitions/greeter_steps.rb:1
    uninitialized constant CucumberGreeter (NameError)
    ./features/step_definitions/greeter_steps.rb:2:in `/^a greeter$/'
    features/greeter_says_hello.feature:8:in `Given a greeter'
  When I send it the greet message    ↩
                              # features/step_definitions/greeter_steps.rb:5
  Then I should see "Hello Cucumber!" ↩
                              # features/step_definitions/greeter_steps.rb:9

Failing Scenarios:
cucumber features/greeter_says_hello.feature:7 # Scenario: greeter says hello

1 scenario (1 failed)
3 steps (1 failed, 2 skipped)
0m0.003s
```

The first step is failing because we haven't defined a CucumberGreeter.
The next two steps are being skipped because the first one failed. Again,
to keep things simple, go ahead and define the missing class right
alongside the step definitions in greeter_steps.rb.

Here is the full listing:

> hello/5/features/step_definitions/greeter_steps.rb

```ruby
class CucumberGreeter
  def greet
    "Hello Cucumber!"
  end
end

Given /^a greeter$/ do
  @greeter = CucumberGreeter.new
end

When /^I send it the greet message$/ do
  @message = @greeter.greet
end

Then /^I should see "([^"]*)"$/ do |greeting|
  @message.should == greeting
end
```

Now we should get different output when we run cucumber features:

```
Feature: greeter says hello
  In order to start learning RSpec and Cucumber
  As a reader of The RSpec Book
  I want a greeter to say Hello
```

```
Scenario: greeter says hello          ↩
                     # features/greeter_says_hello.feature:7
  Given a greeter                     ↩
                     # features/step_definitions/greeter_steps.rb:7
  When I send it the greet message    ↩
                     # features/step_definitions/greeter_steps.rb:11
  Then I should see "Hello Cucumber!" ↩
                     # features/step_definitions/greeter_steps.rb:15

1 scenario (1 passed)
3 steps (3 passed)
0m0.003s
```

This time, the scenario and all of its steps pass. So, now we have a passing RSpec example and a passing Cucumber scenario. You can type rspec spec, and the rspec command will run everything inside the spec directory. If you moved greeter_spec.rb to the spec directory, then you should see output similar to the output you saw at the end of Section 2.2, *Hello RSpec*, on page 12.

There is certainly a lot of detail yet to cover here, but that's why this is a book and not a blog post! In the chapters that follow, you'll learn all about RSpec and Cucumber and how to use them in the context of Behaviour-Driven Development. So, what are you waiting for? All the good stuff is yet to come. Turn the page already!

Chapter 3

Describing Features

To get started doing BDD with RSpec and Cucumber, we're going to write a problem-solving game that we'll call Codebreaker. Our version will be played in a shell, but it is based on a classic pencil and paper game named Bulls and Cows.[1]

We picked a game because we thought it would be more fun than a banking or social networking application. We also wanted something that was small enough to accomplish in a few short chapters but complex enough to provide some interesting edge cases. By the time we get through this tutorial, we'll have planned a small release, planned and executed an iteration, developed some code from the outside in, and have a game we can play at the command line.

We'll develop the game using the process and practices of Behaviour-Driven Development that we introduced in Chapter 1, *Introduction*, on page 3, and that you'll read more about throughout this book. We're going to drive straight on through, stopping only occasionally to review things and answer questions at the end of each chapter. When you're looking for more detail, we'll tell you where you can find it, but we won't get hung up in too much detail during this part of the book so that we can experience the feel of BDD in the trenches.

But before we develop anything, let's start with an overview of the game and its rules.

---

1. http://en.wikipedia.org/wiki/Bulls_and_cows

3.1 Introducing Codebreaker

Codebreaker is a logic game in which a *code-breaker* tries to break a secret code created by a *code-maker*. The code-maker, which will be played by the application we're going to write, creates a secret code of four numbers between 1 and 6.

The code-breaker then gets some number of chances to break the code. In each turn, the code-breaker makes a guess of four numbers (again, 1 to 6). The code-maker then marks the guess with up to four + and - signs.

A + indicates an *exact match*: one of the numbers in the guess is the same as one of the numbers in the secret code and in the same position.

A - indicates a *number match*: one of the numbers in the guess is the same as one of the numbers in the secret code but in a different position.

For example, given a secret code 1234, a guess with 4256 would earn a +-. The + is for the 2 in the second position in the guess, which matches the 2 in the secret code in both number and position: an exact match. The - is for the 4 in the first position in the guess, which matches the 4 in the code but not in the same position: a number match.

The plus signs for the exact matches always come before the minus signs for the number matches and don't align with specific positions in the guess or the secret code.

3.2 Planning the First Release

As you'll read about in Chapter 11, *Writing Software That Matters*, on page 123, one of the three principles of BDD is "Enough is enough." We want to avoid the pitfalls of the Big Design Up Front,[2] but we also want to do enough planning to know we're heading in the right direction. We'll do some of that planning in this chapter, picking out *user stories* for our first iteration.

For the first release, we simply want to be able to play the game. We should be able to type a command in a shell to start it up, submit guesses, and see the mark for each of our guesses until we crack the

---

2. BDUF is designing an application in significant detail before writing the first line of code.

code. Now that may sound like an over-simplification, and it certainly leaves open more questions than it answers, but it gives us a target on which to set our sights, which serves as a basis from which we can start assembling a list of user stories that will get us there.

Selecting Stories

A great way to get started gathering user stories is to do a high-level brain dump of the sorts of things we might like to do. Here are some titles to get started:

- Code-breaker starts game
- Code-breaker submits guess
- Code-breaker wins game
- Code-breaker loses game
- Code-breaker plays again
- Code-breaker requests hint
- Code-breaker saves score

See how each of these is phrased as *role + action*? The role is the *code-breaker* role each time because this game has only one kind of user. In other applications, we might have several different kinds of users, in which case we want to express stories in terms of a specific role (not just a generic *user*), because that impacts how we think about each requirement and why we're implementing code to satisfy it. See the sidebar on the next page for more on this.

These are also high level and don't tell us much about how the system should respond to these actions. Let's take these titles and generate some user stories from them.

A Token for a Conversation

We'll use the simple format described in *Extreme Programming Installed* [JAH02]. The idea is that there should be just enough information to serve as a *token for a conversation* that should take place as we get closer to implementation.[3]

---

3. In Extreme Programming, index cards are the preferred medium for user stories. This keeps them lightweight and reinforces the idea that these are not formal documentation. There is an XP joke that if you can't fit a requirement on an index card, you should get a smaller card.

> **Focus on the Role** _____
>
> Mike Cohn, author of _User Stories Applied_ (Coh04), talked about focusing on the role when writing user stories at the Agile 2006 Conference. The example he gave was that of an airline reservation system, pointing out that the regular business traveler booking a flight wants very different things from such a system than the occasional vacation traveler.
>
> Think about that for a minute. Imagine yourself in these two different roles and the different sorts of details you would want from such a system based on your goals. For starters, the business traveler might want to maintain a profile of regular itineraries, while the vacationer might be more interested in finding package deals that include hotel and car at a discount.
>
> Focusing on this distinction is a very powerful tool in getting down to the details of the features required of a system.

Code-breaker starts game The code-breaker opens a shell, types a command, and sees a welcome message and a prompt to enter the first guess.

Code-breaker submits guess The code-breaker enters a guess, and the system replies by marking the guess according to the marking algorithm.

Code-breaker wins game The code-breaker enters a guess that matches the secret code exactly. The system responds by marking the guess with four + signs and a message congratulating the code-breaker on breaking the code in however many guesses it took.

We can already see some of the challenges ahead: "according to the marking algorithm" is going to require some conversation with the stakeholders. In fact, this is where we'll spend the majority of our time both planning and developing, because the marking algorithm is where much of the complexity lies.

Continuing with stories for the other titles:

Code-breaker loses game After some number of turns, the game tells the code-breaker that the game is over (need to decide how many turns and whether to reveal the code).

Code-breaker plays again After the game is won or lost, the system prompts the code-breaker to play again. If the code-breaker indicates yes, a new game begins. If the code-breaker indicates no, the system shuts down.

Code-breaker requests hint At any time during a game, the code-breaker can request a hint, at which point the system reveals one of the numbers in the secret code.

Code-breaker saves score After the game is won or lost, the code-breaker can opt to save information about the game: who (initials?), how many turns, and so on.

Note the deliberate lack of detail and even some open questions. We'll get into some detail as we choose which of these stories we want to include in the release, and then we'll get more detailed in each iteration within the release. But at each phase, we want to do just enough planning to keep on moving, and no more.

Narrowing Things Down

Now that we have some stories,[4] let's consider them in the context of the stated goal for the initial release: to simply be able to play the game. Looking at the original list of stories, there are only two that are absolutely necessary to meet that goal:

- Code-breaker starts game
- Code-breaker submits guess

We definitely have to be able to start the game somehow so that one is a no-brainer. Once we've started the game, if we can submit a guess and get the mark, then we can submit more guesses. As soon as we get a perfect mark, the game is won, and we hit Ctrl+C to stop the game and start the game back up to play again. What do you think?

Maybe it would be a bit more satisfying to play if the game told us when we won—a bit of positive feedback to motivate us to play again. That sounds like it's pretty important, so let's add the Code-breaker wins game story to our release plan.

Of course, having to hit Ctrl+C and then restart the game to play again is a little cheesy, don't you think? That just won't do, so let's also add

---

4. If we were developing this for commercial distribution, we'd likely have dozens more stories, even for such a simple game.

the Code-breaker plays again story as well. So, now our release plan includes these four stories:

- Code-breaker starts game

- Code-breaker submits guess

- Code-breaker wins game

- Code-breaker plays again

Hmmm. Seeing those together brings up the question of what will happen if the code-breaker doesn't win after some number of guesses. How else will we know when to prompt the code-breaker to play again? Maybe we should add the Code-breaker loses game story. What do you think?

Wait, wait, wait! We're heading down a slippery slope here. Pretty soon we'll be including our entire backlog of stories in the first release! Let's step back for a second. What is the release goal? To be able to play the game. Let's examine that a bit. Why does playing the game matter? Why do we want to be able to play the game?

Context Matters

Perhaps our plan is to sell the game to millions of people and retire young. More likely, it's for a class project for school. OK, which class? If it's a usability class, then hitting Ctrl+C just won't fly. But if it's an algorithms class, then the most important thing is that the marking algorithm works correctly.

The point is that our goal is to write software that matters, and what matters depends entirely on context and is the purview of the stakeholders! In our case, the primary stakeholder is *you*! You're reading this book and trying to learn something about RSpec and Cucumber and the process of BDD. You're also a programmer, so it's quite likely that you are perfectly capable of hitting Ctrl+C.

Given this context, we'll go with Code-breaker starts game and Code-breaker submits guess. Together, those two stories should suffice to get us to the point where we can play the game—unless, of course, we're missing something.

The Hidden Story

It turns out that there *is* one feature of the game that we haven't discussed yet! We won't really see the evidence of it until we submit a guess and the game marks it. Can you guess what it is? Think about how the game will be able to mark the guess. It has to mark it against *something*, right?

The secret code!

The game will need to generate a secret code that is different every time in order for it to be truly enjoyable. Now is this a user story? This is one of those gray areas that challenges the boundaries of what a user story is. Ask one experienced XPer, and you'll hear that this is really part of the Code-breaker starts game story based on the idea that the secret code should be generated when the game starts up.

The next person might argue that it's really part of the Code-breaker submits guess story because that's the first time the user gets any feedback from the system that depends on the guess.

User Stories Are a Planning Tool

We're going to take a third stance and make it a separate story based on practicality. We're going to have a lot to cover in these chapters, and we want to keep things small enough to accomplish in a reasonable time so we can check things off the list as we go. Does that sound selfish? Does that sound like we're putting the developer's needs ahead of those of the stakeholder?

Absolutely not! We're just planning! And user stories are, above all else, a planning tool. Although you can find many definitions of what a user story *is* and therefore *must be* in order to earn the title, here is a simple set of criteria that David learned from Bob Koss at Object Mentor. A user story must have the following characteristics:

Have business value Clearly, the game is no fun unless it generates a different secret code each time.

Be testable That's easy. We just start up a bunch of games and ask for the code. As you'll see when we develop this part, this reveals some interesting questions about designing for testability.

Be small enough to implement in one iteration This is the motivation for separating this story. It's a guideline that allows us to balance implementation concerns with requirements.

So, now we have our release plan with three stories. It's time to start breaking it down into iterations.

3.3 Planning the First Iteration

Acceptance Test–Driven Planning is one of three practices of BDD.[5] It is an extension of Acceptance Test–Driven *Development*, which is a formalization of the notion of customer tests in XP. ATDD involves collaborating with stakeholders on acceptance tests before we write any code.[6]

The difference between ATDP and ATDD is simple. ATDD specifies that we write acceptance tests before we write code, but it doesn't specify when we should write them.

ATDP specifies that the acceptance tests are agreed on *during* or possibly *before*, but no later than, an iteration planning meeting. This lets us consider the acceptance criteria in our estimates, which improves our ability to plan iterations, which is why it's called Acceptance Test–Driven *Planning*.

Narratives in Features

Cucumber lets us describe application features in a simple plain-text format and then use those descriptions to automate interaction with the application. We're going to use Cucumber to express application features in this chapter and then automate them in the next.

Cucumber features have three parts: a title, a brief narrative, and an arbitrary number of scenarios that serve as acceptance criteria. Here's what the title and narrative for the code-breaker starts game feature might look like:

```
Feature: code-breaker starts game

  As a code-breaker
  I want to start a game
  So that I can break the code
```

The title is just enough to remind us who the feature is for, the code-breaker, and what the feature is about, starting a game. Although the narrative is free-form, we generally follow the Connextra format that is described in Chapter 17, *Intro to Cucumber*, on page 243 or variations of it that we'll discuss at different points in the book.

---

5. The other two are Domain-Driven Design and Test-Driven Development.
6. The term *acceptance test* means different things to different people. We'll discuss this in the context of BDD in Chapter 17, *Intro to Cucumber*, on page 243.

With this narrative, we have some understanding of what we want to do with the system, but how will we know when we've started the game? How will we know when we've satisfied this requirement? How will we know when we're done?

Acceptance Criteria

To answer these questions, we'll add acceptance criteria to the feature. Imagine that you sit down to play Codebreaker, fire up a shell, and type the codebreaker command. How do you know it started? Perhaps it says something like "Welcome to Codebreaker!" And then, so you know what to do next, it probably says something like "Enter a guess."

That will be the acceptance criteria for this feature. Here's how we express that in Cucumber:

```
Feature: code-breaker starts game

  As a code-breaker
  I want to start a game
  So that I can break the code

  Scenario: start game
    Given I am not yet playing
    When I start a new game
    Then I should see "Welcome to Codebreaker!"
    And I should see "Enter guess:"
```

The Scenario keyword is followed by a string and then a series of steps. Each step begins with any of five keywords: *Given*, *When*, *Then*, *And*, and *But*.

Given steps represent the state of the world before an event. *When* steps represent the event. *Then* steps represent the expected outcomes.

And and *But* steps take on the quality of the previous step. In the start game scenario, the *And* step is a second *Then*; a second expected outcome. If we wanted to expect that the game says "Welcome to Codebreaker!" but not "What is your quest?" we would add a *But* step saying *But I should not see "What is your quest?"* This would be treated as a *Then*.

See how the Given and When steps in this scenario both use the first person? We choose the first-person form because it makes the narrative feel more compelling. Given x, when *I* y, then *I* should see a message saying "z." This helps keep the focus on how *I* would use the system if *I* were in a given role (the code-breaker).

Given I am not yet playing expresses the context in which the subsequent steps will be executed. When I start a new game is the event or action that occurs because *I* did something. The Thens are the expected outcomes—what we expect to happen as a result of the When.

Let's store this feature in a file. We will go over the details of the project structure later in Chapter 4, *Automating Features with Cucumber*, on page 35, but for now just create a codebreaker directory wherever you like to keep projects on your computer. This will be the root directory for the project, from which we'll type all our shell commands as we progress.

Inside the codebreaker directory, add a subdirectory named features. Create a new file named codebreaker_starts_game.feature in that directory, and copy in the content of the feature, shown earlier.

Now add a subdirectory inside features named support, and inside features/support add a file named env.rb. Even though we'll leave this empty for now, Cucumber needs this file (or any .rb file) in order to know that we're using Ruby.[7]

Now open a shell, cd into the codebreaker project root directory, and type cucumber. You'll see the same text that is in the file with some additional context information and metadata. We'll discuss what all that means in the next chapter when we begin to automate the scenarios.

Submitting a Guess

The next feature we want to tackle in the first iteration is as follows:

`cb/01/features/codebreaker_submits_guess.feature`

```
Feature: code-breaker submits guess

  The code-breaker submits a guess of four numbers.  The game marks the guess
  with + and - signs.

  For each number in the guess that matches the number and position of a number
  in the secret code, the mark includes one + sign. For each number in the guess
  that matches the number but not the position of a number in the secret code,
  the mark includes one - sign.
```

This time we used a free-form narrative instead of the Connextra format. This seems appropriate given that we're describing an algorithm,

---

7. Cucumber supports several different programming languages.

which is a bit more complex than a statement such as "I should see a welcome message." Could we use the Connextra format? Let's give it a try and see.

```
Feature: code-breaker submits guess

  As a code-breaker
  I want to submit a guess
  So that I can try to break the code
```

That doesn't tell us a whole lot, so let's add a scenario:

```
Feature: code-breaker submits guess

  As a code-breaker
  I want to submit a guess
  So that I can try to break the code

  Scenario: all exact matches
    Given the secret code is "1234"
    When I guess "1234"
    Then the mark should be "++++"
```

Even when we add this narrative together with this scenario, we don't really supply enough context information to understand the meaning of the mark. Now look at the original narrative plus a single scenario:

```
Feature: code-breaker submits guess

  The code-breaker submits a guess of four numbers.  The game marks the guess
  with + and - signs.

  For each number in the guess that matches the number and position of a number
  in the secret code, the mark includes one +. For each number in the guess
  that matches the number but not the position of a number in the secret code,
  a - is added to the mark.

  Scenario: all exact matches
    Given the secret code is "1234"
    When I guess "1234"
    Then the mark should be "++++"
```

Wow, what a difference that makes. Now we have an explanation of the mark and an example of how it works in practice. Much clearer, no? So then, why don't we add some prose narrative to the Code-breaker starts game feature as well? Well, we don't really need it. In that case, the scenario tells us everything we need to know in order to understand the context.

So, which should we use? Connextra format? Free-form prose? Some other format? The answer, of course, is that it depends, as we've just seen. In the end, it's good to have a number of tools at our disposal, so we can pick the right one for each job. That's true of RSpec and Cucumber. That's also true of narrative formats.

Adding More Scenarios

With an algorithm as complex as marking a guess, we're going to need more scenarios to demonstrate what the mark should be under different conditions. Let's add a second scenario, shown here without the narrative:

```
Scenario: all exact matches
  Given the secret code is "1234"
  When I guess "1234"
  Then the mark should be "++++"

Scenario: 2 exact matches and 2 number matches
  Given the secret code is "1234"
  When I guess "1243"
  Then the mark should be "++--"
```

The addition of another scenario increases the expression and our understanding of the rules of the algorithm. Of course, we have a long way to go, so let's add some more:

```
Scenario: all exact matches
  Given the secret code is "1234"
  When I guess "1234"
  Then the mark should be "++++"

Scenario: 2 exact matches and 2 number matches
  Given the secret code is "1234"
  When I guess "1243"
  Then the mark should be "++--"

Scenario: 1 exact match and 3 number matches
  Given the secret code is "1234"
  When I guess "1342"
  Then the mark should be "+---"

Scenario: 4 number matches
  Given the secret code is "1234"
  When I guess "4321"
  Then the mark should be "----"
```

If we hadn't seen it before, we can certainly see now that this is not going to scale very well. We have four scenarios, and it's already starting to become difficult to take them all in at a glance. Imagine what this would look like when we add scenarios for three matching numbers, two, one, and then none. We'll likely end up with a couple of dozen scenarios, and it's going to be quite difficult to scan them all and really understand the intent.

Fortunately, Cucumber offers us a few different tools we can use to DRY things up without sacrificing expressiveness and cohesion.[8] You'll read about all of these tools in Chapter 17, *Intro to Cucumber*, on page 243, but the one we're interested in right now is the *scenario outline*.

Scenario Outlines

Cucumber lets us define a single *scenario outline* and then provide tables of input data and expected output. Here's the scenario outline for our submit guess scenarios:

```
Scenario Outline: submit guess
  Given the secret code is "<code>"
  When I guess "<guess>"
  Then the mark should be "<mark>"
```

This looks a lot like the scenario declarations we wrote for the *codebreaker submits guess* feature, with two subtle differences:

- Scenario Outline instead of Scenario

- Variable data placeholders in angle brackets

The words in angle brackets are placeholders for variable data that we'll provide in a tabular format, inspired by FIT (see the sidebar on the following page).

Tabular Data

Here is the first of several tables we'll add, supplying data for scenarios in which all four numbers match:

```
Scenarios: all numbers correct
  | code | guess | mark |
  | 1234 | 1234  | ++++ |
  | 1234 | 1243  | ++-- |
  | 1234 | 1423  | +--- |
  | 1234 | 4321  | ---- |
```

---

8. DRY stands for *Don't Repeat Yourself*. The DRY principle, as described in *The Pragmatic Programmer* [HT00], states that every piece of knowledge in a system should have one authoritative, unambiguous representation.

FIT

Ward Cunningham's Framework for Integration Test (FIT) parses display tables in rich documents written with Microsoft Word or HTML, sends the contents of table cells to the system in development, and compares the results from the system to expected values in the table.*

This allows teams that were already using tools like Word for requirements documentation to turn those documents into executable acceptance tests by specifying expected outputs resulting from prescribed inputs. This works especially well when the acceptance criteria are naturally expressed in a table.

Cucumber's scenario outlines and scenario tables provide a FIT-inspired tabular format for expressing repetitive scenarios like those in our "submit guess" feature, while maintaining the Given, When, and Then language of BDD.

---

*. See http://fit.c2.com/ for more information about FIT.

The Scenarios keyword indicates that what follows are rows of example data. The first row contains column headers that align with the placeholders in the scenario outline. Each subsequent row represents a single scenario.

Following convention, we've named the columns using the same names that are in angle brackets in the scenario outline, but the placeholders and columns are bound by position, not name.

The <code> variable in the *Given* step is assigned the value 1234, from the first column in the first data row (after the headers). It's just as though we wrote Given the secret code is 1234.

The <guess> in the *When* step gets 1234 from the second column, and the <mark> in the *Then* step gets ++++.

With the scenario outline and this first table, we've expressed four scenarios that would have taken sixteen lines in only ten. We've also reduced duplication and created very readable executable documentation in the process. Cucumber lets us supply as many groups of scenarios as we want, supporting a very natural way to group similar scenarios.

Here's the whole feature with fourteen scenarios expressed in a mere twenty-seven lines (beginning with the scenario outline):

```
Feature: code-breaker submits guess

  The code-breaker submits a guess of four numbers.  The game marks the guess
  with + and - signs.

  For each number in the guess that matches the number and position of a number
  in the secret code, the mark includes one + sign. For each number in the guess
  that matches the number but not the position of a number in the secret code,
  the mark includes one - sign.

  Scenario Outline: submit guess
    Given the secret code is "<code>"
    When I guess "<guess>"
    Then the mark should be "<mark>"

    Scenarios: no matches
      | code | guess | mark |
      | 1234 | 5555  |      |

    Scenarios: 1 number correct
      | code | guess | mark |
      | 1234 | 1555  | +    |
      | 1234 | 2555  | -    |

    Scenarios: 2 numbers correct
      | code | guess | mark |
      | 1234 | 5254  | ++   |
      | 1234 | 5154  | +-   |
      | 1234 | 2545  | --   |

    Scenarios: 3 numbers correct
      | code | guess | mark |
      | 1234 | 5234  | +++  |
      | 1234 | 5134  | ++-  |
      | 1234 | 5124  | +--  |
      | 1234 | 5123  | ---  |

    Scenarios: all numbers correct
      | code | guess | mark |
      | 1234 | 1234  | ++++ |
      | 1234 | 1243  | ++-- |
      | 1234 | 1423  | +--- |
      | 1234 | 4321  | ---- |
```

See how easy that is to read and understand? Even a nontechnical team member can read this and figure out what's going on. And therein lies the power of Cucumber. It lets us express requirements in language that the whole team can understand so we can all speak the same language. When we talk about mark, it means the same thing to the CEO as it does to the developer. The same goes for the secret code and a guess.

We now have the acceptance criteria for the two stories we want to include in our first iteration, so the planning meeting has come to a close. In the next chapter, we'll use these same plain-text features to begin to drive out the code for our game, but first let's quickly recap what we've done.

3.4 What We've Learned

In this chapter, we introduced the project that we'll spend the remaining chapters in Part I working on. We planned a release and the first iteration. In the process, we learned about the following:

Selecting stories for a release We did this by narrowing down the stories to those that really matter in the context of the release goals.

Selecting stories for an iteration We picked out two stories that will result in working software sufficient to interact with it in a meaningful way.

Acceptance criteria We wrote Cucumber features and scenarios for each story. We do this during the iteration planning meeting so that we can use what we learn from writing the scenarios to affirm or modify existing estimates. This is known as Acceptance Test–Driven Planning.

Scenario outlines This is one of many tools that Cucumber offers to keep features and scenarios DRY and expressive.

## Chapter 4

Automating Features with Cucumber

In the previous chapter, we selected the stories for the first iteration and wrote them out as features and scenarios in plain text using Cucumber. Now it's time to put those scenarios to work to guide us as we develop code.

At this point, the feature files should be in the features/ directory, each with the .feature file extension. Cucumber recognizes this extension and treats these files as input. Here are the contents of the two files:

cb/02/features/codebreaker_starts_game.feature

```
Feature: code-breaker starts game

  As a code-breaker
  I want to start a game
  So that I can break the code

  Scenario: start game
    Given I am not yet playing
    When I start a new game
    Then I should see "Welcome to Codebreaker!"
    And I should see "Enter guess:"
```

cb/02/features/codebreaker_submits_guess.feature

```
Feature: code-breaker submits guess

  The code-breaker submits a guess of four numbers.  The game marks the guess
  with + and - signs.
```

For each number in the guess that matches the number and position of a number in the secret code, the mark includes one + sign. For each number in the guess that matches the number but not the position of a number in the secret code, the mark includes one - sign.

```
Scenario Outline: submit guess
  Given the secret code is "<code>"
  When I guess "<guess>"
  Then the mark should be "<mark>"

  Scenarios: no matches
    | code | guess | mark |
    | 1234 | 5555  |      |

  Scenarios: 1 number correct
    | code | guess | mark |
    | 1234 | 1555  | +    |
    | 1234 | 2555  | -    |

  Scenarios: 2 numbers correct
    | code | guess | mark |
    | 1234 | 5254  | ++   |
    | 1234 | 5154  | +-   |
    | 1234 | 2545  | --   |

  Scenarios: 3 numbers correct
    | code | guess | mark |
    | 1234 | 5234  | +++  |
    | 1234 | 5134  | ++-  |
    | 1234 | 5124  | +--  |
    | 1234 | 5123  | ---  |

  Scenarios: all numbers correct
    | code | guess | mark |
    | 1234 | 1234  | ++++ |
    | 1234 | 1243  | ++-- |
    | 1234 | 1423  | +--- |
    | 1234 | 4321  | ---- |
```

We should also have an env.rb file in features/support directory. The .rb extension tells Cucumber that we're using Ruby.

If you didn't try to run the features in the previous chapter, try it now. Open a shell to the codebreaker directory, and type cucumber. You should see output that looks just like the text in the .feature files, plus some additional information that we'll talk about as we progress.

4.1 Steps and Step Definitions

When you ran the cucumber command, you should have seen a bunch of code snippets at the end of the output that look something like this:[1]

```
Given /^I am not yet playing$/ do
  pending # express the regexp above with the code you wish you had
end
```

This is a Cucumber *step definition*. If you think of the steps in scenarios as method calls, then step definitions are like method definitions. Go ahead and create a codebreaker_steps.rb file in features/step_definitions/, and add that snippet to it, removing the pending call from the block, like this:

cb/02/features/step_definitions/codebreaker_steps.rb

```
Given /^I am not yet playing$/ do
end
```

---

1. If you don't see the step definition snippets, it's likely because Cucumber doesn't know what programming language you're using. It determines the language based on the types of files in features/step_definitions or features/support. That's why we added the env.rb file to features/support. If you haven't added it already, do it now so you can see the step definition snippets.

Now run cucumber features/codebreaker_starts_game.feature from the project root, and you'll see the following in the output:[2]

```
Feature: code-breaker starts game

  As a code-breaker
  I want to start a game
  So that I can break the code

  Scenario: start game
    Given I am not yet playing
    When I start a new game
    Then I should see "Welcome to Codebreaker!"
    And I should see "Enter guess:"

1 scenario (1 undefined)
4 steps (3 undefined, 1 passed)
0m0.002s
```

You can implement step definitions for undefined steps with these snippets:

```
When /^I start a new game$/ do
  pending # express the regexp above with the code you wish you had
end

Then /^I should see "([^"]*)"$/ do |arg1|
  pending # express the regexp above with the code you wish you had
end
```

The output starts with the content of the file, followed by a summary that tells us that we have one scenario with four steps, including one passing step and three undefined steps and then code snippets for the remaining undefined steps. So, what just happened?

The argument to the cucumber command was the features/codebreaker_ starts_game.feature file. When Cucumber starts up, it loads up all the Ruby files in the same directory as the file and any of its subdirectories. This includes features/step_definitions/codebreaker_steps.rb, where we copied the step definition earlier.

4.2 Step Definition Methods

We can define steps by calling any of the following methods provided by Cucumber: Given(), When(), Then(), And(), or But(). The last two, And()

---

2. We've suppressed some information from the output to make it easier to read. We'll do this throughout the chapter, so don't be surprised if the output in the book doesn't perfectly match the output you see in the shell.

and But(), take on the meaning of the previous Given(), When(), or Then(), so in this example, the And() on the last line of the scenario is treated as a Then().

In this case, we called the Given() method and passed it a Regexp and a block. Cucumber then stores the block in a hash-like structure with the Regexp as its key.

After loading the Ruby files, Cucumber loads and parses the .feature files, matching the steps in scenarios against the stored step definitions. It does this by searching for a Regexp that matches the step and then executes the block stored with that Regexp as its key.

Given

In our case, when Cucumber sees the Given I am not yet playing step in the scenario, it strips off the *Given* and looks for a Regexp that matches the string I am not yet playing. At this point, we have only one step definition, and its Regexp is /^I am not yet playing$/, so Cucumber executes the associated block from the step definition.

Of course, since there is nothing in the block yet, there is nothing that can go wrong, so the step is considered passing. As it turns out, that's exactly what we want in this case. We don't actually want Given I am not yet playing to do anything. We just want it in the scenario to provide context for the subsequent steps, but we're going to leave the associated block empty.

When

The *When* is where the action is. We need to create a new game and then start it. Here's what that might look like:

```
cb/03/features/step_definitions/codebreaker_steps.rb
```

```
Given /^I am not yet playing$/ do
end

When /^I start a new game$/ do
  Codebreaker::Game.new.start
end
```

At this point, we don't have any application code, so we're just writing *the code we wish we had*. We want to keep it simple, and this is about as simple as it can get.

The Code You Wish You Had

In my early days at Object Mentor I (David) attended a TDD class taught by James Grenning. He was refactoring an existing method, and he wrote a statement that called a method that didn't exist yet, saying "start by writing the code you wish you had."

This was a galvanizing moment for me.

It is common to write the code we wish we had doing TDD. We send a message from the code example to an object that does not have a corresponding method. We let the Ruby interpreter tell us that the method does not exist (red) and then implement that method (green).

Doing the same thing within application code, calling the code we wish we had in one module from another module, was a different matter. It was as though an arbitrary boundary had been lifted and suddenly all of the code was my personal servant, ready and willing to bend to my will. It didn't matter whether we were in a test or in the code being tested. What mattered was that we started from the view of the code that was going to use the new code we were about to write.

Over the years this has permeated my daily practice. It is very liberating, and it results in more usable APIs than I would have come up with starting with the object receiving the message.

In retrospect, this also aligns closely with the outside-in philosophy of BDD. If the goal is to provide great APIs, then the best place to design them is from their consumers.

Now run cucumber features/codebreaker_starts_game.feature again, and you should see the following within the output:

```
Scenario: start game
  Given I am not yet playing
  When I start a new game
    uninitialized constant Codebreaker (NameError)
    ./features/step_definitions/codebreaker_steps.rb:5:in `/^I start a new game$/'
    features/codebreaker_starts_game.feature:9:in `When I start a new game'
  Then I should see "Welcome to Codebreaker!"
  And I should see "Enter guess:"

Failing Scenarios:
cucumber features/codebreaker_starts_game.feature:7 # Scenario: start game
```

```
1 scenario (1 failed)
4 steps (1 failed, 2 undefined, 1 passed)
0m0.003s
```

Cucumber shows us the error message, uninitialized constant Codebreaker (NameError), immediately following the step that caused the error. The summary tells us that there is one failing scenario and one failing step. The scenario is considered failing because it has a failing step.

The error message tells us that we need to create a Codebreaker constant. It's coming from the reference to Codebreaker::Game in the step definition we just wrote, which also calls the start(), so let's go ahead and create that. Create a lib directory with a codebreaker subdirectory, and add a game.rb file in lib/codebreaker with the following:

cb/04/lib/codebreaker/game.rb

```ruby
module Codebreaker
  class Game
    def start
    end
  end
end
```

If you run cucumber now, you'll see the same error because Cucumber isn't loading game.rb yet. The conventional approach to this is to have a file in the lib directory named for the top-level module of the app. In our case, that's codebreaker.rb. Create that file now, with the following:

cb/04/lib/codebreaker.rb

```ruby
require 'codebreaker/game'
```

Now add the following to features/support/env.rb:

cb/04/features/support/env.rb

```ruby
$LOAD_PATH << File.expand_path('../../../lib', __FILE__)
require 'codebreaker'
```

Cucumber will load features/support/env.rb, which now requires lib/codebreaker.rb, which, in turn, requires lib/codebreaker/game.rb, which is where we defined the Codebreaker module with the Game with an empty start() method. If you now run cucumber features/codebreaker_starts_game.feature, you should see some different results:

```
Scenario: start game
  Given I am not yet playing
  When I start a new game
  Then I should see "Welcome to Codebreaker!"
  And I should see "Enter guess:"
```

```
1 scenario (1 undefined)
4 steps (2 undefined, 2 passed)
0m0.002s
```

You can implement step definitions for undefined steps with these snippets:

```
Then /^I should see "([^"]*)"$/ do |arg1|
  pending # express the regexp above with the code you wish you had
end
```

Then

With the second step passing, we can move on to the *Then* steps. The last snippet is a single step definition that will handle both the Then and And steps in the scenario, passing whatever is captured by the ([^\"]*) part of the regular expression to the block as the message parameter.

As for what to write in the block, when we say I should see "Welcome to Codebreaker!", we're really saying I should see "Welcome to Codebreaker!" in the console, and *that* means we need a means of capturing messages that the Game sends to STDOUT.

The trick, of course, is that we're running Cucumber in the console, and it is already using STDOUT. We need a fake object that the Game *thinks* is STDOUT, but it really just captures messages for us so we can set expectations about those messages.

4.3 Test Double

A fake object that pretends to be real object is called a *test double*. You're probably familiar with *stubs* and *mocks*. *Test double* is a generic name for them, along with *fakes*, *spies*, and so on, and so on. You'll read all about test doubles in Chapter 14, *RSpec::Mocks*, on page 179.

Given that we'll use a test double for output, here is what we want the step definition to look like:

cb/06/features/step_definitions/codebreaker_steps.rb

```
Then /^I should see "([^"]*)"$/ do |message|
  output.messages.should include(message)
end
```

Again, we're writing the code we wish we had so that we know what code to add. This line suggests that our fake object should have a messages collection. We'll also want it to have a puts() method that the Game can use.

Here's what that looks like:

`cb/06/features/step_definitions/codebreaker_steps.rb`

```ruby
class Output
  def messages
    @messages ||= []
  end

  def puts(message)
    messages << message
  end
end

def output
  @output ||= Output.new
end
```

The output() method uses a caching technique called *memoization*. The first time output() is called, it creates an Output, stores it in an @output variable, and returns it. If it gets called again, it returns the same Output object.

Now we need to give the Game a reference to the Output. Modify the When step as follows:

`cb/06/features/step_definitions/codebreaker_steps.rb`

```ruby
When /^I start a new game$/ do
  game = Codebreaker::Game.new(output)
  game.start
end
```

Run cucumber after making these modifications and additions to code-breaker_steps.rb. You should see the following output:

```
Scenario: start game
  Given I am not yet playing
  When I start a new game
    wrong number of arguments (1 for 0) (ArgumentError)
```

We need to modify the game to accept the output object passed to new:

`cb/07/lib/codebreaker/game.rb`

```ruby
module Codebreaker
  class Game
    def initialize(output)
    end

    def start
    end
  end
end
```

Now run Cucumber again, and this time you should see this:

```
Scenario: start game
  Given I am not yet playing
  When I start a new game
  Then I should see "Welcome to Codebreaker!"
    expected [] to include "Welcome to Codebreaker!"
```

So far, all the failures we've seen have been because of exceptions and errors. We now have our first logical error, so it's time to add some behavior to our Game. For that we're going to shift gears and jump over to RSpec. Before we do, however, let's review what we've just learned.

4.4 What We've Learned

At this point, we've made our way through the second step in the concentric cycles described in Section 1.5, *The BDD Cycle*, on page 9: we now have a Cucumber step, which is failing with a logical failure. And we've also laid quite a bit of foundation.

We've set up the development environment for the Codebreaker game, with a conventional directory layout for Ruby libraries. We expressed the first feature from the outside using Cucumber, with automatable acceptance criteria using the simple language of Given, When, Then.

So far, we've been describing things from the outside with Cucumber. In the next chapter, we'll begin to work our way from the outside in, using RSpec to drive out behavior of individual objects.

## Chapter 5

Describing Code with RSpec

In the previous chapter, we introduced and used Cucumber to describe the behavior of our Codebreaker game from the outside, at the application level. We wrote step definitions for our first Cucumber feature that will handle the steps in the scenario, and we left off with a failing step: we're expecting Game to send a message to our fake Output, but its array of messages is empty.

In this chapter, we're going to use RSpec to *describe* behavior at a much more granular level: the expected behavior of instances of the Game class.

5.1 Getting Started with RSpec

To get going, create a spec directory, with a subdirectory named codebreaker. Now create a file named game_spec.rb in spec/codebreaker/. As we progress, we'll maintain a parallel structure like this in which each source file (for example, lib/codebreaker/game.rb) has a parallel spec file (for example, spec/codebreaker/game_spec.rb). See the *Joe Asks...* on the next page for more on this. Add the following to game_spec.rb:

```
cb/08/spec/codebreaker/game_spec.rb
Line 1  require 'spec_helper'
     2
     3  module Codebreaker
     4    describe Game do
     5      describe "#start" do
     6        it "sends a welcome message"
     7        it "prompts for the first guess"
     8      end
     9    end
    10  end
```

> ### Joe Asks...
> #### Shouldn't We Avoid a One-to-One Mapping?
>
> Perhaps you've heard that a one-to-one mapping between objects and their specs is a BDD no-no. There is some truth to this, but the devil is in the details.
>
> We want to avoid a strict adherence to a structure in which every object has a single example group and every method has a single code example. That sort of structure leads to long examples that take an object through many phases, setting expectations at several stopping points in each example. Examples like these are difficult to write to begin with and much more difficult to understand and debug later.
>
> A one-to-one mapping of spec-file to application-code-file, however, is not only perfectly fine but actually beneficial. It makes it easier to understand where to find the specs for code you might be looking at. It also makes it easier for tools to automate shortcuts like the one in the RSpec TextMate bundle, which switches between spec-file and application-code-file with Ctrl+Shift+Down.

The first two statements are standard Ruby. We require a file named spec_helper.rb on line 1. We'll actually store that file in the spec directory, which RSpec adds to the global $LOAD_PATH. More on that in a minute.

The second statement declares a Ruby module named Codebreaker. This isn't necessary in order to run the specs, but it provides some conveniences. For example, we don't have to fully qualify Game on line 4.

The describe() method hooks into RSpec's API and returns a subclass of RSpec::Core::ExampleGroup. As its name suggests, this is a group of examples of the expected behavior of an object. If you're accustomed to xUnit tools like Test::Unit, you can think of an ExampleGroup as being akin to a TestCase.

The it() method creates an *example*. Technically, it's an instance of the ExampleGroup returned by describe(), but you really don't need to worry about that at this point. We'll get into the details of the underlying framework in Chapter 12, *Code Examples*, on page 137.

Connect the Specs to the Code

Before we can run this, we need to add the spec_helper.rb required on line 1. Create that now, and add the following:

cb/08/spec/spec_helper.rb

```
require 'codebreaker'
```

Similar to what we did with Cucumber's env.rb in the previous chapter, spec/codebreaker/game_spec.rb requires spec/spec_helper.rb, which requires lib/codebreaker.rb, which, in turn, requires lib/codebreaker/game.rb.

Open a shell and cd to the codebreaker project root directory, and run the game_spec.rb file with the rspec command,[1] like this:

```
rspec spec/codebreaker/game_spec.rb --format doc
```

You should see output similar to this:

```
Codebreaker::Game
  #start
    sends a welcome message (PENDING: Not Yet Implemented)
    prompts for the first guess (PENDING: Not Yet Implemented)

Pending:
  Codebreaker::Game#start sends a welcome message
    # Not Yet Implemented
    # ./spec/codebreaker/game_spec.rb:6
  Codebreaker::Game#start prompts for the first guess
    # Not Yet Implemented
    # ./spec/codebreaker/game_spec.rb:7
```

The --format doc option tells RSpec to format the output using the same nesting we see in the nested describe blocks in the file. We see Codebreaker::Game on the first line because we wrapped describe Game do inside the Codebreaker module.

The second line shows the string we passed to describe(), and the third and fourth lines show the strings we passed to it().

"PENDING: Not Yet Implemented" tells us that we have to implement those examples, which we do by passing a block to the it() method. Without the block, the example is considered pending.

---

1. The rspec command is installed when you install the rspec gem.

After RSpec outputs all the strings we passed to describe() and it(), it lists all the pending examples and their locations. This is followed by a summary that tells us how many examples were run, how many failed, and how many are pending.

5.2 Red: Start with a Failing Code Example

In game_spec.rb, we want to do what we've done in the feature: specify that when we start the game, it sends the right messages to the output. Start by modifying game_spec.rb as follows:

cb/09/spec/codebreaker/game_spec.rb

```
require 'spec_helper'

module Codebreaker
  describe Game do
    describe "#start" do
▶      it "sends a welcome message" do
▶        output = double('output')
▶        game = Game.new(output)
▶
▶        output.should_receive(:puts).with('Welcome to Codebreaker!')
▶
▶        game.start
▶      end

      it "prompts for the first guess"
    end
  end
end
```

Just as we did in the scenario, we want a test double to stand in for the real STDOUT. Instead of rolling our own as we did in the scenario, however, we're using RSpec's dynamic test double framework, RSpec::Mocks,[2] to create a dynamic test double on the first line of the example.

Next, we create a Game object, passing it the test double output we created on the previous line. These first two lines are the givens in this example.

The next line sets up a *message expectation*: an expectation that the output object should receive the puts message with the string "Welcome

---

2. See Chapter 14, *RSpec::Mocks*, on page 179 for more about RSpec::Mocks.

to Codebreaker!" as its only argument. If it does, then the expectation will pass. If not, we'll get a failure.

We send the game the start message on the last line. The intent we're expressing is that when we call game.start, the output should receive puts('Welcome to Codebreaker!').

Now run the rspec command again, but this time use the --color flag:

```
rspec spec --color --format doc
```

```
Codebreaker::Game
  #start
    sends a welcome message (FAILED - 1)
    prompts for the first guess (PENDING: Not Yet Implemented)

Pending:
  Codebreaker::Game#start prompts for the first guess
    # Not Yet Implemented
    # ./spec/codebreaker/game_spec.rb:17

Failures:
  1) Codebreaker::Game#start sends a welcome message
     Failure/Error: output.should_receive(:puts).with('Welcome to Codebreaker!')
     (Double "output").puts("Welcome to Codebreaker!")
         expected: 1 time
         received: 0 times
     # ./spec/codebreaker/game_spec.rb:11

Finished in 0.00143 seconds
2 examples, 1 failure, 1 pending
```

And *voila*! We have *red*, a failing example. Sometimes failures are logical failures, and sometimes they're errors. In this case, we have an error. Regardless, once we have red, we want to get to green.

The summary at the bottom of the output tells us we have one failure and one pending example. On the third line, we see FAILED - 1, which tells us that the example is the first failure recorded, the details of which are listed beginning on the line with 1). If we had more failures, they'd each be numbered in sequence.

5.3 Green: Get the Example to Pass

The failure message tells us that output never received puts. Here's what we need to do to get this example to pass:

```
cb/10/lib/codebreaker/game.rb
```

```
module Codebreaker
  class Game
    def initialize(output)
►     @output = output
    end

    def start
►     @output.puts 'Welcome to Codebreaker!'
    end
  end
end
```

Make those changes and run the rspec command again, and you should see this:

```
Codebreaker::Game
  #start
    sends a welcome message
    prompts for the first guess (PENDING: Not Yet Implemented)

Pending:
  Codebreaker::Game#start prompts for the first guess
    # Not Yet Implemented
    # ./spec/codebreaker/game_spec.rb:14

Finished in 0.00144 seconds
2 examples, 0 failures, 1 pending
```

We have our first passing example! We've gone from red to green. The next step in the cycle is to refactor. We don't really have any duplication yet, so let's see whether we've had any impact on the features:

```
Scenario: start game
  Given I am not yet playing
  When I start a new game
  Then I should see "Welcome to Codebreaker!"
  And I should see "Enter guess:"
    expected ["Welcome to Codebreaker!"] to include "Enter guess:"
```

Progress! Now one of the two *Then*s is passing, so it looks like we're about halfway done with this feature. Actually, we're quite a bit more than halfway done, because, as you'll soon see, all the pieces are already in place for the rest.

Next Step

The following failing step is the next thing to work on: And I should see "Enter guess:". Go ahead and add an example for this behavior to game_spec.rb:

cb/11/spec/codebreaker/game_spec.rb

```ruby
require 'spec_helper'

module Codebreaker
  describe Game do
    describe "#start" do
      it "sends a welcome message" do
        output = double('output')
        game = Game.new(output)

        output.should_receive(:puts).with('Welcome to Codebreaker!')

        game.start
      end

      it "prompts for the first guess" do
        output = double('output')
        game = Game.new(output)

        output.should_receive(:puts).with('Enter guess:')

        game.start
      end
    end
  end
end
```

This is very similar to the first example, but we're expecting a different message. We'll come back and DRY that up in a bit, but first let's get it passing. Run the spec, and watch it fail:

```
Codebreaker::Game
  #start
    sends a welcome message
    prompts for the first guess (FAILED - 1)

Failures:
  1) Codebreaker::Game#start prompts for the first guess
     Failure/Error: game.start
     Double "output" received :puts with unexpected arguments
       expected: ("Enter guess:")
            got: ("Welcome to Codebreaker!")
     # ./lib/codebreaker/game.rb:8:in `start'
     # ./spec/codebreaker/game_spec.rb:22

Finished in 0.00199 seconds
2 examples, 1 failure
```

This time, the output didn't receive puts('Enter guess:'). Resolve that as follows:

```
cb/12/lib/codebreaker/game.rb
```

```ruby
module Codebreaker
  class Game
    def initialize(output)
      @output = output
    end

    def start
      @output.puts 'Welcome to Codebreaker!'
▶     @output.puts 'Enter guess:'
    end
  end
end
```

Run the rspec command:

```
Codebreaker::Game
  #start
    sends a welcome message (FAILED - 1)
    prompts for the first guess (FAILED - 2)

Failures:
  1) Codebreaker::Game#start sends a welcome message
     Failure/Error: game.start
     Double "output" received :puts with unexpected arguments
       expected: ("Welcome to Codebreaker!")
            got: ("Enter guess:")
     # ./lib/codebreaker/game.rb:10:in `start'
     # ./spec/codebreaker/game_spec.rb:12

  2) Codebreaker::Game#start prompts for the first guess
     Failure/Error: game.start
     Double "output" received :puts with unexpected arguments
       expected: ("Enter guess:")
            got: ("Welcome to Codebreaker!")
     # ./lib/codebreaker/game.rb:8:in `start'
     # ./spec/codebreaker/game_spec.rb:21

Finished in 0.00219 seconds
2 examples, 2 failures
```

And *ta-da*! Now not only is the second example still failing, but the first example is *failing as well*! Who'da thunk? This may seem a bit confusing if you've never worked with test doubles and message expectations before, but test doubles are like computers. They are extraordinarily obedient, but they are not all that clever. By default, they will expect exactly what you tell them to expect, nothing more and nothing less.

We've told the double in the first example to expect puts( ) with "Welcome to Codebreaker!" and we've satisfied that requirement, but we've only told it to expect "Welcome to Codebreaker!" It doesn't know anything about "Enter guess:"

Similarly, the double in the second example expects "Enter guess:" but the first message it gets is "Welcome to Codebreaker!"

We could combine these two into a single example, but we like to follow the guideline of "one expectation per example." The rationale here is that if there are two expectations in an example that should both fail given the implementation at that moment, we'll only see the first failure. No sooner do we meet that expectation than we discover that we haven't met the second expectation. If they live in separate examples, then they'll both fail, and that will provide us with more accurate information than if only one of them is failing.

We could also try to break the messages up into different steps, but we've already defined how we want to talk to the game object. So, how can we resolve this?

as_null_object

There are a couple of ways we can go about it, but the simplest way is to tell the double output to only listen for the messages we tell it to expect and ignore any other messages.[3] This is based on the Null Object design pattern described in *Pattern Languages of Program Design 3* [MRB97] and is supported by RSpec's double framework with the as_null_object( ) method:

cb/13/spec/codebreaker/game_spec.rb

```
require 'spec_helper'

module Codebreaker
  describe Game do
    describe "#start" do
      it "sends a welcome message" do
        output = double('output').as_null_object
        game = Game.new(output)

        output.should_receive(:puts).with('Welcome to Codebreaker!')

        game.start
      end
```

---

3. Actually, that's not completely true. Unexpected messages are actually recorded because it is sometimes helpful to include them in failure messages.

```
      it "prompts for the first guess" do
▶       output = double('output').as_null_object
        game = Game.new(output)

        output.should_receive(:puts).with('Enter guess:')

        game.start
      end
    end
  end
end
```

Run the rspec command again, and you should see this:

```
Codebreaker::Game
  #start
    sends a welcome message
    prompts for the first guess

Finished in 0.00174 seconds
2 examples, 0 failures
```

Good news. Both examples are now passing. Now that we have green, it's time to refactor!

5.4 Refactor

In the preface to his seminal book on *Refactoring* [FBB+99], Martin Fowler writes, "Refactoring is the process of changing a software system in such a way that it does not alter the external behavior of the code yet improves its internal structure."

How do we know that we're not changing behavior? We run the examples between every change. If they pass, we've refactored successfully. If any fail, we know that the very last change we made caused a problem, and we either quickly recognize and address the problem or roll back that step to get back to green and try again.

Fowler talks about changing the designs of systems, but on a more granular scale, we want to refactor to, for example, eliminate duplication in the implementation *and* examples. Looking back at game_ spec.rb, we can see that the first two lines of each example are identical. Perhaps you noticed this earlier, but we prefer to refactor *in the green* rather than *in the red*. Also, the intent of the examples is expressed in the last two lines of each.

before(:each)

In this case, we have a very clear break between what is context and what is behavior, so let's take advantage of that and move the context to a block that is executed before each of the examples. Modify game_spec.rb as follows:

cb/14/spec/codebreaker/game_spec.rb

```ruby
require 'spec_helper'

module Codebreaker
  describe Game do
    describe "#start" do
▶     before(:each) do
▶       @output = double('output').as_null_object
▶       @game = Game.new(@output)
▶     end

      it "sends a welcome message" do
▶       @output.should_receive(:puts).with('Welcome to Codebreaker!')
▶       @game.start
      end

      it "prompts for the first guess" do
▶       @output.should_receive(:puts).with('Enter guess:')
▶       @game.start
      end
    end
  end
end
```

Just as you might expect from reading this, the block passed to before(:each) will be run before each example. The before block and the example are executed in the same object, so they have access to the same instance variables.

Adding all of those @ symbols can be tedious and error prone, so RSpec offers an alternative approach.

let(:method) {}

When the code in a before block is only creating instance variables and assigning them values, which is most of the time, we can use RSpec's let() method instead. let() takes a symbol representing a method name and a block, which represents the implementation of that method.

Here's the same example, using let():

```
cb/15/spec/codebreaker/game_spec.rb
```
```
require 'spec_helper'

module Codebreaker
  describe Game do
    describe "#start" do
      let(:output) { double('output').as_null_object }
      let(:game)   { Game.new(output) }

      it "sends a welcome message" do
        output.should_receive(:puts).with('Welcome to Codebreaker!')
        game.start
      end

      it "prompts for the first guess" do
        output.should_receive(:puts).with('Enter guess:')
        game.start
      end
    end
  end
end
```

The first call to let() defines a memoized output() method that returns a double object. Memoized means that the first time the method is invoked, the return value is cached and that same value is returned every subsequent time the method is invoked within the same scope. That fact doesn't affect our current example, but it will come in handy a bit later.

Now run the feature again:

```
Feature: code-breaker starts game

  As a code-breaker
  I want to start a game
  So that I can break the code

  Scenario: start game
    Given I am not yet playing
    When I start a new game
    Then I should see "Welcome to Codebreaker!"
    And I should see "Enter guess:"

1 scenario (1 passed)
4 steps (4 passed)
0m0.003s
```

And *voilà*! We now have our first passing code examples and our first passing feature. There were a lot of steps to get there, but in practice this all really takes just a few minutes, even with all the wiring and require statements.

We've also set up quite a bit of infrastructure. You'll see, as we move along, that there is less and less new material needed to add more features, code examples, and application code. It just builds gradually on what we've already developed.

Now that we have a passing feature, it would be nice to see it in action. For that, we'll need to create and execute a simple script. Create a bin in the project root directory (sibling to lib and spec), and add a bin/codebreaker file. If you're on a *nix system, enter this code in that file:

cb/15/bin/codebreaker
```
#!/usr/bin/env ruby
$LOAD_PATH.unshift File.expand_path('../../lib', __FILE__)
require 'codebreaker'

game = Codebreaker::Game.new(STDOUT)
game.start
```

Windows users use the same script without the first line and also add bin/codebreaker.bat with the following:

cb/15/bin/codebreaker.bat
```
@"ruby.exe" "%~dpn0" %*
```

If you're on *nix, now run chmod +x bin/codebreaker so we can execute it, and then run this:

```
$ bin/codebreaker
Welcome to Codebreaker!
Enter guess:
```

Now look at that! Who knew that this little bit of code was actually going to start to make something work? Of course, our Codebreaker game just says hello and then climbs back in its cave, so we have a ways to go before you'll want to show this off to all your friends.

In the next chapter, we'll start to get down to the real fun, submitting guesses and having the game score them. But before we move on, let's review what we've done thus far.

5.5 What We've Learned

We started this chapter with a logical failure in a Cucumber scenario. This was our cue to jump from the outer circle (Cucumber) to the inner circle (RSpec) of the BDD cycle.

We then followed the familiar TDD red/green/refactor cycle using RSpec. Once we had a passing code example, we reran the Cucumber scenario. We saw that we had gotten our first Then step to pass, but there was one more that was failing, so we jumped back down to RSpec, went through another red/green/refactor cycle, and now the whole scenario was passing.

This is the BDD cycle. Driving development from the outside in, starting with business-facing scenarios in Cucumber and working our way inward to the underlying objects with RSpec.

The material in the next chapter, submitting guesses, is going to present some interesting challenges. It will expose you to some really cool features in Cucumber, as well as some thought-provoking discussion about the relationship between Cucumber scenarios and RSpec code examples. So, take a few minutes break, drink up some brain juice, and meet us at the top of the next chapter.

## Chapter 6

Adding New Features

Welcome back! We left off with the Codebreaker game inviting us to guess the secret code but then leaving us hanging at the command line. The next feature we're going to tackle is submitting a guess and getting feedback from the Codebreaker game as to how close the guess is to breaking the secret code.

This feature is going to introduce an algorithm for marking a guess. This is where things start to get really interesting because algorithms tend to cover a lot of possible cases with a small amount of code. As you'll see, we're going to have a lot more scenarios and specs than we did for the Code-breaker starts game feature. Luckily, we have tools in both RSpec and Cucumber to keep things readable and DRY.

6.1 Scenario Outlines in Cucumber

Here's the Cucumber feature we wrote back in Section 3.3, *Planning the First Iteration*, on page 26:

cb/15/features/codebreaker_submits_guess.feature

```
Feature: code-breaker submits guess

  The code-breaker submits a guess of four numbers.  The game marks the guess
  with + and - signs.

  For each number in the guess that matches the number and position of a number
  in the secret code, the mark includes one + sign. For each number in the guess
  that matches the number but not the position of a number in the secret code,
  the mark includes one - sign.

  Scenario Outline: submit guess
    Given the secret code is "<code>"
```

```
When I guess "<guess>"
Then the mark should be "<mark>"

Scenarios: no matches
    | code | guess | mark |
    | 1234 | 5555  |      |

Scenarios: 1 number correct
    | code | guess | mark |
    | 1234 | 1555  | +    |
    | 1234 | 2555  | -    |

Scenarios: 2 numbers correct
    | code | guess | mark |
    | 1234 | 5254  | ++   |
    | 1234 | 5154  | +-   |
    | 1234 | 2545  | --   |

Scenarios: 3 numbers correct
    | code | guess | mark |
    | 1234 | 5234  | +++  |
    | 1234 | 5134  | ++-  |
    | 1234 | 5124  | +--  |
    | 1234 | 5123  | ---  |

Scenarios: all numbers correct
    | code | guess | mark |
    | 1234 | 1234  | ++++ |
    | 1234 | 1243  | ++-- |
    | 1234 | 1423  | +--- |
    | 1234 | 4321  | ---- |
```

The narrative is self-explanatory. After that, we use a scenario outline, which we introduced in Section 3.3, *Scenario Outlines*, on page 31. Briefly, the rows in the scenarios tables provide data for the <placeholders> in the scenario outline. To figure out what our next step is, run the Code-breaker submits guess feature with the following command:

```
cucumber features/codebreaker_submits_guess.feature
```

As we saw earlier, the output includes the contents of the file listed previously, plus a summary and code snippets for any undefined steps. Here is the summary and just a few of the code snippets:

```
14 scenarios (14 undefined)
42 steps (42 undefined)
0m0.031s
```

You can implement step definitions **for** undefined steps with these snippets:

```
Given /^the secret code is "([^"]*)"$/ do |arg1|
  pending # express the regexp above with the code you wish you had
end

When /^I guess "([^"]*)"$/ do |arg1|
  pending # express the regexp above with the code you wish you had
end

Then /^the mark should be "([^"]*)"$/ do |arg1|
  pending # express the regexp above with the code you wish you had
end
```

The summary says we have fourteen scenarios, one for each nonheader row in the tables in each group of scenarios. All fourteen scenarios are considered undefined because we don't have step definitions defined for them. So now, with that help from Cucumber, let's write some step definitions.

Step Definitions

Step definitions for scenario outlines and tables are just like the step definitions we learned about in Chapter 4, *Automating Features with Cucumber*, on page 35. We'll still provide regular expressions that capture input data and a block of code that interacts with the application code.

Copy the first snippet into features/step_definitions/codebreaker_steps.rb, and modify it as follows:

```
cb/16/features/step_definitions/codebreaker_steps.rb
Given /^the secret code is "([^"]*)"$/ do |secret|
  game = Codebreaker::Game.new(output)
  game.start(secret)
end
```

The Regexp captures a group of characters in quotes. This will capture the code (1234, for example) and pass it to the body of the step definition. The first line of the body should look familiar, because it is just like the first step in I start a new game. Then the last line passes in the secret code from the match group.

Now run cucumber again, and you'll see output including this:

```
Scenarios: no matches
  | code | guess | mark |
  | 1234 | 5555  |      |
  wrong number of arguments (1 for 0) (ArgumentError)
  ./features/step_definitions/codebreaker_steps.rb:20:in `start'
```

You should see the ArgumentError for every scenario. This is actually good news, because the error tells us that everything is wired up correctly, and we now know what we have to do next: get the start() method on Game to accept the secret code as an argument.

6.2 Responding to Change

At this point, all the RSpec code examples are passing, but we have failing Cucumber scenarios. We're "in the meantime," so to speak, where changing requirements from the outside are rendering our requirements on the inside incorrect.

Our new step definition wants Game.start() to accept the secret code as an argument, but our RSpec examples assume that start() does not take any arguments. If we just add the argument to start(), then the specs fail with an argument error as well, but with 0 for 1 instead of 1 for 0. To keep the specs passing while we're making changes to support the scenarios, modify start() to accept an argument with a default value, like so:

`cb/17/lib/codebreaker/game.rb`

```
► def start(secret=nil)
    @output.puts 'Welcome to Codebreaker!'
    @output.puts 'Enter guess:'
  end
```

Run the specs, and they should all still pass. Now run the codebreaker_submits_guess scenarios, and you should see this:

```
14 scenarios (14 undefined)
42 steps (28 undefined, 14 passed)
0m0.028s
```

At this point, the scenarios are either passing or undefined, but none is failing, and the specs are passing. Now we can go in and modify the specs to pass a secret code to start(), like this:

`cb/18/spec/codebreaker/game_spec.rb`

```
  it "sends a welcome message" do
    output.should_receive(:puts).with('Welcome to Codebreaker!')
► game.start('1234')
  end

  it "prompts for the first guess" do
    output.should_receive(:puts).with('Enter guess:')
► game.start('1234')
  end
```

Run the examples, and watch them pass. Now modify start() again, this time removing the default value from the method definition:

cb/18/lib/codebreaker/game.rb

```
def start(secret)
  @output.puts 'Welcome to Codebreaker!'
  @output.puts 'Enter guess:'
end
```

Run the examples one more time, and they should still pass. Now run the codebreaker_submits_guess scenarios again, and they should still be passing or undefined. But what about the codebreaker_starts_game scenario?

Assess the Impact on Other Features

Now that we don't have any failures in the feature we're working on or the specs, run cucumber with no arguments to run all (both) of the features. The output should include this:

```
When I start a new game
  wrong number of arguments (0 for 1) (ArgumentError)
  ./features/step_definitions/codebreaker_steps.rb:25:in `start'
```

The step definition for When I start a new game is still calling start() with no argument. Modify that as follows:

cb/19/features/step_definitions/codebreaker_steps.rb

```
When /^I start a new game$/ do
  game = Codebreaker::Game.new(output)
  game.start('1234')
end
```

Now all the specs should be passing, and all the scenarios are either passing or undefined.

A Small Change Goes a Long Way

We still have twenty-eight steps undefined, but we now have fourteen passing steps in codebreaker_submits_guess.feature. These are all the Given steps. Remember, each row in the tables represents a separate scenario. Until we get to the point where the failures are logical failures, as opposed to runtime errors due to structural discrepancies, a small change is likely to impact all of the scenarios at once.

The remaining undefined steps are the When steps that actually submit the guess and the Then steps that set the expectation that the game should mark the guess. Copy the snippet for the When step into code-breaker_steps.rb, and modify it as follows:

cb/20/features/step_definitions/codebreaker_steps.rb

```
When /^I guess "([^"]*)"$/ do |guess|
  @game.guess(guess)
end
```

Similar to the Given step, we capture the guess in the regular expression and pass it on to the Game, this time via the guess() method. This new step is expecting an @game instance variable, so modify the Given step as follows:

cb/20/features/step_definitions/codebreaker_steps.rb

```
Given /^the secret code is "([^"]*)"$/ do |secret|
▶   @game = Codebreaker::Game.new(output)
▶   @game.start(secret)
end
```

Run the features again, and you'll see this in the output:

```
Scenarios: no matches
  | code | guess | mark |
  | 1234 | 5555  |      |
  undefined method `guess' for #<Codebreaker::Game:0x10219f728> (NoMethodError)
```

We wrote the *code we wish we had*, but we don't have it! The Game has no guess() method, so we'll need to add one. Add this to game.rb:

cb/21/lib/codebreaker/game.rb

```
  class Game
    def initialize(output)
      @output = output
    end

    def start(secret)
      @output.puts 'Welcome to Codebreaker!'
      @output.puts 'Enter guess:'
    end

▶   def guess(guess)
▶   end
  end
```

Now run the scenarios:

```
14 scenarios (14 undefined)
42 steps (14 undefined, 28 passed)
0m0.024s
```

You can implement step definitions for undefined steps with these snippets:

```
Then /^the mark should be "([^"]*)"$/ do |arg1|
  pending # express the regexp above with the code you wish you had
end
```

Again, there are no failures, but now there are only fourteen steps undefined. These are the Then steps. Copy the last snippet to codebreaker_steps.rb, and modify it like this:

> cb/22/features/step_definitions/codebreaker_steps.rb

```
Then /^the mark should be "([^"]*)"$/ do |mark|
  output.messages.should include(mark)
end
```

Now run the scenarios again, and you should see this:

```
Scenarios: no matches
  | code | guess | mark |
  | 1234 | 5555  |      |
  expected ["Welcome to Codebreaker!", "Enter guess:"] to include ""
          (Spec::Expectations::ExpectationNotMetError)
```

Fantastic! Instead of an exception or a structural error, we're getting a logical failure on the Then step. Even though this is happening in all fourteen scenarios, this is good news because we know that we have all the step definitions we need and everything is wired up correctly. Now it's time to drill down to RSpec and drive out the solution with isolated code examples.

6.3 What We've Learned

In this chapter, we explored scenario outlines in Cucumber, which allow us to express groups of similar scenarios in a readable, scannable, and DRY format.

We also added a new feature to an existing code base. In doing so, we introduced a change that would lead to many failures at once if we had used brute force and just made the change: adding a parameter to a method signature. Instead of brute force, we assigned a default value to the parameter. This kept the existing specs passing and allowed us to make progress on the Cucumber scenarios. We later removed the default parameter, once it became obsolete.

Although this is just one simple technique, it demonstrates and reinforces the notion that code is always in motion, and we are able to keep it moving with confidence if we keep the examples passing.

## Chapter 7

Specifying an Algorithm

The RSpec code examples we wrote for the Codebreaker starts game feature specified a simple responsibility of the Game: send messages to the output. The next responsibility is more complex. We need to specify the algorithm we're going to use to mark a guess submitted by the codebreaker.

We have fourteen scenarios for this, all of which are failing because the marking algorithm hasn't been written yet. They all have to pass for this feature to be done, so no single scenario is more important than the next. So, which one should we start with?

7.1 Begin with the Simplest Example

From the perspective of business value, the order in which we get the scenarios *within a feature* to pass doesn't really matter. This suggests that we should pick examples that will make it easy for us to progress in small steps.

At any point in this part of the process, we want to find the example that we think would be the simplest to implement. With no examples written yet, the simplest example is probably one in which there are no matches in the guess, so the mark is empty. As it happens, that's the first scenario in the feature as well, but even if it weren't, this would be a good place to start.

Make the following changes to game_spec.rb:

cb/24/spec/codebreaker/game_spec.rb

```ruby
require 'spec_helper'

module Codebreaker
  describe Game do
►   let(:output) { double('output').as_null_object }
►   let(:game)   { Game.new(output) }

    describe "#start" do
      it "sends a welcome message" do
        output.should_receive(:puts).with('Welcome to Codebreaker!')
        game.start('1234')
      end

      it "prompts for the first guess" do
        output.should_receive(:puts).with('Enter guess:')
        game.start('1234')
      end
    end

►   describe "#guess" do
►     context "with no matches" do
►       it "sends a mark with ''" do
►         game.start('1234')
►         output.should_receive(:puts).with('')
►         game.guess('5555')
►       end
►     end
►   end
  end
end
```

We moved the let() statements up a block so they are in scope in the new example. See Section 12.6, *Nested Example Groups*, on page 153 for more about nested example groups and scopes.

The output allows the messages it receives when we call start() because it uses as_null_object. The only message it cares about is the one we specify in the example—that it should receive puts() with an empty string.

Run the rspec command, and you should see this:

```
1) Codebreaker::Game #guess with no matches sends a mark with ''
   Failure/Error: output.should_receive(:puts).with('')
   (Double "output").puts("")
       expected: 1 time
       received: 0 times
   # ./spec/codebreaker/game_spec.rb:27
```

The failure message tells us that output received the messages sent when we called start, but not the empty string we're expecting now. To get this to pass, modify the guess() method as follows:

cb/25/lib/codebreaker/game.rb

```
    def guess(guess)
      @output.puts ''
    end
```

Run the specs again, and they should pass. Now go back and run the features, and you should see that the first scenario is passing, but the rest are failing. One down, thirteen to go.

With the simplest example passing, what example should we write next?

Follow Up with the Next Simplest Example

Again, we want to find an example that would fail given the current implementation and be simple to implement. Given that we started with no matches, the next simplest example would probably be one match, but which kind? We can have an exact match, which is when a number in the guess is in the secret code in the same position, or a number match, which is when a number in the guess is in the secret code but not in the same position.

Thinking briefly about the implementation of each, one might argue that the exact match would be easier to implement because we have to examine only one position in the secret code. Of course, one might also argue that, given the fact that we don't have any examples with exact matches right now, we can determine a number match by simply asking whether the secret contains a specific number. We're going to go with the latter, but please feel free to experiment with this after you've gone through the chapter.

Add the following example:

cb/26/spec/codebreaker/game_spec.rb

```
    describe "#guess" do
      context "with no matches" do
        it "sends a mark with ''" do
          game.start('1234')
          output.should_receive(:puts).with('')
          game.guess('5555')
        end
      end
```

```
    ▶            context "with 1 number match" do
    ▶              it "sends a mark with '-'" do
    ▶                game.start('1234')
    ▶                output.should_receive(:puts).with('-')
    ▶                game.guess('2555')
    ▶              end
    ▶            end
               end
```

Run the specs, and the new example fails with this:

```
1) Codebreaker::Game #guess with 1 number match sends a mark with '-'
   Failure/Error: output.should_receive(:puts).with('-')
   Double "output" received :puts with unexpected arguments
     expected: ("-")
          got: ("")
   # ./spec/codebreaker/game_spec.rb:34
```

The current implementation of guess always sends an empty string to the output. We still want it to do that for the first example, but this new example is expecting a minus sign. Here's a simple solution:

cb/27/lib/codebreaker/game.rb

```
     def start(secret)
  ▶    @secret = secret
       @output.puts 'Welcome to Codebreaker!'
       @output.puts 'Enter guess:'
     end

     def guess(guess)
  ▶    if @secret.include?(guess[0])
  ▶      @output.puts '-'
  ▶    else
         @output.puts ''
  ▶    end
     end
   end
```

The code should be self-explanatory. Run the examples, and you should see them pass. Admittedly, this works only because the matching number in the example is in the first position (index 0) in the guess. If it were anywhere else, our implementation would have to use a different index.

This is one of those moments that makes people who are new to TDD uncomfortable. We know with some certainty that this is not the implementation we want when we're finished, and we might even have a good idea of what that implementation should be. The problem is that we don't have enough examples to really specify what this code *should* do, so any code that we write right now would be speculative.

This should all make sense by the time we get to the end of the chapter, but for now, let's move on to the next step. We just made a failing example pass, so it's time to refactor.

7.2 Refactor to Remove Duplication

As we discussed earlier, refactoring is a technique for improving a design without changing behavior. There are many ways in which we can improve a design. The most common is to remove duplication, so let's start with that. There are two lines in the guess method that are sending messages to output. Let's start by extracting that to a single statement. Modify the guess() method as follows:

cb/28/lib/codebreaker/game.rb

```ruby
    def guess(guess)
      if @secret.include?(guess[0])
►       mark = '-'
      else
►       mark = ''
      end
►     @output.puts mark
    end
```

Now run the specs, and make sure they all still pass. Then, run the scenarios, and you should see that we have two of them passing. Progress!

Looking back at the spec, we have an example for no matches and one number match, so let's add an example for an exact match:

cb/30/spec/codebreaker/game_spec.rb

```ruby
    describe "#guess" do
      context "with no matches" do
        it "sends a mark with ''" do
          game.start('1234')
          output.should_receive(:puts).with('')
          game.guess('5555')
        end
      end

      context "with 1 number match" do
        it "sends a mark with '-'" do
          game.start('1234')
          output.should_receive(:puts).with('-')
          game.guess('2555')
        end
      end
```

```
►        context "with 1 exact match" do
►          it "sends a mark with '+'" do
►            game.start('1234')
►            output.should_receive(:puts).with('+')
►            game.guess('1555')
►          end
►        end
       end
```

Run the specs, and you should see the new example fail with the following message:

```
Failure/Error: output.should_receive(:puts).with('+')
Double "output" received :puts with unexpected arguments
  expected: ("+")
       got: ("-")
# ./spec/codebreaker/game_spec.rb:42
```

We got a - instead of a + because the current implementation gives us a - if the first number in the guess is anywhere in the code. We need to treat an exact match differently from a number match. Modify the guess() method as follows:

cb/31/lib/codebreaker/game.rb

```
    def guess(guess)
►     if guess[0] == @secret[0]
►       mark = '+'
►     elsif @secret.include?(guess[0])
        mark = '-'
      else
        mark = ''
      end
      @output.puts mark
    end
```

Run the specs, and they should all pass, so let's look for more refactoring opportunities.

7.3 Refactor to Express Intent

The changes we just made didn't add any new duplication, but removing duplication is not the only way to improve a design. Take a look at the first and third lines of the guess() method. Do they express intent well? Not really. The first line is asking whether the first number is an exact match, and the third line is asking whether it is a number match. We know that's what it means now because we just implemented the code, but it might not be so clear to anyone else.

Here is a great opportunity to use the Extract Method refactoring to introduce abstractions that more clearly express the intent of the guess() method. You may think of classes and interfaces when we use the word *abstraction*, but here's another way to look at it: names are abstractions. That applies to names of systems, components, packages, namespaces, classes, methods, and even variable names.

With that context, let's extract an exact_match? method, like this:

`cb/32/lib/codebreaker/game.rb`

```
    def guess(guess)
▶     if exact_match?(guess, 0)
        mark = '+'
      elsif @secret.include?(guess[0])
        mark = '-'
      else
        mark = ''
      end
      @output.puts mark
    end

▶   def exact_match?(guess, index)
▶     guess[index] == @secret[index]
▶   end
```

Run the specs, and they should still pass. Next, we'll extract a number_match? method:

`cb/325/lib/codebreaker/game.rb`

```
    def guess(guess)
      if exact_match?(guess, 0)
        mark = '+'
▶     elsif number_match?(guess, 0)
        mark = '-'
      else
        mark = ''
      end
      @output.puts mark
    end

    def exact_match?(guess, index)
      guess[index] == @secret[index]
    end

▶   def number_match?(guess, index)
▶     @secret.include?(guess[index])
▶   end
```

Run the specs again. They should still pass. Now read the code in the guess method out loud. Paraphrasing in English, it sounds something like this: "If we have an exact match in the first position, the mark is a single plus sign. Else, if we have a number match in the first position, the mark is a single minus sign. Else, the mark is empty."

That is what we mean when we talk about self-documenting code.

Gradually Add Complexity

Run the scenarios, and you'll see that three are passing now. The eleven failing scenarios involve more than one match, so we'll move on to multiple matches. Add the following context and example to game_spec.rb:

cb/33/spec/codebreaker/game_spec.rb

```ruby
context "with 2 number matches" do
  it "sends a mark with '--'" do
    game.start('1234')
    output.should_receive(:puts).with('--')
    game.guess('2355')
  end
end
```

Run the specs, and you should see this new example fail with the following message:

```
1) Codebreaker::Game #guess with 2 number matches sends a mark with '--'
   Failure/Error: output.should_receive(:puts).with('--')
   Double "output" received :puts with unexpected arguments
     expected: ("--")
          got: ("-")
   # ./spec/codebreaker/game_spec.rb:49
```

We're getting one minus sign instead of the two that we were expecting because the implementation only deals with the number in the first position, indicated by the index 0 that we're passing to number_match? and exact_match?. Modify the guess method as follows:

cb/34/lib/codebreaker/game.rb

```ruby
    def guess(guess)
►     mark = ''
►     (0..3).each do |index|
        if exact_match?(guess, index)
►         mark << '+'
        elsif number_match?(guess, index)
►         mark << '-'
        end
►     end
      @output.puts mark
    end
```

First, we declare a mark variable and assign it a value of empty string. We then iterate through the four indices representing the positions in the guess. Then, instead of assigning values to mark in the loop, we append to the same string. We're also able to remove the else branch in the conditional because there's no need to append an empty string.

Run the specs, and they should all pass. Run the scenarios, and you should see that twelve are passing, leaving only three failing scenarios to go. The failure messages include the following:

```
expected ["Welcome to Codebreaker!", "Enter guess:", "-+"] to include "+-"

expected ["Welcome to Codebreaker!", "Enter guess:", "-++"] to include "++-"

expected ["Welcome to Codebreaker!", "Enter guess:", "--+"] to include "+--"
```

We want the plus signs to appear before the minus signs, but each of these failures are because of the minus signs showing up first. Let's add an RSpec example that exposes this:

cb/35/spec/codebreaker/game_spec.rb

```ruby
context "with 1 number match and 1 exact match (in that order)" do
  it "sends a mark with '+-'" do
    game.start('1234')
    output.should_receive(:puts).with('+-')
    game.guess('2535')
  end
end
```

The 2 in the first position of the guess is a number match, so it gets a minus sign. The 3 in the third position is an exact match, so it gets a plus sign. Run the specs, and this last example fails the same way as the scenario:

```
1) Codebreaker::Game #guess with 1 number match and 1 exact match (in that order)
     sends a mark with '+-'
   Failure/Error: output.should_receive(:puts).with('+-')
   Double "output" received :puts with unexpected arguments
     expected: ("+-")
          got: ("-+")
   # ./spec/codebreaker/game_spec.rb:57
```

To get this to pass, we have to make sure all the plus signs come before the minus signs. One approach to this would be to split the iteration into two, one that adds plus signs for the exact matches and one that adds minus signs for the number matches.

Modify the guess() method as follows:

`cb/37/lib/codebreaker/game.rb`

```ruby
def guess(guess)
  mark = ''
  (0..3).each do |index|
    if exact_match?(guess, index)
      mark << '+'
    end
  end
  (0..3).each do |index|
    if number_match?(guess, index)
      mark << '-'
    end
  end
  @output.puts mark
end
```

Run the specs, and you'll see that in addition to our last example still failing, we've also introduced a second failure:

```
Codebreaker::Game
  #start
    sends a welcome message
    prompts for the first guess
  #guess
    with no matches
      sends a mark with ''
    with 1 number match
      sends a mark with '-'
    with 1 exact match
      sends a mark with '+' (FAILED - 1)
    with 2 number matches
      sends a mark with '--'
    with 1 number match and 1 exact match (in that order)
      sends a mark with '+-' (FAILED - 2)

1) Codebreaker::Game #guess with 1 exact match sends a mark with '+'
   Failure/Error: output.should_receive(:puts).with('+')
   Double "output" received :puts with unexpected arguments
     expected: ("+")
          got: ("+-")
   # ./spec/codebreaker/game_spec.rb:40

2) Codebreaker::Game #guess with 1 number match and 1 exact match (in that order)
      sends a mark with '+-'
   Failure/Error: output.should_receive(:puts).with('+-')
   Double "output" received :puts with unexpected arguments
     expected: ("+-")
          got: ("+--")
   # ./spec/codebreaker/game_spec.rb:56
```

```
Finished in 0.00237 seconds
7 examples, 2 failures
```

Learning from Rapid Feedback

One of the benefits of progressing in small steps is that when we introduce a new failure, we know exactly what we just did, so we have context in which we can analyze the failure. Both failures are because of one more minus sign than we were expecting in the mark. What about the change we just made would cause that to happen?

If you go back and look at the guess() method before we broke the single iterator into two, the block had an if, elsif, else structure. The elsif branch was the one that was adding minus signs to the mark, and it was executed only if the if branch hadn't already been executed.

Now take a look at the number_match? method. Can you see what's missing? It only looks to see whether the number is in the secret code, but it doesn't ensure that it's not an exact match! A number match is a number in the guess that appears in the secret code in *any other position*. We got the definition of number_match? wrong, so let's fix it. Update the number_match? to reflect this learning:

cb/38/lib/codebreaker/game.rb

```
    def number_match?(guess, index)
      @secret.include?(guess[index]) && !exact_match?(guess, index)
    end
```

Run the specs now, and they'll all pass. Run the scenarios again, and you'll see that they are all passing as well! This feature is *done*!

Not so fast! We skipped over the refactoring step in the last red/green/refactor cycle, so we should review the implementation of the marking algorithm to make sure it is clear and expresses intent well. As it turns out, there is quite a bit that we can do to improve its expressiveness, so we'll save that for the next chapter. In the meantime, let's review what we've learned so far.

7.4   What We've Learned

In this chapter, we drove out the implementation of an algorithm in small steps. We still have some refactoring to do to make it as simple and expressive as we'd like, but the current implementation does pass all of its scenarios and all of its specs.

We started with an example that we believed would be the simplest to implement. We followed that with the next simplest example, and then the next, and so on.

We also learned that we benefit from working in small steps because we know exactly what we just did when we introduce a failure. If we didn't run the specs right after splitting up the iterator, we might not have learned about the problem we introduced until much later, when it would be more difficult to track it down.

In the next chapter, we'll dig a bit deeper into refactoring, exploring techniques and tools we use to refactor with confidence!

## Chapter 8

Refactoring with Confidence

In his book *Refactoring* [FBB+99], Martin Fowler describes refactoring as "a change made to the internal structure of software to make it easier to understand and cheaper to modify without changing its observable behavior."

In this chapter, we're going to examine the guess method that we left in the previous chapter and look for ways we can improve it with the goal of making it easier to understand and cheaper to modify. To do that, we need to recognize problems when we see them. And for that, one must have a nose for smelly code!

8.1 Sniffing Out Code Smells

A *code smell*, according to the c2 wiki,[1] is "a hint that something has gone wrong somewhere in your code." The *Refactoring* book catalogs and categorizes several of them. We're not going to go through every code smell, but we'll examine the guess method and see what smells we might discover. Here is how we left it:

```
cb/38/lib/codebreaker/game.rb
```

```ruby
def guess(guess)
  mark = ''
  (0..3).each do |index|
    if exact_match?(guess, index)
      mark << '+'
    end
  end
```

---

1. http://c2.com/xp/CodeSmell.html

```
    (0..3).each do |index|
      if number_match?(guess, index)
        mark << '-'
      end
    end
    @output.puts mark
end
```

If you just finished reading the previous chapter, this should make pretty good sense to you without much study. Start with an empty string for the mark. For each number in the guess, add a plus sign to the mark if it is an exact match. Then, for each number in the guess, add a minus sign if it is a number match. Then output the result.

Of course, when we explain it like that, it is clear that this method is procedural code embedded in an object structure. Generally speaking, we want to avoid procedural code because it has a tendency to grow in complexity and become progressively difficult to understand and maintain.

If you're familiar with code smells, you may recognize two of them in this method: Temporary Variable and Long Method. Both of these smells are related to procedural methods like this.

Temporary Variable

The mark variable in the guess method is the temporary variable we're talking about. The problem with temp variables is that they tend to change state within a method. As a method grows longer, this makes it easier to introduce bugs based on poor understanding of the state of that variable at any given moment in the method.

Right now, the mark variable has eight opportunities to change state before we send it to the output. If anything goes wrong in either of the iterators, it will be difficult to track down which iteration of which iterator.

We'll clean this up during our refactoring this chapter.

Long Method

A long method is a method that does more than one thing. Think of it as the Single Responsibility Principle applied to a method. The motivation is the same as SRP: we want methods to have only one reason to change as requirements of a system change so that we can make changes in small steps and with confidence.

8.2 One Step at a Time

The refactoring we're about to engage in has many steps. We're going to go one step at a time, running the specs between each step to ensure that we're preserving behavior as we move.

Clarify the Smell

Before we can refactor away the procedural nature of a method, it is sometimes helpful to clarify that nature first. Let's start by rephrasing the procedure a bit:

- Count up the exact matches.

- Count up the number matches.

- Add a plus sign for each exact match.

- Add a minus sign for each number match.

We'll start by clarifying the first step: counting up the exact matches. Make the following modifications to the guess() method:

```
cb/39/lib/codebreaker/game.rb
    def guess(guess)
►     exact_match_count = 0
      mark = ''
      (0..3).each do |index|
        if exact_match?(guess, index)
►         exact_match_count += 1
        end
      end
      (0..3).each do |index|
        if number_match?(guess, index)
          mark << '-'
        end
      end
►     @output.puts '+'*exact_match_count + mark
    end
```

Now we'll introduce a new exact_match_count variable and assign it a value of 0. We increment its value in the first iterator and then use the * operator on the last line to build a string of n plus signs.

A Circuitous Path

Wait. Didn't we just identify temporary variables as a code smell? Why yes, we did. Refactoring is not always linear in that some steps seem to take us further away from our goal even when those steps are in service of our goal. Temporary variables can be a very useful tool in the process of refactoring. . . temporarily. By the time we're done, we'll have eliminated them.

Run the specs, and they all should pass. On to the next step. We'll do the same thing with the number matches:

cb/391/lib/codebreaker/game.rb

```ruby
    def guess(guess)
      exact_match_count = 0
▶     number_match_count = 0
      (0..3).each do |index|
        if exact_match?(guess, index)
          exact_match_count += 1
        end
      end
      (0..3).each do |index|
        if number_match?(guess, index)
▶         number_match_count += 1
        end
      end
▶     @output.puts '+'*exact_match_count + '-'*number_match_count
    end
```

Again, we introduce a temp variable, increment its value in the second iterator, and then use it to build the string on the last line. We don't need the mark variable any longer, so we've removed it. Run the specs, and they should still pass. On to the next step: extract the calculation of exact_match_count to a separate method.

Extract Method

The Extract Method refactoring is a great tool for improving a long method. The process is quite simple. We create a new empty method with the name we want to use, move the code from the source method to the target method, and adjust as necessary. Here is the result:

cb/392/lib/codebreaker/game.rb

```ruby
    def guess(guess)
      number_match_count = 0
      (0..3).each do |index|
        if number_match?(guess, index)
          number_match_count += 1
        end
      end
▶     @output.puts '+'*exact_match_count + '-'*number_match_count
    end
```

```
►     def exact_match_count
►       exact_match_count = 0
►       (0..3).each do |index|
►         if exact_match?(guess, index)
►           exact_match_count += 1
►         end
►       end
►       exact_match_count
►     end
```

We created a new method named exact_match_count. Then we moved the declaration of the exact_match_count temp variable to the top of the new method, followed by the first iterator from the guess method. Then we return the value of the temp variable at the end of the method. The last line of the guess() method didn't change, but its reference to exact_match_count now points to the method instead of a local, temp variable.

Run the specs, and you'll see several failures like this one:

```
1) Codebreaker::Game #guess with no matches sends a mark with ''
   Failure/Error: game.guess('5555')
   wrong number of arguments (0 for 1)
   # ./lib/codebreaker/game.rb:30:in `guess'
```

Run the specs with the --backtrace flag, like this:

```
rspec spec --backtrace
```

This tells RSpec to print out a full backtrace for each failure. In this case, the first two lines are the same in each backtrace, and they point us to the third line of the new exact_match_count() method. There is no guess variable in the scope of the method, so it finds the guess() method on the object, which requires a single argument.

To resolve this error, let's pass the guess from the guess() method to the exact_match_count() method, like this:

cb/393/lib/codebreaker/game.rb

```
    def guess(guess)
      number_match_count = 0
      (0..3).each do |index|
        if number_match?(guess, index)
          number_match_count += 1
        end
      end
►     @output.puts '+'*exact_match_count(guess) + '-'*number_match_count
    end
```

```
▶    def exact_match_count(guess)
       exact_match_count = 0
       (0..3).each do |index|
         if exact_match?(guess, index)
           exact_match_count += 1
         end
       end
       exact_match_count
     end
```

Now the guess on line 3 of the exact_match_count() method points to the argument. Run the specs, and they should all pass again. As we discussed in Section 7.3, *Learning from Rapid Feedback*, on page 77, running the specs between every step provides rapid feedback when there are failures and makes it much easier to isolate them than it would if we learned about the failures later in the process.

Next step!

Let's do the same thing with number_match_count. We'll extract a number_match_count() method, this time including the guess in the method definition:

cb/394/lib/codebreaker/game.rb

```
     def guess(guess)
▶      @output.puts '+'*exact_match_count(guess) + '-'*number_match_count(guess)
     end

     def exact_match_count(guess)
       exact_match_count = 0
       (0..3).each do |index|
         if exact_match?(guess, index)
           exact_match_count += 1
         end
       end
       exact_match_count
     end

▶    def number_match_count(guess)
▶      number_match_count = 0
▶      (0..3).each do |index|
▶        if number_match?(guess, index)
▶          number_match_count += 1
▶        end
▶      end
▶      number_match_count
▶    end
```

Run the specs, and they should all pass.

Watch Out for New Smells

As we're refactoring, the design is gradually changing before our very noses. We need to keep them open, constantly sniffing for new code smells. We've cleaned up the guess() method quite a bit, but we've also introduced even more duplication between the two new methods.

We can reduce the duplication using Ruby's inject iterator in each of the new methods.[2] Start with the exact_match_count method:

cb/40/lib/codebreaker/game.rb

```
    def exact_match_count(guess)
►     (0..3).inject(0) do |count, index|
►       count + (exact_match?(guess, index) ? 1 : 0)
►     end
    end
```

If you're new to Ruby, you might find inject a bit confusing. We're going to use it in this case because it helps us get rid of our own temp variables by providing one as a block argument.

What happens is that the count variable is initialized with the 0 passed to inject and passed into the block as the first block argument. The second block argument is the next value in the collection we're iterating on: 0 the first time, 1 the second, and so on.

With each iteration, inject assigns the return value of the block to the count variable.

And now the same with number_match_count:

cb/40/lib/codebreaker/game.rb

```
    def number_match_count(guess)
►     (0..3).inject(0) do |count, index|
►       count + (number_match?(guess, index) ? 1 : 0)
►     end
    end
```

Here is the result of all the refactoring we've done so far:

cb/41/lib/codebreaker/game.rb

```
def guess(guess)
  @output.puts '+'*exact_match_count(guess) + '-'*number_match_count(guess)
end

def exact_match_count(guess)
  (0..3).inject(0) do |count, index|
```

---

2. See *Programming Ruby* [TFH05] to learn more about inject().

```
      count + (exact_match?(guess, index) ? 1 : 0)
    end
  end

  def number_match_count(guess)
    (0..3).inject(0) do |count, index|
      count + (number_match?(guess, index) ? 1 : 0)
    end
  end

  def exact_match?(guess, index)
    guess[index] == @secret[index]
  end

  def number_match?(guess, index)
    @secret.include?(guess[index]) && !exact_match?(guess, index)
  end
```

Isn't that expressive? And look how much cleaner everything is! The guess method is no longer procedural, and we've reduced all of the temp variables to those provided as block arguments by Ruby's iterators. All in all, this is a big improvement, but there's more we can do. Do you see any other code smells?

Large Class

Similar to the Long Method smell, the Large Class smell is not really about size; it's about responsibilities. Our Game violates the Single Responsibility Principle by taking on multiple concerns: it formats output, sends messages to output, and marks each guess. It was violating SRP since we first introduced the guess() method, but that violation and its solution are much more clear now.

We have four methods that all deal with marking a guess. These methods clearly belong together. We might even be tempted to put a comment above the first one indicating that the next four methods deal with marking the guess. This is a strong hint that we're missing an abstraction in our design.

Extract Class

The Extract Class refactoring is the remedy for an SRP violation. The steps are as follows:

1. Create an empty Marker class inside the Game class. We'll move it out to its own file later, but it's easier to do the refactoring if everything is in one file.

2. Add an initializer to the Marker that accepts the secret code and assigns it to an instance variable named @secret.

3. Copy the four calculation methods directly into the new Marker class. Don't delete the originals yet.

4. Create a new Marker in the guess method, passing the @secret instance variable to Marker.new.

5. Call exact_match_count and number_match_count on the Marker object.

6. Remove the original copies of the four calculation methods from the Game.

If you follow those steps correctly, the specs should pass between every step, and the end result should look like this:

cb/411/lib/codebreaker/game.rb

```ruby
  def guess(guess)
►    marker = Marker.new(@secret)
►    @output.puts '+'*marker.exact_match_count(guess) +
►                 '-'*marker.number_match_count(guess)
  end

  class Marker
►    def initialize(secret)
►      @secret = secret
►    end

    def exact_match_count(guess)
      (0..3).inject(0) do |count, index|
        count + (exact_match?(guess, index) ? 1 : 0)
      end
    end

    def number_match_count(guess)
      (0..3).inject(0) do |count, index|
        count + (number_match?(guess, index) ? 1 : 0)
      end
    end

    def exact_match?(guess, index)
      guess[index] == @secret[index]
    end

    def number_match?(guess, index)
      @secret.include?(guess[index]) && !exact_match?(guess, index)
    end
  end
end
```

Now that we have this structure, of course, we can smell some new odors. First, doesn't it seem odd that we have to pass the guess to the exact_match_count and number_match_count() methods from the guess() method in the Game?

Also, notice how we assign the secret to an instance variable that we access directly from the instance methods, whereas we're slinging the guess around from method to method. The fact that they operate at two different levels of abstraction made sense in the context of the Game object, but it no longer does in the context of the Marker.

To resolve both of these issues, let's start by passing the guess to the initializer of the Marker, like this:

`cb/412/lib/codebreaker/game.rb`

```
    def guess(guess)
▶     marker = Marker.new(@secret, guess)
      @output.puts '+'*marker.exact_match_count(guess) +
                    '-'*marker.number_match_count(guess)
    end

    class Marker
      def initialize(secret, guess)
▶       @secret, @guess = secret, guess
      end
    end
```

Now change all the references to guess inside the Marker to point to the @guess instance variable:

`cb/413/lib/codebreaker/game.rb`

```
    def exact_match_count(guess)
      (0..3).inject(0) do |count, index|
▶       count + (exact_match?(@guess, index) ? 1 : 0)
      end
    end

    def number_match_count(guess)
      (0..3).inject(0) do |count, index|
▶       count + (number_match?(@guess, index) ? 1 : 0)
      end
    end

    def exact_match?(guess, index)
▶     @guess[index] == @secret[index]
    end

    def number_match?(guess, index)
▶     @secret.include?(@guess[index]) && !exact_match?(@guess, index)
    end
```

Now we can start removing the guess from the signatures of each of the methods. Start with the exact_match_count() method, removing it from the call to that method and the method declaration itself:

cb/414/lib/codebreaker/game.rb

```ruby
    def guess(guess)
      marker = Marker.new(@secret, guess)
►     @output.puts '+'*marker.exact_match_count +
                   '-'*marker.number_match_count(guess)
    end

    class Marker
►     def exact_match_count
        (0..3).inject(0) do |count, index|
          count + (exact_match?(@guess, index) ? 1 : 0)
        end
      end
    end
```

Run the specs, and they should all pass. Now do the same with the number_match_count, exact_match?, and number_match? methods, running the specs between each change. They should pass every time. The end result should look like this:

cb/415/lib/codebreaker/game.rb

```ruby
def guess(guess)
  marker = Marker.new(@secret, guess)
  @output.puts '+'*marker.exact_match_count +
               '-'*marker.number_match_count
end

class Marker
  def initialize(secret, guess)
    @secret, @guess = secret, guess
  end

  def exact_match_count
    (0..3).inject(0) do |count, index|
      count + (exact_match?(index) ? 1 : 0)
    end
  end

  def number_match_count
    (0..3).inject(0) do |count, index|
      count + (number_match?(index) ? 1 : 0)
    end
  end

  def exact_match?(index)
    @guess[index] == @secret[index]
  end
```

```
  def number_match?(index)
    @secret.include?(@guess[index]) && !exact_match?(index)
  end
end
```

There! Now we have good decoupling of concepts and good cohesion within each object. The Marker is responsible only for marking. We kept the plus and minus signs inside the Game, which is currently responsible for all the messages that get sent to output. Had we moved those into the Marker, we would have violated the DRY principle by having that responsibility represented in two locations.

Now that we have the Marker in pretty good shape, let's move it to its own file. Create a marker.rb file in lib/codebreaker/, open the Codebreaker module, and copy the Marker into that file. Don't forget to remove it from the Game class. Now require that file from lib/codebreaker.rb, like this:

cb/42/lib/codebreaker.rb

```
require 'codebreaker/game'
require 'codebreaker/marker'
```

Run the specs to make sure everything is still wired up correctly. They should all pass. So should all of the scenarios. Go ahead and run them to make sure everything is still working correctly.

8.3 Updating Specs After Refactoring

After refactorings that introduce new methods and classes like Extract Method and Extract Class, the RSpec code examples may no longer reflect the responsibilities of the objects they specify. In our case, we have no specs for the Marker, and we have a bunch of examples for the Game that are more closely aligned with the Marker than they are with the Game.

We want the specs to serve as documentation of the responsibilities of the objects they exercise, so let's move some things around. First, let's add some examples for the Marker behavior. Add a marker_spec.rb file to spec/codebreaker/, and add the following code:

cb/42/spec/codebreaker/marker_spec.rb

```
require 'spec_helper'

module Codebreaker
  describe Marker do
```

```ruby
describe "#exact_match_count" do
  context "with no matches" do
    it "returns 0" do
      marker = Marker.new('1234','5555')
      marker.exact_match_count.should == 0
    end
  end

  context "with 1 exact match" do
    it "returns 1" do
      marker = Marker.new('1234','1555')
      marker.exact_match_count.should == 1
    end
  end

  context "with 1 number match" do
    it "returns 0" do
      marker = Marker.new('1234','2555')
      marker.exact_match_count.should == 0
    end
  end
  context "with 1 exact match and 1 number match" do
    it "returns 1" do
      marker = Marker.new('1234','1525')
      marker.exact_match_count.should == 1
    end
  end
end

describe "#number_match_count" do
  context "with no matches" do
    it "returns 0" do
      marker = Marker.new('1234','5555')
      marker.number_match_count.should == 0
    end
  end

  context "with 1 number match" do
    it "returns 1" do
      marker = Marker.new('1234','2555')
      marker.number_match_count.should == 1
    end
  end

  context "with 1 exact match" do
    it "returns 0" do
      marker = Marker.new('1234','1555')
      marker.number_match_count.should == 0
    end
  end
```

```
        context "with 1 exact match and 1 number match" do
          it "returns 1" do
            marker = Marker.new('1234','1525')
            marker.number_match_count.should == 1
          end
        end
      end
    end
end
```

We're really only interested in the exact_match_count and number_match_count() methods because those are the only methods being used by the Game. Run that new spec file with this command:

```
rspec spec/codebreaker/marker_spec.rb --format nested
```

The output should look like this:

```
Codebreaker::Marker
  #exact_match_count
    with no matches
      returns 0
    with 1 exact match
      returns 1
    with 1 number match
      returns 0
    with 1 exact match and 1 number match
      returns 1
  #number_match_count
    with no matches
      returns 0
    with 1 number match
      returns 1
    with 1 exact match
      returns 0
    with 1 exact match and 1 number match
      returns 1
```

See how nicely that documents the behavior of these methods of the Marker in different contexts?

Now comes the question of what to do with the examples we wrote for the guess() method on the Game. We used them to drive out the implementation of the marking algorithm in small steps, and they served that purpose well. They also served us well during the refactoring we just did because we were able to get rapid feedback after each change, and when there were failures, we were able to isolate them quickly.

That said, the responsibility of the Game object has changed. It's still responsible for sending a mark to the output, but it's no longer responsible for calculating the mark. With that, let's remove the existing examples for guess and add one that documents its responsibility. Modify game_spec.rb so it looks like this:

```
cb/42/spec/codebreaker/game_spec.rb
```

```ruby
require 'spec_helper'

module Codebreaker
  describe Game do
    let(:output) { double('output').as_null_object }
    let(:game)   { Game.new(output) }

    describe "#start" do
      it "sends a welcome message" do
        output.should_receive(:puts).with('Welcome to Codebreaker!')
        game.start('1234')
      end

      it "prompts for the first guess" do
        output.should_receive(:puts).with('Enter guess:')
        game.start('1234')
      end
    end

    describe "#guess" do
      it "sends the mark to output" do
        game.start('1234')
        output.should_receive(:puts).with('++++')
        game.guess('1234')
      end
    end
  end
end
```

Run the specs, and they should all pass. If you run them with --format nested, you'll see documentation of the responsibilities of both objects.

Are We Done Yet?

Refactoring can be addictive. Every time we do one refactoring, our attention is drawn to an area of the code we may not have focused on before. Or perhaps we were focused on it, but the new structure exposes new smells. We could certainly do more refactoring now if we wanted to, but eventually we have to stop and move on.

At this point, we've made excellent progress, and the code is clear and well factored. Of course, we could do more, and we *will* in the next chapter, but for now let's move on to a new topic.

8.4 Exploratory Testing

Exploratory testing is a practice in which we discover the behavior of an application by interacting with it directly. It is the opposite of the process we've been learning about, in that we're looking to see what the app actually does and then question whether that is the correct behavior.

It has a rich history and is a deep craft in its own right, the breadth of which is outside the scope of this book. For our purposes, we want you to simply fire up the Codebreaker game and enter guesses and analyze the outcomes.

Now that the game can mark a guess for us, we just need a minor adjustment to bin/codebreaker, and we can begin interacting with the game. Here's the script for *nix users:

cb/42/bin/codebreaker

```ruby
#!/usr/bin/env ruby
$LOAD_PATH.unshift File.expand_path('../../lib', __FILE__)
require 'codebreaker'

game = Codebreaker::Game.new(STDOUT)
game.start('1234')
while guess = gets.chomp
  game.guess(guess)
end
```

Windows users use the same script without the first line and also add bin/codebreaker.bat with the following:

cb/42/bin/codebreaker.bat

```
@"ruby.exe" "%~dpn0" %*
```

Clearly, the game won't be too much fun because it has the same code every time, but at least at this point, you can try it and maybe even show your friends.

Perhaps you're wondering why we'd want to do exploratory testing if we've already tested the app. Well, we haven't. Remember that BDD is a design practice, not a testing practice. We're using executable examples of how we want the application to behave. But just as Big Design Up Front fails to allow for discovery of features and designs that naturally emerge through iterative development, driving out behavior with examples fails to unearth all of the corner cases that we'll naturally discover by simply using the software.

As you explore the Codebreaker game, try to find the flaws in the marking algorithm. You'll know what the not-so-secret code is, so try different inputs and see what happens. What happens when you input non-numeric characters? How about too many or too few? What about duplicates in the guess that match one of the numbers in the secret code?

As you're doing this, flaws will appear for a variety of reasons. Perhaps there are missing scenarios or code examples. Some flaws may stem from naive design choices. The reasons for these flaws are not important. What *is* important is that the investment we've made to get this far has been very, very small compared to an exhaustive up-front requirements-gathering process. An interactive session with working software is worth a thousand meetings.

8.5 What We've Learned

In this chapter, we took a closer look at refactoring and how it impacts the resulting design. We were able to refactor with confidence because we ran the specs between each step, so we always knew right away when we introduced a problem.

We looked at two structural refactorings in detail: Extract Method and Extract Class. We also talked about a few specific code smells: Temporary Variable, Long Method, and Large Class.

Refactoring is not a direct path; some of the steps seem to take us further in the wrong direction, even though they really help us to set up a step we are about to make. We can often make it easier to remove a code smell by clarifying it first.

Each step in a refactoring draws our attention to different parts of the design. This process often reveals new code smells that had either gone unnoticed or hadn't been there before.

After a refactoring, we should look at our specs and make sure they still document responsibilities correctly. Documentation is a key value of executable code examples.

Lastly, we discussed using exploratory testing as a means of discovering bugs and misconceptions, rather than trying to think of everything in a vacuum before we've written any code.

In the next chapter, we'll address a couple of fallacies in our marking that may have been discovered in exploratory testing. So, put down this book for a few minutes, and go explore! See you at the top of the next chapter.

## Chapter 9

Feeding Back What We've Learned

At the end of the previous chapter, we asked you to do some exploratory testing. How did it go? Did you discover anything odd? Did you find any bugs? Any requirements that we may have missed in our initial planning?

One issue you may have encountered is the way in which the Marker handles duplicate matches. If the secret code is 1234 and the guess is 1155, we get a mark of +-. We didn't really discuss what should happen in a case like this earlier, but now that we see it, it does make us question what the correct mark should be.

In this chapter, we'll examine this question and document the results in Cucumber scenarios. Then we'll write code examples and evolve the Marker to handle these new requirements. In the process, we'll do a bit more refactoring, which we'll discover is made far simpler by the refactoring we've already done.

9.1 Use Cucumber for Collaboration

As we just saw, with a secret code of 1234 and a guess of 1155, we're getting a mark of +-. Without even looking at the code, we can guess that this is happening because the Marker evaluates the 1 in the first position of the guess as an exact match with the 1 in the first position in the secret code, and then it evaluates the 1 in the second position of the guess as a number match with the same number in the first position of the code.

Does that seem right?

Document New Requirements with Cucumber

It's tempting, when this sort of question comes up, to make assumptions about how things should work. Fight that temptation! This is exactly what Cucumber is for. We can sit down with the customer and sketch out some scenarios and talk about them. Cucumber's simple use of Given, When, Then is a great facilitator for this sort of conversation. And in our case, our use of Cucumber's scenario outlines makes it even easier.

That said, we will now fast-forward past that conversation, having decided on the following rules, as expressed in the narrative and some new scenarios in codebreaker_submits_guess.feature:

cb/43/features/codebreaker_submits_guess.feature

```
Feature: code-breaker submits guess

  The code-breaker submits a guess of four numbers.  The game marks the guess
  with + and - signs.

  For each number in the guess that matches the number and position of a number
  in the secret code, the mark includes one + sign. For each number in the guess
  that matches the number but not the position of a number in the secret code,
  the mark includes one - sign.

▶  Each position in the secret code can only be matched once.  For example, a
▶  guess of 1134 against a secret code of 1234 would get three plus signs: one
▶  for each of the exact matches in the first, third and fourth positions.  The
▶  number match in the second position would be ignored.

  Scenario Outline: submit guess
    Given the secret code is "<code>"
    When I guess "<guess>"
    Then the mark should be "<mark>"

  Scenarios: no matches
    | code | guess | mark |
    | 1234 | 5555  |      |

  Scenarios: 1 number correct
    | code | guess | mark |
    | 1234 | 1555  | +    |
    | 1234 | 2555  | -    |

  Scenarios: 2 numbers correct
    | code | guess | mark |
    | 1234 | 5254  | ++   |
    | 1234 | 5154  | +-   |
    | 1234 | 2545  | --   |
```

Scenarios: 3 numbers correct
code	guess	mark
1234	5234	+++
1234	5134	++-
1234	5124	+--
1234	5123	---

Scenarios: all numbers correct
code	guess	mark
1234	1234	++++
1234	1243	++--
1234	1423	+---
1234	4321	----

▶   Scenarios: matches with duplicates
▶ | code | guess | mark |
▶ | 1234 | 1155 | + |
▶ | 1234 | 5115 | - |
▶ | 1134 | 1155 | ++ |
▶ | 1134 | 5115 | +- |
▶ | 1134 | 5511 | -- |
▶ | 1134 | 1115 | ++ |
▶ | 1134 | 5111 | +- |

Now run the scenarios with the cucumber command, and you should see the following failures (output abbreviated for clarity):

```
Scenarios: matches with duplicates
  | code | guess | mark |
  | 1234 | 1155  | +    |
  expected ["Welcome to Codebreaker!", "Enter guess:", "+-"] to include "+"
  | 1234 | 5115  | -    |
  expected ["Welcome to Codebreaker!", "Enter guess:", "--"] to include "-"
  | 1134 | 1155  | ++   |
  | 1134 | 5115  | +-   |
  | 1134 | 5511  | --   |
  | 1134 | 1115  | ++   |
  expected ["Welcome to Codebreaker!", "Enter guess:", "++-"] to include "++"
  | 1134 | 5111  | +-   |
  expected ["Welcome to Codebreaker!", "Enter guess:", "+--"] to include "+-"

21 scenarios (4 failed, 17 passed)
63 steps (4 failed, 59 passed)
0m0.039s
```

The failing scenarios all fail in similar ways. They each get a symbol in the mark for every 1 that appears in the guess even when there are fewer 1s in the secret code. We need to modify the marking algorithm so that each position in the code can be matched only once. It also seems that the extra mark is always an extra minus sign, so let's focus on the number_match_count method first.

Write a Code Example That Exposes the Problem

Add the following context and example to the examples for number_match_count in marker_spec.rb:

cb/43/spec/codebreaker/marker_spec.rb

```
module Codebreaker
  describe Marker do
    describe "#number_match_count" do
▶       context "with 1 exact match duplicated in guess" do
▶         it "returns 0" do
▶           marker = Marker.new('1234','1155')
▶           marker.number_match_count.should == 0
▶         end
▶       end
      end
    end
end
```

The first argument to Marker.new is the secret code, and then second is the guess. We expect the 1 in the first position of the secret code to be accounted for in the exact_match_count, so the 1 in the second position of the guess should not be matched against it. Run this new example with the rspec command, and you should see the following failure:

```
1) Codebreaker::Marker #number_match_count with 1 exact match
     duplicated in guess returns 0
   Failure/Error: marker.number_match_count.should == 0
   expected: 0,
        got: 1 (using ==)
```

Let's review the implementation of the Marker:

cb/43/lib/codebreaker/marker.rb

```
module Codebreaker
  class Marker
    def initialize(secret, guess)
      @secret, @guess = secret, guess
    end

    def exact_match_count
      (0..3).inject(0) do |count, index|
        count + (exact_match?(index) ? 1 : 0)
      end
    end

    def number_match_count
      (0..3).inject(0) do |count, index|
```

```
      count + (number_match?(index) ? 1 : 0)
    end
  end

  def exact_match?(index)
    @guess[index] == @secret[index]
  end

  def number_match?(index)
    @secret.include?(@guess[index]) && !exact_match?(index)
  end
  end
end
```

Our implementation of number_match? is not robust enough to handle this new requirement. It looks for any number that's in the secret and not in the same position, but it doesn't account for whether that number has been matched already. This is why we occasionally get two matches for one number in the secret code.

9.2 Experimenting with a New Implementation

We need a new way to count up the number matches. We *could* modify the design such that we keep track of each number in the secret code and disqualify it for future matches once it's been matched, but that would require returning to the more procedural approach we left behind in the previous chapter.

Take a Step Back

Let's look at this from a different angle. We already know the number of exact matches. That's easy because we just have to evaluate one position at a time. We can do that in any order, and we don't need to know whether positions have been matched before or not.

What if we count up *all* the matches without regard for whether they're in the same position and then subtract the number of exact matches? If that total is three, for example, and there are two exact matches, then we know that we have one number match remaining. Make sense?

Phrased differently, the count of number matches is the total match count less the exact match count. We can express that very cleanly in Ruby like this:

```
def number_match_count
  total_match_count - exact_match_count
end
```

Assuming that's correct, how do we count the total matches? The simplest approach would probably be to iterate through the numbers in the guess, removing matches from the secret as they are found.

For example, if the secret is 1234 and the guess is 1145, we start by evaluating the 1 in the first position of the guess. There is a 1 in the secret, so we remove it, leaving 234. Now we look at the 1 in the second position in the guess. There is no longer a 1 in the secret, so we move on to the 4 in the third position of the guess. There is a 4 in the secret, so we remove it, leaving 23. Finally, we look at the 5 in the last position of the guess. There is no match in the secret, so we are done. We've removed two numbers from the secret, so that's the total count of matches.

That seems like it might work, but it's a very different implementation from the one we have now. One of the benefits of having the specs we have is that we can experiment with alternate implementations very cheaply, and we'll quickly know whether we're on the right path. Let's give it a whirl.

Experiment *in the Green*

We're going to experiment with a new implementation, and we want to use our existing code examples as a safety net to ensure that we're preserving behavior as we do. We have a failing example now, so we want to disable it temporarily while we're working. That way, if we introduce any new failures, we won't confuse them with this one. Let's declare this example *pending*, like this:

`cb/44/spec/codebreaker/marker_spec.rb`

```
context "with 1 exact match duplicated in guess" do
  it "returns 0" do
    pending("refactor number_match_count")
    marker = Marker.new('1234', '1155')
    marker.number_match_count.should == 0
  end
end
```

Similar to when we called the it() method with no block, RSpec treats this example as pending: execution stops after the pending statement, and then RSpec lists the example as pending in the output. This gets the example out of the way while keeping it on our radar. You can read more about different ways to declare pending examples in Section 12.2, *Pending Examples*, on page 142.

Run the specs, and you should see one pending example and zero failures. Now let's write our experimental implementation and see how it goes. Modify marker.rb as follows:

cb/45/lib/codebreaker/marker.rb

```
def number_match_count
  total_match_count - exact_match_count
end

def total_match_count
  count = 0
  @guess.map do |n|
    if @secret.include?(n)
      @secret.delete_at(@secret.index(n))
      count += 1
    end
  end
  count
end
```

We iterate through the numbers in the @guess, asking the @secret each time if it includes that number. If it does, we ask the @secret for the index of the number and then tell it to delete at that index.

Run the specs, and you'll see a bunch of failures. The failure message in the first one gives us a pretty big hint as to what the problem is:

```
1) Codebreaker::Game #guess sends the mark to output
   Failure/Error: game.guess('1234')
   undefined method `delete_at' for "1234":String
   # ./lib/codebreaker/marker.rb:22:in `total_match_count'
```

The implementation is assuming an array API, but the @secret and @guess variables are actually strings. Let's split the strings into arrays, like this:

cb/46/lib/codebreaker/marker.rb

```
    def total_match_count
      count = 0
►     secret = @secret.split('')
►     @guess.split('').map do |n|
►       if secret.include?(n)
►         secret.delete_at(secret.index(n))
          count += 1
        end
      end
      count
    end
```

Run the specs, and they should all pass—except for the pending example, that is, so remove the pending statement from the previous example, and run them all again. They should all pass, even the one that was pending!

Next, run the Cucumber scenarios, and they should pass, too. Great! We only spent a few minutes thinking about a new implementation, tried it out, made a small adjustment when a bunch of examples failed, and *voila*!

You Can Always Roll Back

Things don't always work out quite this cleanly. Sometimes we'll try to experiment like this and run into failure after failure after failure.

When that happens to you, and it *will*, don't let it go on too long before rolling back to the last point at which all examples were passing. Then you can proceed forward again in smaller steps.

One More Refactoring

Now that we have a new implementation, it can use a little bit of cleanup. Rather than going through this together, we'll show you where we ended up after a bit of refactoring but leave the actual refactoring as an exercise for you.

Here is the code we ended up with:

`cb/47/lib/codebreaker/marker.rb`

```ruby
def total_match_count
  secret = @secret.split('')
  @guess.split('').inject(0) do |count, n|
    count + (delete_first(secret, n) ? 1 : 0)
  end
end

def delete_first(code, n)
  code.delete_at(code.index(n)) if code.index(n)
end
```

There's always more we *can* do, but at this point we have solved for duplicate matches, and the code is well factored, readable, and maintainable.

A Bit of Glue

We are not going to develop any more Codebreaker implementation together, but before we move on, here is some prototype code you can add to bin/codebreaker so you can have some fun trying to break a randomly generated code:

`cb/47/bin/codebreaker`

```ruby
#!/usr/bin/env ruby
$LOAD_PATH.unshift File.expand_path('../../lib', __FILE__)
require 'codebreaker'

▶ def generate_secret_code
▶   options = %w[1 2 3 4 5 6]
▶   (1..4).map { options.delete_at(rand(options.length))}.join
▶ end

  game = Codebreaker::Game.new(STDOUT)
▶ secret_code = generate_secret_code
▶ at_exit { puts "\n***\nThe secret code was: #{secret_code}\n***" }
▶ game.start(secret_code)
  while guess = gets.chomp
    game.guess(guess)
  end
```

This adds a method to generate a random secret code so you can tease your brain trying to break the code. We also added a little at_exit hook that prints the code out at the end, so you can see what you were up against when you're unable to do so.

To be clear, this is *not* production code and is not intended to be shipped. It's just a prototype development aid we're slapping in place so that we can enjoy the fruits of our labors and do more exploratory testing.

9.3 What We've Learned

In this chapter, we took lessons that we learned from exploratory testing and fed them back into the process. We documented the new requirements in Cucumber scenarios and used them as our starting point for continued development.

In the process of analyzing what we learned, we stepped back and thought about a different implementation that might be superior to the one we had. We experimented with the new implementation, using our existing scenarios and code examples to ensure that we preserved behavior. When we ran the code examples, we learned about the error we made in our implementation right away and were able to quickly fix the error and continue progressing.

This is a small demonstration of how code examples serve as regression tests over the life of an application. If we've written them well and kept them focused on small, isolated bits of behavior, they run very fast and provide us with practical feedback very quickly.

Note that our experiment was on a very small bit of lower-level functionality. This would have been much more challenging if the marking algorithm were still expressed in a single method in the Game.

This brings us to the end of this first part of the book. We hope that you now have a sense of what it's like to use Cucumber and RSpec together to discover requirements, flesh them out at the high level, and design objects that provide solutions for them. These are the daily practices of a developer working on a Behaviour-Driven Development project, but developer practices are only one component of BDD as a whole.

In the next part of the book, we'll provide a bit of background on BDD, including what came before and where we are today. You'll learn about the motivations for BDD and the basic principles behind the process that have led us to the practices we just covered.

Part II

Behaviour-Driven Development

## Chapter 10

The Case for BDD

Most of the software we write will never get used. It's nothing personal—it's just that as an industry we are not very good at giving people what they want. It turns out that the underlying reason for this is that traditional software methods are set up to fail—they actually work against us. Heroic individuals deliver software *in spite of* their development process rather than because of it. In this chapter, we look at how and why projects fail and shine a spotlight on some of the challenges facing Agile development.

10.1 How Traditional Projects Fail

Traditional projects fail for all sorts of reasons. A good way to identify the different failure modes is to ask your project manager what keeps them up at night. (It's nice to do this from time to time anyway—it helps their self-esteem.) It is likely your project manager will come up with a list of fears similar to ours.

Delivering Late or Over Budget

We estimate, we plan, we have every contingency down to the nth degree, and then much to our disappointment, real life happens. When we slip the first date, no one minds too much. After all, it will only be a couple of weeks. If it goes on for long enough—slipping week by week and month by month—enough people will have left and joined that we can finally put the project out of its misery. Eighteen months to two years is usually enough. This is software that doesn't matter.

Delivering the Wrong Thing

Most of us use software that was delivered late and over budget—on our desktops, in our mobile phones, in our offices and homes. In fact, we have become used to systems that update themselves with bug fixes and new features in the form of service packs and system updates or websites that grow new features over time. But none of us use software that doesn't solve the problem we have.

It is surprising how much project management effort is spent looking after the schedule or budget when late software is infinitely more useful than irrelevant software. This is software that doesn't matter.

Unstable in Production

Hooray! The project came in on time and on budget, and the users looked at it and decided they like it, so we put it into production. The problem is it crashes twice a day. We think it's a memory thing or a configuration thing or a clustering thing or an infrastructure thing or—who are we kidding? We don't really know what's causing it except that it's rather embarrassing and it's costing us a lot of money. If only we had spent more time testing it. People will use this once and then give up when it keeps crashing. This is software that doesn't matter.

Costly to Maintain

There are a number of things we don't need to consider if we are writing disposable software. Maintainability is one of them. However, if we expect to follow Release 1 with a Release 2, Release 3, or even a Professional Super-Cow Power Edition, then we can easily paint ourselves into a corner by not considering downstream developers.

Over time, the rate at which they can introduce new features will diminish until they end up spending more of their time tracking down unexpected regressions and unpicking spaghetti code than actually getting work done. At some point, the software will cost more to improve than the revenue it can generate. This is software that doesn't matter.

10.2 Why Traditional Projects Fail

Most of these failure modes happen with smart people trying to do good work. For the most part, software people are diligent and well-intentioned, as are the stakeholders they are delivering to, which makes it especially sad when we see the inevitable "blame-storming" that follows in the wake of another failed delivery. It also makes it unlikely that project failures are the results of incompetence or inability—there must be another reason.

How Traditional Projects Work

Most software projects go through the familiar sequence of Planning, Analysis, Design, Code, Test, Deploy. Your process may have different names, but the basic activities in each phase will be fairly consistent. (We are assuming some sort of business justification has already happened, although even that isn't always the case.)

We start with the *Planning phase*. How many people do we need? For how long? What resources will they need? Basically, how much will it cost to deliver this project, and how soon will we see anything?

Then we move into an *Analysis phase*. This is where we articulate in detail the problem we are trying to solve, ideally without prescribing how it should be solved, although this is almost never the case.

Then we have a *Design phase*. This is where we think about how we can use a computer system to solve the problem we articulated in Analysis. During this phase we think about design and architecture, large- and small-scale technical decisions, and the various standards around the organization, and we gradually decompose the problem into manageable chunks for which we can produce functional specifications.

Now we move onto the *Coding phase*, where we write the software that is going to solve the problem, according to the specifications that came out of the Design phase. A common assumption by the program board at this stage is that all the "hard thinking" has been done by this stage. This is why so many organizations think it's OK to have their programming and testing carried out by offshore, third-party vendors.

Now, because we are responsible adults, we have a *Testing phase* where we test the software to make sure it does what it was supposed to do. This phase contains activities with names like *user acceptance testing* or *performance testing* to emphasize that we are getting closer to the users now and the final delivery.

Eventually, we reach the *Deployment phase* where we deploy the application into production. With a suitable level of fanfare, the new software glides into production and starts making us money!

All these phases are necessary. You can't start solving a problem you haven't articulated, you can't start implementing a solution you haven't described, you can't test software that doesn't exist, and you can't (or at least shouldn't) deploy software that hasn't been tested. Of course, in reality, you can do any of these things, but it usually ends in tears.

How Traditional Projects Really Work

We have delivered projects in pretty much this way since we first started writing computer systems. There have been various attempts at improving the process and making it more efficient and less error-prone, using documents for formalized hand-offs, creating templates for the documents that make up those hand-offs, assembling review committees for the templates for the documents, establishing standards and formalized accreditation for the review committees, and so on. You can certainly see where the effort has gone.

The reason for all this ceremony around hand-offs, reviews, and such is that the later in the software delivery life cycle we detect a defect—or introduce a change—the more expensive it is to put right. And it's not just a little more; in fact, empirical evidence over the years has shown that it is exponentially more expensive the later you find out. With this in mind, it makes sense to front-load the process. We want to make sure we have thought through all the possible outcomes and covered all the angles early on so we aren't surprised by "unknown unknowns" late in the day.

But this isn't the whole story. However diligent we are at each of the development phases, anyone who has delivered software in a traditional way will attest to the amount of work that happens "under the radar."

The program team signs off the project plan, resplendent in its detail, dependencies, resource models, and Gantt charts. Then the analysts start getting to grips with the detail of the problem and say things like, "Hmm, this seems to be more involved than we thought. We'd better replan; this is going to be a biggie."

Then the architects start working on their functional specifications, which uncover a number of questions and ambiguities about the requirements. What happens if this message isn't received by that other system? Sometimes the analysts can immediately answer the question, but more often it means we need more analysis and hence more time from the analysts. Better update that plan. And get it signed off. And get the new version of the requirements document.

You can see how this coordination cost can rapidly mount up. Of course, it really kicks off during the testing phase. When the tester raises a defect, the programmer throws his hands in the air and says he did what was in the functional spec, the architect blames the business analyst, and so on, right back up the chain. It's easy to see where this exponential cost comes from.

As this back-and-forth becomes more of a burden, we become more afraid of making changes, which means people do work outside of the process and documents get out of sync with one another and with the software itself. Testing gets squeezed, people work late into the night, and the release itself is usually characterized by wailing and gnashing of teeth, bloodshot eyes, and multiple failed attempts at deciphering the instructions in the release notes.

If you ask experienced software delivery folks why they run a project like that, front-loading it with all the planning and analysis, then getting into the detailed design and programming, and only really integrating and testing it at the end, they will gaze into the distance, looking older than their years, and patiently explain that this is to mitigate against the exponential cost of change—the principle that introducing a change or discovering a defect becomes exponentially more expensive the later you discover it. The *top-down* approach seems the only sensible way to hedge against the possibility of discovering a defect late in the day.

A Self-fulfilling Prophecy

To recap, projects become exponentially more expensive to change the further we get into them, because of the cumulative effect of keeping all the project artifacts in sync, so we front-load the process with lots of risk-mitigating planning, analysis, and design activities to reduce the likelihood of rework.

Now, how many of these artifacts—the project plan, the requirements specification, the high- and low-level design documents, the software itself—existed before the project began? That's right, *exactly none!* So, all that effort—that exponentially increasing effort—occurs *because we run projects the way we do!* So, now we have a chicken-and-egg situation, or a *reinforcing loop* in systems thinking terminology. The irony of the traditional project approach is that *the process itself causes the exponential cost of change!*

Digging a little deeper, it turns out the curve originates in civil engineering. It makes sense that you might want to spend a lot of time in the design phases of a bridge or a ship. You wouldn't want to get two-thirds of the way through building a hospital only to have someone point out it is in the wrong place. Once the reinforced concrete pillars are sunk, things become very expensive to put right!

However, these rules apply to software development only *because we let them!* Software is, well, soft. It is supposed to be the part that's easy to change, and with the right approach and some decent tooling, it can be very malleable. So, by using the metaphor of civil engineering and equating software with steel and concrete, we've done ourselves a disservice.

10.3 Redefining the Problem

It's not all doom and gloom, though. There are many teams out there delivering projects on time and within budget and delighting their stakeholders, and they manage to do it again and again. It's not easy. It takes discipline and dedication and relies on a high degree of communication and collaboration, but it is possible. People who work like this tend to agree it is also a lot of fun!

Behaviour-Driven Development is one of a number of *Agile* methodologies. Specifically, it is a *second-generation* Agile methodology, building on the work of the really smart guys. Let's look at how these Agile methods came about and how they address traditional project risks, and then we can see how BDD allows us to concentrate on writing software that matters.

A Brief History of Agile

Since we first started delivering software as projects, there have been software professionals asking themselves the same questions. Why do so many software projects fail? Why are we so *consistently* bad at delivering software? Why does it seem to happen more on larger projects with bigger teams? And can anything be done about it?

Independently they developed a series of lightweight methodologies whose focus was on delivering working software to users, rather than producing reams of documents or staging ceremonial reviews to show how robust their processes were. They found they could cut through a lot of organizational red tape just by putting everyone in the same room.

Then in early 2001 a few of these practitioners got together and produced a short manifesto describing their common position. You might well have seen it before, but it is worth reproducing here because it describes the common ground so perfectly.[1]

The Agile Manifesto

We are uncovering better ways of developing software by doing it and helping others do it. Through this work we have come to value:

Individuals and interactions *over processes and tools*
Working software *over comprehensive documentation*
Customer collaboration *over contract negotiation*
Responding to change *over following a plan*

That is, while there is value in the things on the right, we value the things on the left more.

The Agile Manifesto is empirical—it's based on real experience: "We are uncovering better ways...*by doing it.*" Also notice that it doesn't *dismiss* traditional ideas like documentation and contracts—a criticism often leveled at Agile methods—but rather it expresses a preference for something different: something lighter weight and more directly relevant to the customer or stakeholder.

How Agile Methods Address Project Risks

The authors of the manifesto go further than just the few lines quoted previously. They also documented the principles underpinning their thinking. Central to these is a desire to "deliver working software frequently, from a couple of weeks to a couple of months, with a preference to the shorter timescale."

Imagine for a moment you could do this, namely, delivering production-quality software *every two weeks* to your stakeholders, on your current project, in your current organization, with your current team, starting tomorrow. How would this address the traditional delivery risks we outlined at the start of the chapter?

---

1. You can find the Agile Manifesto online at http://agilemanifesto.org.

No Longer Delivering Late or Over Budget

Since we are delivering the system in tiny, one- or two-week *iterations* or mini-projects, using a small, fixed-size team, it is easy to calculate our project budget: it is simply the burn rate of the team times the number of weeks, plus some hardware and licenses.

Provided we start with a reasonable guess at the overall size of the project (that is, how much we are prepared to invest in solving the business problem in the first place) and we prioritize the features appropriately, then the team can deliver the really important stuff in the early iterations. (Remember, we are delivering by feature, not by module.) So, as we get toward the point when the money runs out, we should by definition be working on lower-priority features. Also, we can measure how much we actually produce in each iteration, known as our *velocity* or *throughput*, and use this to predict when we are really likely to finish.

If, as we approach the deadline, the stakeholders are still having new ideas for features and seeing great things happening, they may choose to fund the project for a further few iterations. Conversely, they may decide *before the deadline* that enough of the functionality has been delivered that they want to finish up early and get a release out. This is another option they have.

No Longer Delivering the Wrong Thing

We are delivering working software to the stakeholders every two weeks (say), which means we are delivering demonstrable features. We don't have a two-week "database schema iteration" or "middleware iteration."

After each iteration, we can demonstrate the new features to the stakeholders, and they can make any tweaks or correct any misunderstandings while the work is still fresh in the development team's mind. These regular, small-scale micro-corrections ensure that we don't end up several months down the line with software that simply doesn't do what the stakeholders wanted.

To kick off the next iteration, we can get together with the stakeholders to reassess the priorities of the features in case anything has changed since last time.[2] This means any new ideas or suggestions can get scheduled, and the corresponding amount of work can be descoped (or extra time added).

---

2. In practice, the planning session often follows directly after the showcase for the previous iteration.

No Longer Unstable in Production

We are delivering every iteration, which means we have to get good at building and deploying the application. In fact, we rely heavily on process automation to manage this for us. It is not uncommon for an experienced Agile team to produce more than 100 good software builds every week.

In this context, releasing to production or testing hardware can be considered just another build to just another environment. Application servers are automatically configured and initialized; database schemas are automatically updated; code is automatically built, assembled, and deployed over the wire; and all manner of tests are automatically executed to ensure the system is behaving as expected.

In fact, in an Agile environment, the relationship between the development team and the downstream operations and DBA folks is often much healthier and more supportive.

No Longer Costly to Maintain

This last one is one of the biggest tangible benefits of an Agile process. After their first iteration, the team is effectively in maintenance mode. They are adding features to a system that "works," so they have to be very careful.

Assuming they can solve the issues of safely changing existing code so as not to introduce regression defects, their working practices should be exactly the same as downstream support developers. It is not uncommon for an Agile development team to be working on several versions of an application simultaneously, adding features to the new version, providing early live support to a recently released version, and providing bug fixing support to an older production version (because we still make mistakes, and the world still moves on!).

10.4 The Cost of Going Agile

So, this is great news! By rethinking the way we approach project delivery, we've managed to comprehensively address all our traditional project risks. Instead of seeing a project as a linear sequence of activities that ends up with a big delivery, we find things work better if we deliver frequently in short iterations. So, why isn't everyone doing this?

The obvious but unpopular answer is *because it's really hard!* Or rather, it's really hard to do well. Delivering production-quality software week after week takes a lot of discipline and practice. For all their systemic faults, traditional software processes cause you to focus on certain aspects of a system at certain times. In an Agile process, the training wheels come off, and the responsibility now lies with you. That autonomy comes at a cost!

If we want to deliver working software frequently—as often as every week on many projects—there are a number of new problems we need to solve. Luckily, Agile has been around for long enough that we have an answer to many of these problems, or at least we understand them well enough to have an opinion about them. Let's look at some of the challenges of Agile, and then we will see how BDD addresses them.

Outcome-Based Planning

The only thing we really know at the beginning of a project is that we don't know very much and that what we do know is subject to change. Much like steering a car, we know the rough direction, but we don't know every detailed nuance of the journey, such as exactly when we will turn the steering wheel or by how many degrees. We need to find a way to estimate the cost of delivering a project among all this uncertainty and accept that the fine details of the requirements are bound to change, and that's OK.

Streaming Requirements

If we want to deliver a few features every week or two, we must start describing requirements in a way that supports this. The traditional requirements process tends to be document-based, where the business analyst takes on the role of author and produces a few kilos of requirements.

Instead of this batch delivery of requirements, we need to come up with a way to describe features that we can feed into a more streamlined delivery process.

Evolving Design

In a traditional process, the senior techies would come up with The Design (with audible capitals, most likely based on The Standards). Before we were allowed to start coding, they would have produced high-level designs, detailed designs, and probably class diagrams describing every interaction. Each stage of this would be signed off. In an Agile world, the design needs to flex and grow as we learn more about the problem and as the solution takes shape. This requires rethinking the process of software design.

Changing Existing Code

Traditional programming is like building little blocks for later assembly. We write a module and then put it to one side while we write the next one, and so on, until all the modules are written. Then we bring all the modules together in a (usually painful) process called *integration*. An Agile process requires us to keep revisiting the same code as we evolve it to do new things.

Because we take a feature-wise approach to delivery rather than a module-wise one, we will often need to add new behavior to existing code. This isn't because we got it "wrong" the first time but because the code is currently exactly fit for purpose, and we need the application to do more now. *Refactoring*, the technique of restructuring code without changing its observable behavior, is probably the place where most advances have been made in terms of tool support and automation, especially with statically typed languages like Java and C#.

Frequent Code Integration

Integrating code ahead of a testing cycle is a thankless and fraught task. All the individual modules "work"—just not together! Imagine doing this every single month. Or every week. What about potentially several times *every day*? This is the frequency of integration an iterative process demands: it's frequent enough that it is known as *continuous integration*.

Continual Regression Testing

Whenever we add a new feature, it might affect many parts of the code base. We are doing feature-wise development, so different parts of the code base are evolving at different rates, depending on the kind of feature we are implementing. When we have a single feature, the system is easy to test. When we add the hundredth feature, we suddenly have to regression test the previous ninety-nine. Imagine when we add the two hundredth feature—or the one thousandth! We need to get really good at regression testing; otherwise, we will become ever slower at adding features to our application.

Frequent Production Releases

This is one of the hardest challenges of Agile software delivery, because it involves coordination with the downstream operations team. Things are suddenly outside of the team's control. All the other aspects—streaming requirements, changing design and code, frequent integration, and regression testing—are behaviors we can adopt ourselves.

Getting software into formally controlled environments puts us at odds with the corporate governance structures. But if we can't get into production frequently, there is arguably little value in all the other stuff. It may still be useful for the team's benefit, but software doesn't start making money until it's in production. Remember, we want to be writing software that matters!

Co-located Team

To make this all work, you can't afford for a developer to be waiting around for her manager to talk to someone else's manager to get permission for her to talk to them. The turnaround is just too slow. There are organizational and cultural changes that need to happen in order to shorten the feedback cycles to minutes rather than days or weeks.

The kind of interactions we require involve the whole team sitting together, or at least as near one another as possible. It simply isn't effective to have the programmers in one office, the project managers in another, and the testers elsewhere, whether along the corridor or in a different continent.

10.5 What We've Learned

There are a number of different ways in which traditional software projects fail, and these failures are intrinsic to the way the projects are run. The result of "process improvement" on traditional projects is simply to reinforce these failure modes and ironically make them even more likely.

An analysis of this approach to running software projects leads back to the exponential cost curve that originated in the world of civil engineering, where things are made of steel and concrete. Being aware of this, a number of experienced IT practitioners had been spending some time wondering what software delivery might look like if they ignored the constraints of thinking like civil engineers.

They realized that taking an iterative, collaborative approach to software delivery could systemically eliminate the traditional risks that project managers worry about. They called this approach Agile.

It isn't all plain sailing, however, and adopting an Agile approach introduces its own challenges. There is no free lunch!

In the next chapter, we will see how BDD addresses these challenges and where RSpec and Cucumber fit into the picture.

## Chapter 11

Writing Software That Matters

Although BDD started as a simple reframing of Test-Driven Development, it has grown into a fully fledged software methodology in its own right. In this chapter, we look at the mechanics of BDD and see how RSpec and Cucumber fit into the picture.

11.1 A Description of BDD

Behaviour-Driven Development is about implementing an application by describing its behavior from the perspective of its stakeholders.

This description of BDD implies a number of things. First, it suggests we need to understand the world from the point of view of our stakeholders if we are to deliver anything useful. We need to understand their domain, the challenges and opportunities they face, and the words they use to describe the behavior they want from an application. We use techniques from *Domain-Driven Design* to help with this.

Second, it implies there is more than one stakeholder. We don't just look at the world from the point of view of an end user or the person paying the bills but anyone with an interest in the project.

11.2 The Principles of BDD

When we describe BDD as writing "software that matters," we mean software that has value to a stakeholder, that is neither too little to solve the problem nor over-engineered, and that we can demonstrate works.

We sum this up using the following *three principles of BDD*:

Enough is enough Up-front planning, analysis, and design all have a diminishing return. We shouldn't do less than we need to get started, but any more than that is wasted effort. This also applies to process automation. Have an automated build and deployment, but avoid trying to automate *everything*.

Deliver stakeholder value If you are doing something that isn't either delivering value or increasing your ability to deliver value, stop doing it, and do something else instead.

It's all behavior Whether at the code level, the application level, or beyond, we can use the same thinking and the same linguistic constructs to describe behavior at any level of granularity.

11.3 The Project Inception

Before we get into the day-to-day delivery of a project, we need to understand what it is all about. To do this, we get all the *stakeholders* together to establish a *vision* or *purpose* for the project: what is it we are trying to achieve here? This should be a single pithy statement, something like this: *improve our supply chain* or *understand our customers better*.

BDD defines a stakeholder as *anyone who cares* about the work we are undertaking, whether they are the people whose problem we are trying to solve—known as the *core stakeholders*—or the people who are going to help solve it—who we call the *incidental stakeholders*. This latter group includes the operations folk who will monitor the application, the support team who will diagnose problems and add new features, the legal and security experts who will ensure the application is fit for the purpose from an organizational risk perspective, and in fact all the people representing what we usually call *nonfunctional requirements*. From a BDD perspective, there is no such thing as a nonfunctional requirement, just a feature with an incidental stakeholder. Even the people in the delivery team are stakeholders. (Who would you say is the stakeholder for having an automated build?)

It is the core stakeholders' responsibility to define the vision and the incidental stakeholders' to help them understand what's possible, at what cost, and with what likelihood. This is the objective of the up-front thinking—that and nothing more.

Now we can't just go off and start coding *improve our supply chain.* We need to understand what that means first, so we work with the core stakeholders—the people whose vision it is—to identify *outcomes* or *goals*. How will they know when this project has achieved its purpose? What will they be able to do that they can't do now? There should only be a few of these, or the project will quickly lose its focus. If you find yourself looking at more than a handful of outcomes, either you are going too low level too quickly or this may be a bigger problem than you think and should be broken out into a program of smaller projects.

For the supply chain example, some outcomes might be *the ordering process is easier* or *better access to suppliers' information.* Some people recommend these outcomes should be *SMART* (see the sidebar on page 127), but this becomes less important as you build trust between the core stakeholders and the delivery team.

To achieve these outcomes, we are going to need some software. We describe the sorts of things the software needs to do as *feature sets* or *themes.* The terms are synonymous, so use whichever feels best for you. Themes are things like *reporting* or *customer registration*, again too high level to start coding but specific enough to have some useful conversations around.

Finally, we are in a position to talk about the specific *features* or *stories* that make up these themes. (See the sidebar on page 129 for a discussion of stories and features.)

This is the level where we will actually be working day-to-day—these describe the behavior we will implement in software.

You can see how this gives us traceability right back to a specific stakeholder need. Each feature is there only because it is adding value to a feature set. Each feature set is contributing to one or more of the outcomes, and each outcome is part of the overall purpose of the project. Too often Agile teams dive straight into the feature or story level without taking the time to think about the overall shape of the delivery.

At this stage, you could be forgiven for thinking this looks a lot like traditional top-down decomposition. The difference is that we stop before a traditional analysis phase would, again remembering to only do just enough.

It is dangerous to get too hung up on the detail of features because it can create false expectations with your stakeholders. Remember, they came to us with a need or problem, so success for them will be if we can meet that need and solve that problem. By focusing on the details, we inadvertently shift their attention so that they now associate success with delivering the features we drove out during the planning.

A better use of our efforts during an inception is to try to identify and mitigate the "gotchas." Where are the risky areas—in terms of technology or integration points, an unknown business domain, access to key stakeholders, market conditions, external dependencies—that are likely to derail our nascent project? Keeping a log of these risks and assumptions is at least as important as the breakdown of the project objectives.

11.4 The Cycle of Delivery

The BDD delivery cycle starts with a stakeholder discussing a requirement with a business analyst.[1] The requirement might be a problem they want solved or an idea they've had. The analyst helps the stakeholder articulate the requirement in terms of *features* that make sense to the stakeholder—using their own domain terms—and maybe further into small, verifiable chunks known as *stories*, which represent no more than a few days work.

Next the stakeholder and business analyst work with a tester to determine the stories' scope. What does *done* look like for each story? We don't want to overdesign the solution because that's a waste of effort, but likewise we don't want to do too little; otherwise, we won't be meeting the stakeholder's original need.

Where the business analyst thinks in abstract terms (*it should be possible to withdraw money from a checking account*), the tester is typically thinking in terms of concrete scenarios. *If I have $100 in an account and I withdraw $80, what happens? What about if I try to withdraw $120? What happens if I have an overdraft facility on the account? What if I try to go past my overdraft limit?*

By identifying which scenarios are important to the story before development starts, the stakeholder can specify exactly how much they want the programmers to do or how much development effort they want

---

1. The terms *stakeholder, business analyst,* and so on, describe roles rather than individuals. On a small team, the same person may take on more than one role at different times. You can think of them as different hats people can wear.

SMART Outcomes

The acronym SMART is used to describe outcomes or objectives that have certain characteristics, namely, that they are *Specific*, *Measurable*, *Achievable*, *Relevant*, and *Timeboxed*:

Specific means there is enough detail to know that something is done. *Snappier user experience* is not specific, whereas *Faster response time for the four most common user journeys* is.

Measurable means you can determine whether the objective was reached, for example *10 percent reduction in response times.*

Achievable helps reduce unrealistic expectations. *All credit card transactions should be instantaneous* is unlikely to happen.

Relevant manages the issue of people trying to cram in every conceivable feature just in case. *We want clear, concise reporting and a puppy.*

Timeboxed simply means we know when to call time if we haven't achieved an outcome; otherwise, it could just trundle on forever or for as long as someone is prepared to keep paying.

The emphasis on the SMARTness of objectives or outcomes happens a lot in command-and-control cultures where success is measured in terms of reaching individual targets. More enlightened companies focus on improving throughput and trusting people to act with integrity.

Non-SMART, vaguely worded outcomes allow the participants—both the stakeholders and the delivery team—to be adaptable in what they deliver so they can all focus on doing the best they can with the resources and time they have. This allows the stakeholders to invest incrementally in a project: as long as they are seeing value delivered they continue to invest; otherwise, they can stop the project and assign the team to solving another challenge.

to invest in delivering the feature. The developers will only implement enough to satisfy the agreed scenarios, *and no more*.

The final task before the programmers start implementing the story is to automate the scenarios where it makes sense to do so. In the same way, Test-Driven Development[2] uses code examples to drive the design; these automated scenarios will drive the high-level direction of the development effort.

One of the most important characteristics of BDD is that the scenarios are easy to automate yet are still easily understandable to the stakeholder. Defining and automating these scenarios is the realm of Cucumber.

Now at last we can finally get down to the coding part of the delivery cycle. A developer—or ideally a pair of developers—uses RSpec to code by example to get the scenario working. We start by writing a code example[3] to describe the behavior we want, then we implement the code to make that example work, and then we refactor. The RSpec portions of this book describe exactly how we do this, so we don't need to say anything more here.

Eventually we end up with just enough software to make the scenario work, and then we iterate through the other scenarios until we are done. This then brings us full circle, such that we can demonstrate the working scenarios back to the stakeholder, and the story is done.

Now imagine we could run a mini-project that just contained a single story—something simple enough to develop in a couple of days—and do just enough analysis to understand that story and then design an application to *only do that one thing*! How hard could that be? We could easily implement it and test that it works and then deploy it into an environment where we could showcase it to the stakeholder who asked us for it.

It would mean we didn't spend weeks poring over database schemas or entity-relationship diagrams, we didn't go to town with UML code

---

2. BDD calls Test-Driven Development *coding by example*, which places the emphasis on using examples to drive out the behavior of the code. The fact that these examples become tests once the code is written is a secondary concern.

3. Agile testing expert Brian Marick refers to a code example as an *exemplar*, which is technically a more correct term. An exemplar is an example intended to demonstrate a specific point. We prefer calling them examples because it is a more familiar term.

Stories In, Features Out

Many people use the words *feature* and *story* interchangeably, but there is a subtle difference. A feature is something that delivers cohesive value to a stakeholder. A story is a piece of demonstrable functionality that shouldn't take more than a few days to implement. So, the feature is more useful from the point of view of the stakeholder, and the story is more useful from the point of view of the team delivering the feature.

Often a feature can be delivered as a single story, but sometimes the feature doesn't naturally decompose to that level. For example, if we are capturing an email address, there might be some validation around that address. This could get quite involved and would take more than a few days of effort. In this case, we could separate out the "happy path"—where all the data is valid—and the most important validation cases into one story and some of the less common but still useful validations into another story. Or we might separate out the security concerns into another story (whose stakeholder would be the security folks), so we would look at cross-site scripting or SQL injection attacks as different aspects of the same feature.

As long as your stories are roughly the same size, this decomposition of features into stories provides the same kind of tracking data as having artificial constructs like *story points* or *ideal days*, terms that can feel uncomfortable to your stakeholders. It is more natural to say, "We've broken that feature into these three stories that tackle different aspects," rather than "This feature is seven points, and this one is four points" or "This week we delivered nine ideal days" (to which the correct response is "Eh?").

It is important to remember that we still decompose along boundaries that make sense to the stakeholder, so we wouldn't break a feature into the database stuff, then the UI stuff, and then the wiring-up stuff. Instead, we would deliver different groups of scenarios.

As we deliver the stories, we arrange any artifacts—such as Cucumber scenario files and step implementations—by feature, because over time it doesn't really matter which story the behavior was implemented in so much as which feature benefited from that story. We call this arrangement "stories in, features out": the input happens to be delivered in stories, but the result is cohesive features.

generation tools, and we certainly didn't write down a detailed functional specification of every last aspect of the feature. We also haven't delivered very much yet!

OK, so now we are going to get a little ambitious. Instead of a single story, we are going to deliver a handful of stories together. In fact, we are going to try to deliver about as many as we think we could reasonably do in a week. In effect, we are going to run a tiny one-week project that we call an *iteration*.[4]

As with any project, our estimates will most likely be wrong. Instead of delivering the seven stories we planned, we might make only five. Or we might have a great week and have capacity to spare for an extra bonus story! In any event, we will know at the end of the week how much we actually did deliver, *and we can use this to predict our throughput for next week!* But that comes later.

Right now we are more interested in what our stakeholders think about the work we've done, so we arrange a showcase. This feedback happens very close to when the work occurred—because we are only showcasing the work we completed in the last iteration—and usually involves the stakeholder saying, "That's *very nearly* exactly what I wanted, but can I change some stuff?"

And now we are ready to plan the next mini-project. We have feedback from our stakeholders, a backlog of stories, and a priority order.

This then is how we work, from day to day and from week to week. We have frequent, regular contact with our stakeholders who get to provide fine-grained steering in the form of feedback and reprioritization. But what does a story look like close up?

11.5 What's in a Story?

Up to now we haven't said anything about the anatomy of a story—just about how they fit into the delivery process. Now it's time to take a look

---

4. You don't have to work in iterations, and if you do, they don't have to be one-week long. We have seen teams using iterations lasting from half a day (no, really!) to four weeks. Some teams don't use iterations at all but have a constant flow of stories that they track using techniques borrowed from Lean manufacturing, such as *kanban* flow control and *finger charts*. The important thing is to ensure you have regular feedback from your stakeholders and a way of measuring throughput.

inside and see how the structure of the story enables us to concentrate on writing software that matters.

A story consists of a number of components:

A title so we know which story we are talking about.

A narrative that tells us what this story is about. There are a couple of common formats for this, but you can use anything that captures the essentials. At the very least, it should identify the *stakeholder* for this story, a description of the *feature* they want, and the reason they want it—the *benefit* they expect to gain by us delivering this behavior.

The most common format for this is known as the Connextra format, after the company where it was first used: *as a [stakeholder], I want [feature] so that [benefit]*.

A recent variant that is becoming popular looks like this: *in order to [benefit], a [stakeholder] wants to [feature]*. The content is exactly the same, but there is a subtle shift in emphasis by putting the benefit first. It helps keep the focus on the outcome rather than the detail of the feature.

Acceptance criteria so we know when we are done. In BDD, the acceptance criteria take the form of a number of *scenarios* made up of individual *steps*.

Before we can begin implementing a story, we need to drive out this level of detail. As we mentioned earlier, this doesn't need to happen during the inception (and probably shouldn't!), but it *does* need to happen before we do anything that requires an understanding of "done," such as scheduling work during iteration/sprint planning. Some teams ensure they have one or two iterations worth of stories prepared as they go; others drive out the detail of scenarios during a weekly planning session. Our recommendation is to try different approaches and go with what works for you and your team.

The business analyst (again remembering this is a role, not necessarily a specific person) should ensure the story uses the language of the stakeholders so everyone is using a consistent vocabulary. In his book *Domain-Driven Design* [Eva03], Eric Evans uses the phrase *ubiquitous language* to describe this shared vocabulary. The idea is that the domain words find their way right into the code base, as the names of objects, methods, variables, and even modules and namespaces. This allows the code to more accurately model the domain, which in turn enables us to solve problems in that domain more effectively.

Now we get into the acceptance criteria—the scenarios—that define "done" for this story. Which ones do we care about (and by omission which ones don't we care about)? This discussion should be a team effort, but the acceptance criteria are "owned" by the tester, or rather by someone in the tester role.

Each scenario has a title. You can think of scenario names like the titles of *Friends* episodes, so they are all "The one where..." for example *[The one where] the account is locked* or *[the one where] the password is invalid.*[5]

We use the slightly artificial structure of *givens*, *events*, and *outcomes* to describe these scenarios. This doesn't mean that every scenario has exactly one Given, When, and Then in that order. Rather, it means that each step is *either* setting something up in a known state (a given) *or* exercising some behavior (an event) *or* verifying something happened (an outcome). Trying to do more than one of these in a single step usually ends up in confusion.

This separation is useful because *it is only the event we care about.* For the setup, the givens, it doesn't matter how we get the world into a known state. We could poke values into a database, drive a UI, read values in from a flat file—it doesn't matter. What matters is that the event steps have no idea how this happened and interact with the application in exactly the same way the stakeholder would. Similarly, it doesn't matter how you verify the outcomes, just that you do. This might involve poking around in a DOM, checking database values, or doing any manner of other checks. It is possible to get hung up on thinking of scenarios as full-blown integration tests so that all the setup steps need to use the same UI as the user might. Now there is definitely a benefit in having these integration tests, and tools like Cucumber and constructs like scenarios are a pretty good way to do this, but this is not the (primary) purpose of a BDD scenario.

---

5. You don't need to use the actual words "The one where..." in the scenario title; it just helps with the names.

11.6 What We've Learned

Behaviour-driven development has grown from an experiment in re-framing TDD to make it easier to understand into a fully fledged Agile methodology.

BDD is based on three core principles, namely:

- **Enough is enough**. We should work to achieve the stakeholder's expectations but avoid doing more than we need to do.

- **Deliver stakeholder value**. There are multiple stakeholders—both core and incidental—and everything we do should be about delivering demonstrable value to them.

- **It's all behavior**. Just as we can describe the application's behavior from the perspective of the stakeholders, we can describe low-level code behavior from the perspective of other code that uses it.

At the start of a project or a release, we carry out some sort of inception activities to understand the purpose of the work we are doing and to create a shared vision. This is about the deliberate discovery of risks and potential pitfalls along the way.

The day-to-day rhythm of delivery involves decomposing requirements into features and then into stories and scenarios, which we automate to act as a guide to keep us focused on what we need to deliver. These automated scenarios become acceptance tests to ensure the application does everything we expect.

BDD stories and scenarios are specifically designed to support this model of working and in particular to be both easy to automate and clearly understandable by their stakeholders.

Part III

RSpec

Chapter 12

Code Examples

In this part of the book, we'll explore the details of RSpec's built-in expectations, mock objects framework, command-line tools, IDE integration, and extension points.

Our goal is to make Test-Driven Development a more joyful and productive experience with tools that elevate the design and documentation aspects of TDD to first-class citizenship. Here are some words you'll need to know as we reach for that goal:

subject code The code whose behavior we are specifying with RSpec.

expectation An expression of how the subject code is expected to behave. You'll read about state-based expectations in Chapter 13, *RSpec::Expectations*, on page 157, and you'll learn about interaction expectations in Chapter 14, *RSpec::Mocks*, on page 179.

code example An executable example of how the subject code can be used and its expected behavior (expressed with expectations) in a given context. In BDD, we write the code examples before the subject code they document.

The *example* terminology comes from Brian Marick, whose website is even named http://exampler.com. Using *example* instead of *test* reminds us that writing them is a design and documentation practice, even though once they are written and the code is developed against them, they become regression tests.

example group A group of code examples.

spec, aka **spec file** A file that contains one or more example groups.

> ### Familiar Structure, New Nomenclature
>
> If you already have some experience with Test::Unit or similar tools in other languages and/or TDD, the words we're using here map directly to words you're already familiar with:
>
> - *Assertion* becomes *expectation*.
> - *Test method* becomes *code example*
> - *Test case* becomes *example group*
>
> In addition to finding these new names used throughout this book, you'll find them in RSpec's code base as well.

In this chapter, you'll learn how to organize executable *code examples* in *example groups* in a number of different ways, run arbitrary bits of code before and after each example, and even share examples across groups.

12.1 Describe It!

RSpec provides a domain-specific language for specifying the behavior of objects. It embraces the metaphor of describing behavior the way we might express it if we were talking to a customer or another developer. A snippet of such a conversation might look like this:

You: *Describe a new account.*

Somebody else: *It should have a balance of zero.*

Here's that same conversation expressed in RSpec:

```
describe "A new Account" do
  it "should have a balance of 0" do
    account = Account.new
    account.balance.should == Money.new(0, :USD)
  end
end
```

We use the describe() method to define an example group. The string we pass to it represents the facet of the system that we want to describe (a new account). The block holds the code examples that make up that group.

The it() method defines a code example. The string passed to it describes the specific behavior we're interested in specifying about that facet (should have a balance of zero). The block holds the example code that exercises the subject code and sets expectations about its behavior.

Using strings like this instead of legal Ruby class names and method names provides a lot of flexibility. Here's an example from RSpec's own code examples:

```
it "matches when actual < (expected + delta)" do
  be_close(5.0, 0.5).matches?(5.49).should be_true
end
```

This is an example of the behavior of code, so the intended audience is someone who can read code. With Test::Unit, we might name the method test_matches_when_value_is_less_than_target_plus_delta, which is pretty readable, but the ability to use nonalphanumeric characters makes the name of this example more expressive.

To get a better sense of how you can unleash this expressiveness, let's take a closer look at the describe() and it() methods.

The describe Method

The describe() method takes an arbitrary number of arguments and an optional block and returns a subclass of RSpec::Core::ExampleGroup. We typically use only one or two arguments, which represent the facet of behavior that we want to describe. They might describe an object, perhaps in a predefined state or perhaps a subset of the behavior we can expect from that object. Let's look at a few examples, with the output they produce so we can get an idea of how the arguments relate to each other:

```
describe "A User" { ... }
=> A User

describe User { ... }
=> User

describe User, "with no roles assigned" { ... }
=> User with no roles assigned

describe User, "should require password length between 5 and 40" { ... }
=> User should require password length between 5 and 40
```

The first argument can be either a reference to a class or module or a string. The second argument is optional and should be a string. Using the class/module for the first argument provides an interesting benefit: when we wrap ExampleGroup in a module, we'll see that module's name in the output. For example, if User is in the Authentication module, we could do something like this:

```
module Authentication
  describe User, "with no roles assigned" do
```

The resulting report would look like this:

```
Authentication::User with no roles assigned
```

So, by wrapping the ExampleGroup in a module, we see the fully qualified name Authentication::User, followed by the contents of the second argument. Together, they form a descriptive string, and we get the fully qualified name for free. This is a nice way to help RSpec help *us* understand where things live as we're looking at the output.

You can also nest example groups, which can be a very nice way of expressing things in both input and output. For example, we can nest the input like this:

```
describe User do
  describe "with no roles assigned" do
    it "is not allowed to view protected content" do
```

This produces output like this:

```
User
  with no roles assigned
    is not allowed to view protected content
```

The context Method

The context() method is an alias for describe(), so they can be used interchangeably. We tend to use describe() for things and context() for context.

The User example, shown earlier, for example, could be written like this:

```
describe User do
  context "with no roles assigned" do
    it "is not allowed to view protected content" do
```

The output would be the same as when we used describe() on the second line, but context() can make it easier to scan a spec file and understand what relates to what.

What's It All About?

Similar to describe(), the it() method takes a single string, an optional hash, and an optional block. The string should be a sentence that, when prefixed with "it," represents the detail that will be expressed in code within the block. Here's an example specifying a stack:

```
describe Stack do
  before(:each) do
    @stack = Stack.new
    @stack.push :item
  end

  describe "#peek" do
    it "should return the top element" do
      @stack.peek.should == :item
    end

    it "should not remove the top element" do
      @stack.peek
      @stack.size.should == 1
    end
  end

  describe "#pop" do
    it "should return the top element" do
      @stack.pop.should == :item
    end

    it "should remove the top element" do
      @stack.pop
      @stack.size.should == 0
    end
  end
end
```

This is also exploiting RSpec's nested example groups feature to group the examples of pop() separately from the examples of peek().

When run with the --format documentation command-line option, this would produce the following output:

```
Stack
  #peek
    should return the top element
    should not remove the top element
  #pop
    should return the top element
    should remove the top element


Finished in 0.00154 seconds
4 examples, 0 failures
```

Looks a bit like a specification, doesn't it? In fact, if we reword the example names without the word *should* in them, we can get output that looks even more like documentation:

```
Stack
  #peek
    returns the top element
    does not remove the top element
  #pop
    returns the top element
    removes the top element


Finished in 0.00157 seconds
4 examples, 0 failures
```

What? No *should*? Remember, the goal here is readable sentences. *Should* was the tool that Dan North used to get people writing sentences but is not itself essential to the goal.

The ability to pass free text to the it() method allows us to name and organize examples in meaningful ways. As with describe(), the string can even include punctuation. This is especially useful when we're dealing with code-level concepts in which symbols have important meaning that can help us understand the intent of the example.

12.2 Pending Examples

In *Test Driven Development: By Example* [Bec02], Kent Beck suggests keeping a list of tests that you have yet to write for the object you're working on, crossing items off the list as you get tests passing, and adding new tests to the list as you think of them.

With RSpec, you can do this right in the code by calling the it() method with no block. Let's say that we're in the middle of describing the behavior of a newspaper:

```
describe Newspaper do
  it "should be black" do
    Newspaper.new.colors.should include('black')
  end

  it "should be white" do
    Newspaper.new.colors.should include('white')
  end

  it "should be read all over"
end
```

RSpec will consider the example with no block to be pending. Running these examples produces the following output:

```
Newspaper
  should be black
  should be white
  should be read all over (PENDING: Not Yet Implemented)

Pending:
  Newspaper should be read all over
    # Not Yet Implemented
    # ./newspaper_spec.rb:17

Finished in 0.00191 seconds
3 examples, 0 failures, 1 pending
```

As you add code to existing pending examples and add new ones, each time you run all the examples, RSpec will remind you how many pending examples you have, so you always know how close you are to being done!

Another case for marking an example pending is when you're in the middle of driving out an object, you have some examples passing, and you add a new failing example. You look at the code, see a change you want to make, and realize that the design really doesn't support what you want to do to make this example pass.

There are a couple of different paths people choose at this juncture. One is to comment out the failing example so you can refactor *in the green* and then uncomment the example and continue. This works great until you're interrupted in the middle of this near the end of the day on Friday, and three months later you look back at that file and find examples you commented out three months ago.

Instead of commenting the example out, you can mark it pending like this:

```
describe "onion rings" do
  it "should not be mixed with french fries" do
    pending "cleaning out the fryer"
    fryer_with(:onion_rings).should_not include(:french_fry)
  end
end
```

In this case, even though the example block gets executed, it stops execution on the line with the pending() declaration. The subsequent code is not run, there is no failure, and the example is listed as pending in the output, so it stays on your radar. When you've finished refactoring, you can remove the pending declaration to execute the code example as normal. This is, clearly, much better than commenting out failing examples and having them get lost in the shuffle.

A third way to indicate a pending example can be quite helpful in handling bug reports. Let's say you get a bug report and the reporter is kind enough to provide a failing example. Or you create a failing example yourself to prove the bug exists. You don't plan to fix it this minute, but you want to keep the code handy. Rather than commenting the code, you could use the pending() method to keep the failing example from being executed.

You can also, however, wrap the example code in a block and pass that to the pending method, like this:

```
describe "an empty array" do
  it "should be empty" do
    pending("bug report 18976") do
      [].should be_empty
    end
  end
end
```

When RSpec encounters this block, it actually executes the block. If the block fails or raises an error, RSpec proceeds as with any other pending example.

If, however, the code executes without incident, RSpec raises a Pending-ExampleFixedError, letting you know that you have an example that is pending for no reason:

```
F

Failures:
  1) an empty array should be empty FIXED
     Expected pending 'bug report 18976' to fail. No Error was raised.
     # ./pending_fixed.rb:4

Finished in 0.00088 seconds
1 example, 1 failure
```

The next step is to remove the pending wrapper and rerun the examples with your formerly pending, newly passing example added to the total of passing examples.

So, now you know three ways to identify pending examples, each of which can be helpful in your process in different ways:

- Add pending examples as you think of new examples that you want to write.

- Disable examples without losing track of them (rather than commenting them out).

- Wrap failing examples when you want to be notified that changes to the system cause them to pass.

Now that you know how to postpone writing examples, let's talk about what happens when you actually write some!

12.3 Hooks: Before, After, and Around

If we were developing a stack, we'd want to describe how a stack behaves when it is empty, almost empty, almost full, and full. And we'd want to describe how the push(), pop(), and peek() methods behave under each of those conditions.

If we multiply the four states by the three methods, we're going to be describing twelve different scenarios that we'll want to group together by either state or method. We'll talk about grouping by method later this chapter. Right now, let's talk about grouping things by *initial state*, using RSpec's before() hook.

before(:each)

To group examples by initial state, or *context*, RSpec provides a before() method that can run either one time before :all the examples in an example group or once before :each of the examples. In general, it's better to use before(:each) because that re-creates the context before each example and keeps state from leaking from example to example. Here's how this might look for the stack examples:

`describeit/stack.rb`
```
describe Stack do
  context "when empty" do
    before(:each) do
      @stack = Stack.new
    end
  end
```

```ruby
    context "when almost empty (with one element)" do
      before(:each) do
        @stack = Stack.new
        @stack.push 1
      end
    end

    context "when almost full (with one element less than capacity)" do
      before(:each) do
        @stack = Stack.new
        (1..9).each { |n| @stack.push n }
      end
    end

    context "when full" do
      before(:each) do
        @stack = Stack.new
        (1..10).each { |n| @stack.push n }
      end
    end
end
```

As we add examples to each of these example groups, the code in the block passed to before(:each) will be executed before each example is executed, putting the environment in the same known starting state before each example in that group.

before(:all)

In addition to before(:each), we can also say before(:all). This gets run once and only once in its own instance of Object,[1] but its instance variables get copied to each instance in which the examples are run. A word of caution in using this: in general, we want to have each example run in complete isolation from one another. As soon as we start sharing state across examples, unexpected things begin to happen.

Consider a stack. The pop() method removes the top item from a stack, which means the second example that uses the same stack *instance* is starting off with a stack that has one less item than in the before(:all) block. When that example fails, this fact is going to make it more challenging to understand the failure.

Even if it seems to you that sharing state won't be a problem right now in any given example, this is sure to change over time. Problems created by sharing state across examples are notoriously difficult to find. If we

---

1. In nested example groups in rspec-1.x, it gets run once per example group.

have to be debugging at all, the last thing we want to be debugging is the examples.

So, what is before(:all) actually good for? One example might be opening a network connection of some sort. Generally, this is something we wouldn't be doing in the isolated examples that RSpec is really aimed at. If we're using RSpec to drive higher-level examples, however, then this might be a good case for using before(:all).

after(:each)

Following the execution of each example, before(:each)'s counterpart after(:each) is executed. This is rarely necessary because each example runs in its own scope, and the instance variables consequently go out of scope after each example.

There are cases, however, when after(:each) can be quite useful. If you're dealing with a system that maintains some global state that you want to modify just for one example, a common idiom for this is to set aside the global state in an instance variable in before(:each) and then restore it in after(:each), like this:

```
before(:each) do
  @original_global_value = $some_global_value
  $some_global_value = temporary_value
end

after(:each) do
  $some_global_value = @original_global_value
end
```

after(:each) is guaranteed to run after each example, even if there are failures or errors in any before blocks or examples, so this is a safe approach to restoring global state.

after(:all)

We can also define some code to be executed after(:all) of the examples in an example group. This is even more rare than after(:each), but there are cases in which it is justified. Examples include closing down browsers, closing database connections, closing sockets, and so on— basically, any resources that we want to ensure get shut down but not after every example.

around(:each)

RSpec provides an around() hook to support APIs that require a block. The most common use case for this is database transactions:

```
around do |example|
  DB.transaction { example.run }
end
```

RSpec passes the current running example to the block, which is then responsible for calling the example's run() method. You can also pass the example to a method within the block as a block itself:

```
around do |example|
  DB.transaction &example
end
```

One pitfall of this structure is that the block is responsible for handling errors and cleaning up after itself. In the previous example, we assume that the transaction() method does this, but that is not always the case. Consider the following:

```
around do |example|
  do_some_stuff_before
  example.run
  do_some_stuff_after
end
```

If the example fails or raises an error, do_some_stuff_after() will not be executed, and the environment may not be correctly torn down. We could get around that with a begin/ensure/end structure, like this:

```
around do |example|
  begin
    do_some_stuff_before
    example.run
  ensure
    do_some_stuff_after
  end
end
```

But now this hook has a lot of responsibility, and the readability is starting to wane. For cases like this, we recommend sticking to before and after hooks:

```
before { do_some_stuff_before }
after  { do_some_stuff_after }
```

after hooks are guaranteed to run even if there is an error in an example or a before, so this removes the burden of error handling we have in around hooks and is arguably more readable.

So, we've now explored before and after :each and before and after :all. These methods are very useful in helping to organize our examples by removing duplication—not just for the sake of removing duplication but with the express purpose of improving clarity and thereby making the examples easier to understand.

But sometimes we want to share things across a wider scope. The next two sections will address that problem by introducing helper methods and shared examples.

12.4 Helper Methods

Another approach to cleaning up our examples is to use helper methods that we define right in the example group, which are then accessible from all the examples in that group. Imagine that we have several examples in one example group, and at one point in each example we need to perform some action that is somewhat verbose.

```ruby
describe Thing do
  it "should do something when ok" do
    thing = Thing.new
    thing.set_status('ok')
    thing.do_fancy_stuff(1, true, :move => 'left', :obstacles => nil)
    ...
  end

  it "should do something else when not so good" do
    thing = Thing.new
    thing.set_status('not so good')
    thing.do_fancy_stuff(1, true, :move => 'left', :obstacles => nil)
    ...
  end
end
```

Both examples need to create a new Thing and assign it a status. This can be extracted out to a helper like this:

```ruby
describe Thing do
  def create_thing(options)
    thing = Thing.new
    thing.set_status(options[:status])
    thing
  end

  it "should do something when ok" do
    thing = create_thing(:status => 'ok')
    thing.do_fancy_stuff(1, true, :move => 'left', :obstacles => nil)
    ...
  end
```

```
it "should do something else when not so good" do
  thing = create_thing(:status => 'not so good')
  thing.do_fancy_stuff(1, true, :move => 'left', :obstacles => nil)
  ...
  end
end
```

One idiom you can apply to clean this up even more is to yield self from initializers in your objects. Assuming that Thing's initialize() method does this and set_status() does as well, you can write the previous like this:

```
describe Thing do
  def given_thing_with(options)
    yield Thing.new do |thing|
      thing.set_status(options[:status])
    end
  end

  it "should do something when ok" do
    given_thing_with(:status => 'ok') do |thing|
      thing.do_fancy_stuff(1, true, :move => 'left', :obstacles => nil)
      ...
    end
  end

  it "should do something else when not so good" do
    given_thing_with(:status => 'not so good') do |thing|
      thing.do_fancy_stuff(1, true, :move => 'left', :obstacles => nil)
      ...
    end
  end
end
```

Obviously, this is a matter of personal taste, but you can see that this cleans things up nicely, reducing the noise level in each of the examples. Of course, with almost all benefits come drawbacks. In this case, the drawback is that we have to look elsewhere to understand the meaning of given_thing_with. This sort of indirection can make under-standing failures quite painful when overused.

A good guideline to follow is to keep things consistent within each code base. If all the code examples in your system look like the earlier one, even your new teammates who might not be familiar with these idioms will quickly learn and adapt. If there is only one example like this in the entire code base, then that might be a bit more confusing. So, as you strive to keep things clean, be sure to keep them consistent as well.

Sharing Helper Methods

If we have helper methods we want to share across example groups, we can define them in one or more modules and then include the modules in the example groups we want to have access to them.

```
module UserExampleHelpers
  def create_valid_user
    User.new(:email => 'email@example.com', :password => 'shhhhh')
  end

  def create_invalid_user
    User.new(:password => 'shhhhh')
  end
end

describe User do
  include UserExampleHelpers

  it "does something when it is valid" do
    user = create_valid_user
    # do stuff
  end

  it "does something when it is not valid" do
    user = create_invalid_user
    # do stuff
  end
```

If we have a module of helper methods that we'd like available in all of our example groups, we can include the module in the configuration (see Section 16.2, *Configuration*, on page 224 for more information):

```
RSpec.configure do |config|
  config.include(UserExampleHelpers)
end
```

So, now that we can share helper methods across example groups, how about sharing *examples*?

12.5 Shared Examples

When we expect instances of more than one class to behave in the same way, we can use a shared example group to describe it once and then include that example group in other example groups. We declare a shared example group with the shared_examples_for() method.

```
shared_examples_for "any pizza" do
  it "tastes really good" do
    @pizza.should taste_really_good
  end
```

```
    it "is available by the slice" do
      @pizza.should be_available_by_the_slice
    end
  end
end
```

Once a shared example group is declared, we can include it in other example groups with the it_behaves_like() method.

```
describe "New York style thin crust pizza" do
  before(:each) do
    @pizza = Pizza.new(:region => 'New York', :style => 'thin crust')
  end

  it_behaves_like "any pizza"

  it "has a really great sauce" do
    @pizza.should have_a_really_great_sauce
  end
end

describe "Chicago style stuffed pizza" do
  before(:each) do
    @pizza = Pizza.new(:region => 'Chicago', :style => 'stuffed')
  end

  it_behaves_like "any pizza"

  it "has a ton of cheese" do
    @pizza.should have_a_ton_of_cheese
  end
end
```

That produces this:

```
New York style thin crust pizza
  has a really great sauce
  behaves like any pizza
    tastes really good
    is available by the slice

Chicago style stuffed pizza
  has a ton of cheese
  behaves like any pizza
    tastes really good
    is available by the slice
```

The it_behaves_like() method generates a nested example group named "behaves like" followed by the first argument: "behaves like any pizza." The block passed to shared_examples_for() is then evaluated in the context of that group, so any methods, examples, before hooks, and so on, that are defined in the block are added to the group.

Like any other nested group, the one generated by it_behaves_like() inherits the methods and hooks defined in the outer group. In this case, we get the before() hooks that define @pizza in each of the groups.

The report shows "behaves like any pizza," and its examples are nested in each of the top-level groups.

This example also hints at a couple of other features that RSpec brings us to help make the examples as expressive as possible: custom expectation matchers and arbitrary predicate matchers. These will be explained in detail in later chapters, so if you haven't skipped ahead to read about them yet, consider yourself teased.

12.6 Nested Example Groups

Nesting example groups is a great way to organize examples within one spec. Here's a simple example:

```
describe "outer" do
  describe "inner" do
  end
end
```

As we discussed earlier in this chapter, the outer group is a subclass of ExampleGroup. In this example, the inner group is a *subclass of the outer group*. This means that any helper methods and/or before and after declarations, included modules, and so on, declared in the outer group are available in the inner group.

If we declare before and after blocks in both the inner and outer groups, they'll be run as follows:

1. Outer before
2. Inner before
3. Example
4. Inner after
5. Outer after

To demonstrate this, copy this into a Ruby file:

```
describe "outer" do
  before(:each) { puts "first" }
  describe "inner" do
    before(:each) { puts "second" }
    it { puts "third"}
    after(:each) { puts "fourth" }
  end
  after(:each) { puts "fifth" }
end
```

If you run that with the rspec command, you should see output like this:

```
first
second
third
fourth
fifth
```

Because they are all run in the context of the same object, we can share state across the before blocks and examples. This allows us to do a progressive setup. For example, let's say we want to express a given in the outer group, an event (or *when*) in the inner group, and the expected outcome in the examples themselves. We could do something like this:

```ruby
describe Stack do
  before(:each) do
    @stack = Stack.new(:capacity => 10)
  end
  describe "when full" do
    before(:each) do
      (1..10).each {|n| @stack.push n}
    end
    describe "when it receives push" do
      it "should raise an error" do
        lambda { @stack.push 11 }.should raise_error(StackOverflowError)
      end
    end
  end
  describe "when almost full (one less than capacity)" do
    before(:each) do
      (1..9).each {|n| @stack.push n}
    end
    describe "when it receives push" do
      it "should be full" do
        @stack.push 10
        @stack.should be_full
      end
    end
  end
end
```

At this point, you might be thinking, "w00t! Now *that* is DRY!" Or, perhaps, "Oh my God, it's so complicated!" Either way, you're right. It *is* DRY,*and* it's so complicated. In the end, you have to find what works for you, and this structure is one option that is available to you. Handle with care.

Nested examples, however, are quite useful for organization of concepts even when we don't use them to build up state. Consider this variation:

```
describe Stack do
  describe "when full" do
    before(:each) do
      @stack = Stack.new(:capacity => 10)
      (1..10).each {|n| @stack.push n}
    end
    describe "when it receives push" do
      it "should raise an error" do
        lambda { @stack.push 11 }.should raise_error(StackOverflowError)
      end
    end
  end
  describe "when almost full (one less than capacity)" do
    before(:each) do
      @stack = Stack.new(:capacity => 10)
      (1..9).each {|n| @stack.push n}
    end
    describe "when it receives push" do
      it "should be full" do
        @stack.push 10
        @stack.should be_full
      end
    end
  end
end
```

Or this one, with no setup:

```
describe Stack do
  describe "when full" do
    describe "when it receives push" do
      it "should raise an error" do
        stack = Stack.new(:capacity => 10)
        (1..10).each {|n| stack.push n}
        lambda { stack.push 11 }.should raise_error(StackOverflowError)
      end
    end
  end
  describe "when almost full (one less than capacity)" do
    describe "when it receives push" do
      it "should be full" do
        stack = Stack.new(:capacity => 10)
        (1..9).each {|n| stack.push n}
        stack.push 10
        stack.should be_full
      end
    end
  end
end
```

Now this is probably the most readable of all three examples. The nested describe blocks provide documentation and conceptual cohesion, and each example contains all the code it needs. The great thing about this approach is that if you have a failure in one of these examples, you don't have to look anywhere else to understand it. It's all right there.

On the flip side, this is the least DRY of all three examples. If we change the stack's constructor, we'll have to change it in two places here and many more in a complete example. So, you need to balance these concerns. Sadly, there's no one true way. And if there were, we'd all be looking for new careers, so let's be glad for the absence of the silver bullet.

12.7 What We've Learned

In this chapter, we covered quite a bit about the approach RSpec takes to structuring and organizing executable code examples. We learned that we can do the following:

- Declare an example group using the describe() method

- Declare an example using the it() method

- Declare an example to be *pending* by either omitting the block or using the pending() method inside the block

- Nest example groups for cohesive organization

- Declare code to be run before, after, and around examples with hooks

- Define helper methods within an example group that are available to each example in that group

- Share examples across multiple groups

But what about the stuff that goes inside the examples? We've used a couple of expectations in this chapter, but we haven't really discussed them. The next chapters will address these lower-level details, as well as introduce some of the peripheral tooling that is available to help you nurture your inner BDD child and evolve into a BDD ninja.

## Chapter 13

RSpec::Expectations

One of our goals in BDD is *getting the words right*. We want to derive language, practices, and processes that support communication between all members of a team, regardless of each person's understanding of technical issues. This is why we like to use nontechnical words like *Given*, *When*, and *Then*.

We also talk about *expectations* instead of *assertions*. The dictionary defines the verb "to assert" as "to state a fact or belief confidently and forcefully." This is something we do in a courtroom. We assert that it was *Miss Peacock* in the *kitchen* with a *rope* because that's what we believe to be true.

In executable code examples, we are setting an *expectation* of what *should* happen rather than what *will* happen. In fact, we've embedded the word *should* right into RSpec's expectation framework. For example, if we are expecting the result of a calculation to be the number 5, here's how we express this in RSpec:

```
result.should equal(5)
```

This is an example of an RSpec *expectation*, a statement that expresses that at a specific point in the execution of a code example, something should be in some state. Here are some other expectations that come with RSpec:

```
message.should match(/on Sunday/)
team.should have(11).players
lambda { do_something_risky }.should raise_error(
  RuntimeError, "sometimes risks pay off ... but not this time"
)
```

In this chapter, you'll learn about all of RSpec's built-in expectations and the simple framework that RSpec uses to express them. You'll also learn how to extend RSpec with your own domain-specific expectations. With little effort, you'll be able to express things like this:

```
judge.should disqualify(participant)
registration.should notify_applicant("person@domain.com", /Dear Person/)
```

To better understand RSpec's expectations, let's get familiar with their different parts. We'll start off by taking a closer look at the should() and should_not() methods, followed by a detailed discussion of various types of *matchers*. As you'll see, RSpec supports matchers for common operations that you might expect, like equality, and some more unusual expressions as well.

13.1 should, should_not, and matchers

RSpec achieves a high level of expressiveness and readability by exploiting open classes in Ruby to add the methods should() and should_not() to every object in the system. Each method accepts either a *matcher* or a Ruby expression using a specific subset of Ruby operators. A matcher is an object that tries to match against an expected outcome.

Let's take a look at an example using the equal matcher, which you can access through the method equal(expected):

```
result.should equal(5)
```

When the Ruby interpreter encounters this line, it begins by evaluating equal(5). This is an RSpec method that returns a matcher object configured to match for equality with the value 5. The matcher then becomes the argument to result.should.

Behind the scenes, the should() method calls matcher.matches?, passing self (the result object) as the argument. Because should() is added to every object, it can be *any* object. Similarly, the matcher can be *any* object that responds to matches?(object).

If matches?(self) returns true, then the expectation is met and execution moves on to the next line in the example. If matches?(self) returns false, should() asks the matcher for a failure message and raises an ExpectationNotMetError with that message.

should_not() works the opposite way. If matches?(self) returns false, then the expectation is met, and execution moves on to the next line in the example. If it returns true, then an ExpectationNotMetError is raised with a message returned by matcher.failure_message_for_should_not.

Note that should() calls matcher.failure_message_for_should, while should_not() uses matcher.failure_message_for_should_not, allowing the matcher to provide meaningful messages in either situation. Clear, meaningful feedback is one of RSpec's primary goals.

The should() and should_not() methods can also take any of several operators such as == and =~. You can read more about those in Section 13.6, *Operator Expressions*, on page 173. Right now, let's take a closer look at RSpec's built-in matchers.

13.2 Built-in Matchers

RSpec ships with several built-in matchers with obvious names that you can use in your examples. In addition to equal(expected), others include the following:

```
include(item)
respond_to(message)
raise_error(type)
```

By themselves, they seem a bit odd, but in context they make a bit more sense:

```
prime_numbers.should_not include(8)
list.should respond_to(:length)
lambda { Object.new.explode! }.should raise_error(NameError)
```

We will cover each of RSpec's built-in matchers, starting with those related to equality.

Equality: Object Equivalence and Object Identity

Although we're focused on behavior, many of the expectations we want to set are about the state of the environment after some event occurs. The two most common ways of dealing with post-event state are to specify that an object should have values that match our expectations (object equivalence) and to specify that an object *is* the very same object we are expecting (object identity).

Most xUnit frameworks support something like assert_equal to mean that two objects are equivalent and assert_same to mean that two objects are really the same object (object identity). This comes from languages like Java, in which there are really only two constructs that deal with equality: the == operator, which, in Java, means the two references point to the same object in memory, and the equals method, which defaults to the same meaning as == but is normally overridden to mean equivalence.

Note that you have to do a mental mapping with assertEqual and assertSame. In Java, assertEqual means equal, and assertSame means ==. This is OK in languages with only two equality constructs, but Ruby is a bit more complex than that. Ruby has four constructs that deal with equality.

```
a == b
a === b
a.eql?(b)
a.equal?(b)
```

Each of these has different semantics, sometimes differing further in different contexts, and can be quite confusing.[1] So, rather than forcing you to make a mental mapping from expectations to the methods they represent, RSpec lets you express the exact method you mean to express.

```
a.should == b
a.should === b
a.should eql(b)
a.should equal(b)
```

The most common of these is should ==, because the majority of the time we're concerned with value equality, not object identity. Here are some examples:

```
(3 * 5).should == 15


person = Person.new(:given_name => "Yukihiro", :family_name => "Matsumoto")
person.full_name.should == "Yukihiro Matsumoto"
person.nickname.should == "Matz"
```

In these examples, we're only interested in the correct values. Sometimes, however, we'll want to specify that an object is the exact object that we're expecting.

```
person = Person.create!(:name => "David")
Person.find_by_name("David").should equal(person)
```

This puts a tighter constraint on the value returned by find_by_name(), requiring that it must be the exact same object as the one returned

---

1. See http://www.ruby-doc.org/core/classes/Object.html#M001057 for the official documentation about equality in Ruby.

by create!(). Although this may be appropriate when expecting some sort of caching behavior, the tighter the constraint, the more brittle the expectation. If caching is not a real requirement in this example, then saying Person.find_by_name("David").should == person is good enough and means that this example is less likely to fail later when things get refactored.

Do Not Use !=

Although RSpec supports the following:

```
actual.should == expected
```

it does *not* support this:

```
# unsupported
actual.should != expected
```

For the negative, you should use this:

```
actual.should_not == expected
```

The reason for this is that == is a method in Ruby, just like to_s(), push(), or any other method named with alphanumeric characters. The result is that the following:

```
actual.should == expected
```

is interpreted as this:

```
actual.should.==(expected)
```

This is not true for !=. Ruby interprets this:

```
actual.should != expected
```

as follows:

```
!(actual.should.==(expected))
```

This means that the object returned by should() receives == whether the example uses == or !=. And *that* means that short of doing a text analysis of each example, which would slow things down considerably, RSpec cannot know that the example really means != when it receives ==. And because RSpec doesn't know, it won't tell you, which means you'll be getting false responses. So, stay away from != in examples.

Floating-Point Calculations

Floating-point math can be a pain in the neck when it comes to setting expectations about the results of a calculation. And there's little more frustrating than seeing "expected 5.25, got 5.251" in a failure message, especially when you're only looking for two decimal places of precision.

To solve this problem, RSpec offers a be_close matcher that accepts an expected value *and* an acceptable delta. So, if you're looking for precision of two decimal places, you can say the following:

```
result.should be_close(5.25, 0.005)
```

This will pass as long as the given value is within .005 of 5.25.

Multiline Text

Imagine developing an object that generates a statement. You could have one big example that compares the entire generated statement to an expected statement. Something like this:

```
expected = File.open('expected_statement.txt','r') do |f|
  f.read
end
account.statement.should == expected
```

This approach of reading in a file that contains text that has been reviewed and approved and then comparing generated results to that text is known as the "Golden Master" technique and is described in detail in J.B. Rainsberger's *JUnit Recipes* [Rai04].

This serves very well as a high-level code example, but when we want more granular examples, this can sometimes feel a bit like brute force, and it can make it harder to isolate a problem when the wheels fall off.

Also, there are times that we don't really care about the entire string, just a subset of it. Sometimes we only care that it is formatted a specific way but don't care about the details. Sometimes we care about a few details but not the format.

In any of these cases, we can expect a matching regular expression using either of the following patterns:

```
result.should match(/this expression/)
result.should =~ /this expression/
```

In the statement example, we might do something like this:

```
statement.should =~ /Total Due: \$37\.42/m
```

One benefit of this approach is that each example is, by itself, less brittle and less prone to fail due to unrelated changes. RSpec's own code examples are filled with expectations like this related to failure messages, where we want to specify certain things are in place but don't want the expectations to fail because of inconsequential formatting changes.

Ch, ch, ch, ch, changes

Ruby on Rails extends Test::Unit with some Rails-specific assertions. One such assertion is assert_difference(), which is most commonly used to express that some event adds a record to a database table, like this:

```
assert_difference 'User.admins.count', 1 do
  User.create!(:role => "admin")
end
```

This asserts that the value of User.admins.count will increase by 1 when you execute the block. In an effort to maintain parity with the Rails assertions, RSpec offers this alternative:

```
expect {
  User.create!(:role => "admin")
}.to change{ User.admins.count }
```

You can also make that more explicit if you want by chaining calls to by(), to() and from().

```
expect {
  User.create!(:role => "admin")
}.to change{ User.admins.count }.by(1)
```

```
expect {
  User.create!(:role => "admin")
}.to change{ User.admins.count }.to(1)
```

```
expect {
  User.create!(:role => "admin")
}.to change{ User.admins.count }.from(0).to(1)
```

This does not work only with Rails. You can use it for any situation in which you want to express a side effect of some event. Let's say you want to specify that a real estate agent gets a $7,500 commission on a $250,000 sale:

```
expect {
  seller.accept Offer.new(250_000)
}.to change{agent.commission}.by(7_500)
```

Now you could express the change by explicitly stating the expected starting and ending values, like this:

```
agent.commission.should == 0
seller.accept Offer.new(250_000)
agent.commission.should == 7_500
```

This is pretty straightforward and might even be easier to understand at first glance. Using expect to change, however, does a nice job of identifying what the event is and what the expected outcome is. It also functions as a wrapper for more than one expectation if you use the from() and to() methods, as in the previous examples.

So, which approach should you choose? It really comes down to a matter of personal taste and style. If you're working solo, it's up to you. If you're working on a team, have a group discussion about the relative merits of each approach.

Expecting Errors

When first learning Ruby, you might get a sense that the language is reading your mind. Say you need a method to iterate through the keys of a Ruby hash so you type hash.each_pair {|k,v| puts k} just to see if it works, and, of course, it does! And this makes you happy!

Ruby is filled with examples of great, intuitive APIs like this, and it seems that developers who write their own code in Ruby strive for the same level of *obvious*, inspired by the beauty of the language. We all want to provide that same feeling of happiness to developers that they get just from using the Ruby language directly.

Well, if we care about making developers happy, we should also care about providing meaningful feedback when the wheels fall off. We want to provide error classes and messages that provide context that will make it easier to understand what went wrong.

Here's a great example from the Ruby library:

```
$ irb
irb(main):001:0> 1/0
ZeroDivisionError: divided by 0
  from (irb):1:in `/'
  from (irb):1
```

The fact that the error is named ZeroDivisionError probably tells you everything you need to know to understand what went wrong. The message "divided by 0" reinforces that. RSpec supports the development of informative error classes and messages with the raise_error() matcher.

If a checking account has no overdraft support, then it should let us know:

```
account = Account.new 50, :dollars
expect {
  account.withdraw 75, :dollars
```

```
}.to raise_error(
  InsufficientFundsError,
  /attempted to withdraw 75 dollars from an account with 50 dollars/
)
```

The raise_error() matcher will accept zero, one, or two arguments. If you want to keep things generic, you can pass zero arguments, and the example will pass as long as any subclass of Exception is raised.

```
expect { do_something_risky }.to raise_error
```

The first argument can be any of a String message, a Regexp that should match an actual message, or the class of the expected error.

```
expect {
  account.withdraw 75, :dollars
}.to raise_error(
  "attempted to withdraw 75 dollars from an account with 50 dollars"
)

expect {
  account.withdraw 75, :dollars
}.to raise_error(/attempted to withdraw 75 dollars/)

expect {
  account.withdraw 75, :dollars
}.to raise_error(InsufficientFundsError)
```

When the first argument is an error class, it can be followed by a second argument that is either a String message or a Regexp that should match an actual message.

```
expect {
  account.withdraw 75, :dollars
}.to raise_error(
  InsufficientFundsError,
  "attempted to withdraw 75 dollars from an account with 50 dollars"
)

expect {
  account.withdraw 75, :dollars
}.to raise_error(
  InsufficientFundsError,
  /attempted to withdraw 75 dollars/
)
```

Which of these formats you choose depends on how specific you want to get about the type and the message. Sometimes you'll find it useful to have several code examples that get into details about messages, while others may just specify the type.

If you look through RSpec's own code examples, you'll see many that look like this:

```
expect {
  @mock.rspec_verify
}.to raise_error(MockExpectationError)
```

Since there are plenty of other examples that specify details about the error messages raised by message expectation failures, this example only cares that a MockExpectationError is raised.

Expecting a Throw

Like raise() and rescue(), Ruby's throw() and catch() allow us to stop execution within a given scope based on some condition. The main difference is that we use throw/catch to express expected circumstances as opposed to exceptional circumstances.

Let's say we're writing an app to manage registrations for courses at a school, and we want to handle the situation in which two students both try to register for the last available seat at the same time. Both were looking at screens that say the course is still open, but one of them is going to get the last seat, and the other is going to be shut out.

We *could* handle that by raising a CourseFullException, but a full course is not really exceptional. It's just a different state. We could ask the Course if it has availability, but unless that query blocks the database, that state could change after the question is asked and before the request to grab the seat is made.

This is a great case for try/catch, and here's how we can spec it:

> expectations/course_full.rb

```
course = Course.new(:seats => 20)
20.times { course.register Student.new }
lambda {
  course.register Student.new
}.should throw_symbol(:course_full)
```

Like the raise_error() matcher, the throw_symbol() matcher will accept zero, one, or two arguments. If you want to keep things generic, you can pass zero arguments, and the example will pass as long as anything is thrown.

The first (optional) argument to throw_symbol() must be a Symbol, as shown in the previous example.

The second argument, also optional, can be anything, and the matcher will pass only if both the symbol and the thrown object are caught. In our current example, that would look like this:

```
expectations/course_full.rb
```
```
course = Course.new(:seats => 20)
20.times { course.register Student.new }
lambda {
  course.register Student.new
}.should throw_symbol(:course_full, 20)
```

13.3 Predicate Matchers

A Ruby predicate method is one whose name ends with "?" and returns a Boolean response. One example that is built right into the language is array.empty?. This is a simple, elegant construct that allows us to write code like this:

```
do_something_with(array) unless array.empty?
```

When we want to set an expectation that a predicate should return a specific result, however, the code isn't quite as pretty.

```
array.empty?.should == true
```

Although that does express our intention, it doesn't read that well. What we really want to say is that the "array should be empty," right? Well, say it then!

```
array.should be_empty
```

Believe it or not, that will work as you expect. The expectation will be met, and the example will pass if the array has an empty? method that returns true. If array does not respond to empty?, then we get a NoMethodError. If it does respond to empty? but returns false, then we get an ExpectationNotMetError.

This feature will work for any Ruby predicate. It will even work for predicates that accept arguments, such as the following:

```
user.should be_in_role("admin")
```

This will pass as long as user.in_role?("admin") returns true.

How They Work

RSpec overrides method_missing to provide this nice little bit of syntactic sugar. If the missing method begins with "be_," RSpec strips off the "be_" and appends "?"; then it sends the resulting message to the given object.

Taking this a step further, there are some predicates that don't read as fluidly as we might like when prefixed with "be_". instance_of?(type), for example, becomes be_instance_of. To make these a bit more readable, RSpec also looks for things prefixed with "be_a_" and "be_an_". So, we also get to write be_a_kind_of(Player) or be_an_instance_of(Pitcher).

Even with all of this support for prefixing arbitrary predicates, there will still be cases in which the predicate just doesn't fit quite right. For example, you wouldn't want to say parser.should be_can_parse("some text"), would you? Well, we wouldn't want to have to say anything quite so ridiculous, so RSpec supports writing custom matchers with a simple DSL that you'll read about in Section 16.7, *Custom Matchers*, on page 229.

13.4 Be True in the Eyes of Ruby

In Ruby, there are two values that evaluate to false in a Boolean expression. One of them is, of course, false. The other is nil. Every other value is evaluated as true. Even 0:

```
puts "0 evals to true" if 0
```

RSpec's be_true and be_false matchers can be used to specify methods that should return values that Ruby will evaluate as true or false, as opposed to the actual values true and false:

```
true.should be_true
0.should be_true
"this".should be_true

false.should be_false
nil.should be_false
```

For the rare cases in which we care that methods return the values true or false, we can use the equal() matcher:

```
true.should equal(true)
false.should equal(false)
```

Up until now we've been discussing expectations about the state of an object. The object should be_in_some_state. But what about when the state we're interested in is not in the object itself but in an object that it owns?

13.5 Have Whatever You Like

A hockey team should have five skaters on the ice under normal conditions. The word *character* should have nine characters in it. Perhaps a Hash should have a specific key. We *could* say Hash.has_key?(:foo).should be_true, but what we really want to say is Hash.should have_key(:foo).

RSpec combines expression matchers with a bit more method_missing goodness to solve these problems for us. Let's first look at RSpec's use of method_missing. Imagine that we have a simple RequestParameters class that converts request parameters to a hash. We might have an example like this:

```
request_parameters.has_key?(:id).should == true
```

This expression makes sense, but it just doesn't read all that well. To solve this, RSpec uses method_missing to convert anything that begins with have_ to a predicate on the target object beginning with has_. In this case, we can say this:

```
request_parameters.should have_key(:id)
```

In addition to the resulting code being more expressive, the feedback that we get when there is a failure is more expressive as well. The feedback from the first example would look like this:

```
expected true, got false
```

whereas the have_key example reports this:

```
expected #has_key?(:id) to return true, got false
```

This will work for absolutely any predicate method that begins with "has_". But what about collections? We'll take a look at them next.

Owned Collections

Let's say we're writing a fantasy baseball application. When our app sends a message to the home team to take the field, we want to specify that it sends nine players out to the field. How can we specify that? Here's one option:

```
field.players.select {|p| p.team == home_team }.length.should == 9
```

If you're an experienced Rubyist, this might make sense right away, but compare that to this expression:

```
home_team.should have(9).players_on(field)
```

Here, the object returned by have() is a matcher, which does not respond to players_on(). When it receives a message, it doesn't understand (like players_on()), it delegates it to the target object, in this case the home_team.

This expression reads like a requirement and, like arbitrary predicates, encourages useful methods like players_on().

At any step, if the target object or its collection doesn't respond to the expected messages, a meaningful error gets raised. If there is no players_on method on home_team, you'll get a NoMethodError. If the result of that method doesn't respond to length or size, you'll get an error saying so. If the collection's size does not match the expected size, you'll get a failed expectation rather than an error.

Unowned Collections

In addition to setting expectations about owned collections, there are going to be times when the object you're describing *is* itself a collection. RSpec lets us use have to express this as well:

```
collection.should have(37).items
```

In this case, items is pure syntactic sugar. What's happening to support this is safe but a bit sneaky, so it is helpful for you to understand what is happening under the hood, lest you be surprised by any unexpected behavior. We'll discuss the inner workings of have a bit later in this section.

Strings

Strings are collections too! They're not quite like arrays, but they do respond to a lot of the same messages as collections do. Because strings respond to length and size, you can also use have to expect a string of a specific length.

```
"this string".should have(11).characters
```

As in unowned collections, characters is pure syntactic sugar in this example.

Precision in Collection Expectations

In addition to being able to express an expectation that a collection should have some number of members, you can also say that it should have *exactly* that number, *at least* that number or *at most* that number.

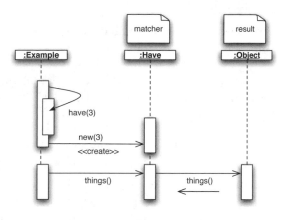

Figure 13.1: HAVE MATCHER SEQUENCE

```
day.should have_exactly(24).hours
dozen_bagels.should have_at_least(12).bagels
internet.should have_at_most(2037).killer_social_networking_apps
```

have_exactly is just an alias for have. The others should be self-explanatory. These three will work for all the applications of have described in the previous sections.

How It Works

The have method can handle a few different scenarios. The object returned by have is an instance of RSpec::Matchers::Have, which gets initialized with the expected number of elements in a collection. So, the following expression:

```
result.should have(3).things
```

is the equivalent of this expression:

```
result.should(Have.new(3).things)
```

In Figure 13.1, we can see how this all ties together. The first thing to get evaluated is Have.new(3), which creates a new instance of Have, initializing it with a value of 3. At this point, the Have object stores that number as the expected value.

Next, the Ruby interpreter sends things to the Have object. Then method_missing is invoked because Have doesn't respond to things. Have overrides method_missing to store the message name (in this case things) for later use and then returns self. So, the result of have(3).things is an instance of Have that knows the name of the collection you are looking for and how many elements should be in that collection.

The Ruby interpreter passes the result of have(3).things to should(), which, in turn, sends matches?(self) to the matcher. It's the matches? method in which all the magic happens.

First, it asks the target object (result) if it responds to the message that it stored when method_missing was invoked (things). If so, it sends that message and, assuming that the result is a collection, interrogates the result for its length or its size (whichever it responds to, checking for length first). If the object does not respond to either length or size, then you get an informative error message. Otherwise, the actual length or size is compared to the expected size, and the example passes or fails based on the outcome of that comparison.

If the target object does not respond to the message stored in method_missing, then Have tries something else. It asks the target object if it, itself, can respond to length or size. If it will, it assumes that you are actually interested in the size of the target object and not a collection that it owns. In this case, the message stored in method_missing is ignored, the size of the target object is compared to the expected size, and, again, the example passes or fails based the outcome of that comparison.

Note that the target object can be anything that responds to length or size, not just a collection. As explained in our discussion of strings, this allows you to express expectations like "this string".should have(11).characters.

In the event that the target object does not respond to the message stored in method_missing, length, or size, then Have will send the message to the target object and let the resulting NoMethodError bubble up to the example.

As you can see, there is a lot of magic involved. RSpec tries to cover all the things that can go wrong and give you useful messages in each case, but there are still some potential pitfalls. If you're using a custom collection in which length and size have different meanings, you might get unexpected results. But these cases are rare, and as long as you are aware of the way this all works, you should certainly take advantage of its expressiveness.

13.6 Operator Expressions

Generally, we want to be very precise about our expectations. We would want to say that "2 + 2 should equal 4," not that "2 + 2 should be greater than 3." There are exceptions to this, however. Writing a random generator for numbers between 1 and 10, we would want to make sure that 1 appears roughly 1,000 in 10,000 tries. So, we set some level of tolerance, say 2 percent, which results in something like "count for 1s should be greater than or equal to 980 and less than or equal to 1,f020."

An example like that might look like this:

```
it "should generate a 1 10% of the time (plus/minus 2%)" do
  result.occurrences_of(1).should be_greater_than_or_equal_to(980)
  result.occurrences_of(1).should be_less_than_or_equal_to(1020)
end
```

Certainly it reads like English, but it's just a bit verbose. Wouldn't it be nice if, instead, we could use commonly understood operators like >= instead of be_greater_than_or_equal_to? As it turns out, we can!

Thanks to some magic that we get for free from the Ruby language, RSpec is able to support the following expectations using standard Ruby operators:

```
result.should == 3
result.should =~ /some regexp/
result.should be < 7
result.should be <= 7
result.should be >= 7
result.should be > 7
```

RSpec can do this because Ruby interprets these expressions like this:

```
result.should.==(3)
result.should.=~(/some regexp/)
result.should(be.<(7))
result.should(be.<=(7))
result.should(be.>=(7))
result.should(be.>(7))
```

RSpec exploits that interpretation by defining == and =~ on the object returned by should() and <, <=, >, and >= on the object returned by be.

13.7 Generated Descriptions

Sometimes we end up with an example docstring that is nearly an exact duplication of the expectation expressed in the example. Here's an example:

```
describe "A new chess board" do
  before(:each) do
    @board = Chess::Board.new
  end

  it "should have 32 pieces" do
    @board.should have(32).pieces
  end
end
```

When we run this with the rspec command, the output looks like this:

```
A new chess board
  should have 32 pieces
```

In this case, we can rely on RSpec's automatic example-name genera-tion to produce the name you're looking for:

```
describe "A new chess board" do
  before(:each) { @board = Chess::Board.new }
  specify { @board.should have(32).pieces }
end
```

This produces the same output we saw earlier:

```
A new chess board
  should have 32 pieces
```

This example uses the specify() method instead of it() because specify is more readable when there is no docstring. Both it() and specify() are actually aliases of the example() method, which creates an example.

Each of RSpec's matchers generates a description of itself, which gets passed on to the example. If the example (or it or specify) method does not receive a docstring, it uses the last of these descriptions that it receives. In this example, there is only one: "should have 32 pieces."

It turns out that it is somewhat rare that the autogenerated names express exactly what you would want to express in the descriptive string passed to example. Our advice is to always start by writing exactly what you want to say and only resort to using the generated descrip-tions when you actually see that the string and the expectation line up precisely.

Here's an example in which it might be clearer to leave the string in place:

```
it "should be eligible to vote at the age of 18" do
  @voter.birthdate = 18.years.ago
  @voter.should be_eligible_to_vote
end
```

Even though the autogenerated description would read "should be eligible to vote," the fact that he is eighteen today is very important to the requirement being expressed. On the other hand, consider this example:

```
describe RSpecUser do
  before(:each) do
    @rspec_user = RSpecUser.new
  end
  it "should be happy" do
    @rspec_user.should be_happy
  end
end
```

This expectation would produce a string identical to the one that is being passed to it, so this is a good candidate for taking advantage of autogenerated descriptions.

13.8 Subjectivity

The *subject* of an example is the object being described. In the happy RSpecUser example, the subject is an instance of RSpecUser, instantiated in the before block.

RSpec offers an alternative to setting up instance variables in before blocks like this, in the form of the subject() method. You can use this method in a few different ways, ranging from explicit and consequently verbose to implicit access that can make things more concise. First let's discuss explicit interaction with the subject.

Explicit Subject

In an example group, you can use the subject() method to define an explicit subject by passing it a block, like this:

```
describe Person do
  subject { Person.new(:birthdate => 19.years.ago) }
end
```

Then you can interact with that subject like this:

```
describe Person do
  subject { Person.new(:birthdate => 19.years.ago) }
  specify { subject.should be_eligible_to_vote }
end
```

Delegation to Subject

Once a subject is declared, the example will delegate should() and should_not() to that subject, allowing you to clean that up even more:

```
describe Person do
  subject { Person.new(:birthdate => 19.years.ago) }
  it { should be_eligible_to_vote }
end
```

Here the should() method has no explicit receiver, so it is received by the example itself. The example then calls subject() and delegates should() to it. Note that we used it() in this case, rather than specify(). Read that aloud and compare it to the previous example, and you'll see why.

The previous example reads "Specify subject should be eligible to vote," whereas this example reads "It should be eligible to vote." Getting more concise, yes? It turns out that, in some cases, we can make things even more concise using an implicit subject.

Implicit Subject

In the happy RSpecUser example, we created the subject by calling new on the RSpecUser class without any arguments. In cases like this, we can leave out the explicit subject declaration, and RSpec will create an *implicit subject* for us:

```
describe RSpecUser do
  it { should be_happy }
end
```

Now *that* is concise! Can't get much more concise than this. Here, the subject() method used internally by the example returns a new instance of RSpecUser.

Of course, this works only when all the pieces fit. The describe() method has to receive a class that can be instantiated safely without any arguments to new(), and the resulting instance has to be in the correct state.

One word of caution: seeing things so concise like this breeds a desire to make everything else concise. Be careful to *not* let the goal of keeping things concise get in the way of expressing what you really want to express. Delegating to an implicit subject takes a lot for granted, and it should be used only when all the pieces really fit, rather than coercing the pieces to fit.

13.9 What We've Learned

In this chapter, we've covered the following:

- should( ) and should_not( )
- RSpec's built-in matchers
- Predicate matchers
- Operator expressions
- Generated descriptions
- Declaring an explicit subject( )
- Using the implicit subject( )

For most projects, you'll probably find that you can express what you want to using just the tools that come along with RSpec. But what about those cases where you think to yourself, "If only RSpec had this one additional matcher"? We'll address that question in Chapter 16, *Extending RSpec*, on page 223, along with a number of other techniques for extending RSpec and tuning its DSL toward your specific projects.

In the meantime, there's still quite a bit more material to cover without extending things at all. In the next chapter, we'll introduce you to RSpec's built-in mock objects framework, a significant key to thinking in terms of behavior.

Chapter 14

RSpec::Mocks

BDD developers specify what code *does*, not what it *is*. We do this from the outside in, starting with Cucumber features to specify how an application should behave when viewed from the outside. We write step definitions that interact with objects that sit at the surface of the app and set expectations about the responses they get back from those same objects.[1]

In all but the most trivial applications, these surface-level objects delegate work to other objects below the surface. Those subsurface objects then delegate some or all of the work to other objects, and they to more objects, and so on, and so on.

From a design standpoint, this all makes perfect sense. We all understand the value of separation of concerns and its impact on the maintainability of an application. But this does present a bit of a chicken-and-egg problem from a development standpoint. We want to progress in small, verifiable steps, but how can we know that an individual object is properly executing its role if an object it delegates work to doesn't exist yet?

Enter *test doubles*.

A test double stands in for a collaborator in an example. If we want the CheckingAccount object to log messages somewhere but we have yet to develop a logger, we can use a double in its place.

---

[1] You learned about step definitions in Section 4.1, *Steps and Step Definitions*, on page 37, and you can read more about them in Chapter 17, *Intro to Cucumber*, on page 243.

We hear doubles referred to as mocks, stubs, fakes, imposters, or any number of other names depending on how they are used, and there is quite a lot of literature describing different names and patterns and the differences between them. When we boil it all down, however, we end up with just a few underlying concepts:

- Test doubles

- Test-specific extensions

- Method stubs

- Message expectations

Method stubs and message expectations are method-level concepts that we can apply to either test doubles or test-specific extensions, which are both object-level concepts. We'll explore each of these in depth and talk about how and when we use them.

14.1 Test Doubles

A test double is an object that stands in for another object in an example. We often refer to them by names like mock objects, test stubs, fakes, and so on. In fact, this chapter is called RSpec::Mocks because that's the name of the RSpec library that we use to generate test doubles. In spite of the fact that all these names have different implications, they tend to get used somewhat interchangeably because the behavior that makes an object a mock as opposed to a stub is *expressed at the method level*. See the sidebar on the next page for more on this.

To create a double, just use the double() method, like this:

```
thingamajig_double = double('thing-a-ma-jig')
```

The string argument is optional but highly recommended because it is used in failure messages. There are also stub() and mock() methods, which produce the same kind of object:

```
stub_thingamajig = stub('thing-a-ma-jig')
mock_thingamajig = mock('thing-a-ma-jig')
```

We can use those to make the spec clearer when appropriate. We'll discuss what that means a bit later. For now, just know that all three methods provide an instance of the RSpec::Mocks::Mock class, which provides facilities for generating method stubs and message expectations.

> ## Test Double Nomenclature
>
> The terminology around test doubles has evolved over the years, and there is quite a lot of overlap, which can be confusing. Some folks in the London XP community had experimented with the idea of self-verifying expectations back in 1999. They needed a name for it and coined the term *mock object*. Over time we've tended to use *mock* to mean any sort of test double regardless of whether we're using it to verify expectations.
>
> Gerard Meszaros introduced the term *test double* in his book *XUnit Test Patterns* (Mes07), in which he also identified a number of test double patterns, including mock objects, test stubs, fakes, spies, and so on. All of the patterns supported by RSpec can be found in Meszaros' writing.
>
> As you learn about test doubles, mocks, stubs, fakes, spies, and so on, keep in mind that we're usually talking about methods rather than objects, and there are generally only two kinds of objects we use: test doubles and test-specific extensions.*
>
> All of the other patterns we'll talk about and you'll read about elsewhere are *usually* variations of method stubs and method expectations and can be applied to either test doubles or test-specific extensions.
>
> ─────────────
>
> *. See Section 14.4, *Test-Specific Extensions*, on page 185.

14.2 Method Stubs

A *method stub* is a method that we can program to return predefined responses during the execution of a code example. Consider the following:

```
Line 1  describe Statement do
2         it "uses the customer's name in the header" do
3           customer = double('customer')
4           customer.stub(:name).and_return('Aslak')
5           statement = Statement.new(customer)
6           statement.generate.should =~ /^Statement for Aslak/
7         end
8       end
```

This example specifies that a statement uses its customer's name to generate part of the statement. The customer double stands in for a real Customer. Thanks to Ruby's dynamic typing, the customer can be of any class, as long as it responds to the right methods.

We create a test double using the double() method on line 3. On line 4, we create a method stub using the stub() method. It takes a single argument: a symbol representing the name of the method that we want to stub. We follow that with a call to and_return(), which tells the double to return 'Aslak' in response to the name() message.[2]

Here is a simple implementation that will pass this example:

```
Line 1   class Statement
2          def initialize(customer)
3            @customer = customer
4          end
5
6          def generate
7            "Statement for #{@customer.name}"
8          end
9        end
```

When the example is executed, the code on line 6 in the example sends the generate() message to the Statement object. This is the object in development and is a real Statement.

When the Statement executes the generate() method, it asks the @customer for its name(). The customer is not the focus of this example. It is an immediate collaborator of the Statement, and we're using a test double to stand in for a real Customer in order to control the data in the example. We programmed it to return 'Aslak', so the result is "Statement for Aslak," and the example passes.

Of course, we could also implement the generate() method like this:

```
Line 1   def generate
2          "Statement for Aslak"
3        end
```

That is, after all, the simplest thing we could do to get the example to pass. This is what traditional TDD instructs us to do first. What it instructs us to do next varies from practitioner to practitioner. One approach is to triangulate, in other words, add another example that uses a different value, forcing the implementation to generalize the value in order to pass both examples.

---

2. This sort of method chaining is called a *fluent interface* and is quite common in all of Ruby's most common test double frameworks. In fact, earlier versions of RSpec used fluent interfaces to set expectations like result.should.equal(4).

Another approach is to view the 'Aslak' in the implementation as duplication with the 'Aslak' in the example. Following the DRY principle, we remove that duplication by generalizing the implementation.

Neither of these approaches is ideal. Triangulation requires an extra example that specifies the same essential behavior. DRY is certainly a worthy justification, but it requires that we take that extra step. Experience shows that this approach will periodically result in hard-coded values remaining in implementation code. There is, however, a third option!

14.3 Message Expectations

A message expectation, aka mock expectation, is a method stub that will raise an error if it is never called. In RSpec, we create a message expectation using the should_receive() method, like this:

```
describe Statement do
  it "uses the customer's name in the header" do
    customer = double('customer')
    customer.should_receive(:name).and_return('Aslak')
    statement = Statement.new(customer)
    statement.generate.should =~ /^Statement for Aslak/
  end
end
```

Using should_receive() instead of stub() sets an expectation that the customer double should receive the name() message. The subsequent and_return() works just like before: it is an instruction to return a specific value in response to name().

In this example, if the generate() method fails to ask the customer double for its name, then the example will fail with Double "customer" expected :name with (any args) once, but received it 0 times . If the generate() method calls customer.name(), then the customer double returns the programmed value, execution continues, and the example passes.

Tight Coupling

Clearly, this example is highly coupled to the implementation, but this coupling is easily justified. We are specifying that the statement uses the customer's name! If that is the requirement that we are expressing in this example, then setting a message expectation is perfectly reasonable.

On the flip side, we want to avoid setting message expectations that are not meaningful in the context of an example. Generally speaking, we only want to use message expectations to express the intent of the example. To explain what we mean, let's look at an example that uses both a method stub and a method expectation.

Mixing Method Stubs and Message Expectations

Extending the statement examples, let's add a requirement that any time a statement is generated, a log entry gets created. Here's one way we might express that:

```
describe Statement do
  it "logs a message on generate()" do
    customer = stub('customer')
    customer.stub(:name).and_return('Aslak')
    logger   = mock('logger')
    statement = Statement.new(customer, logger)

    logger.should_receive(:log).with(/Statement generated for Aslak/)

    statement.generate
  end
end
```

Now we have three participants in the example: the statement, which is the subject of the example; the logger, which is the primary collaborator; and the customer, which is a secondary collaborator. The logger is the primary collaborator because the example's docstring states that the Statement logs a message on generate().

By using the mock() method to generate the logger double and the stub() method to generate the customer double, we're helping to express that these objects are playing different roles in the example. This is a wonderful technique, embedding intent right in the code in the example.

Given, Then, When?

The logger.should_receive() statement is the only expectation in the example, and it comes *before* the event, the When. The resulting flow is a bit different from the Given, When, Then flow that we're accustomed to seeing. Here it's Given, Then, When: *Given* a statement constructed with a customer and logger, *Then* the logger should receive log() *When* the statement receives generate().

This change in flow can be a bit jarring for those experienced in writing code examples yet new to message expectations, so much so that some in the community are beginning to solve the problem with new libraries that take different approaches. See the sidebar on the next page for more on this.

Of course, what we don't see is that there is an automatic and implicit verification step that happens at the end of each example. This is facilitated by the test double framework hooking into the life cycle of the examples, listening for the end of each example, and then verifying that any expectations set in the example were met. So, the flow is really Given, Expect, When, Then, but since we never see the Then, it is admittedly a bit magical.

Thus far, we've only talked about setting method stubs and message expectations on test double objects. This is a very useful technique when the collaborators we need either don't exist yet or are very expensive to set up or use in a code example. But sometimes the collaborator we need already exists, requires little or no setup, and exposes only trivial behavior. For cases like this, we can add support for method stubs and message expectations directly to the real object using a technique called *test-specific extensions*.

14.4 Test-Specific Extensions

As the name suggests, a test-specific extension is an extension of an object that is specific to a particular test, or *example* in our case. We call them test-specific extensions because it is very similar to the *test-specific subclass* pattern described by Meszaros, in which a subclass of a real class is used to extend instances to support test-double-like behavior.

Thanks to Ruby's metaprogramming model, we can get the same result by extending existing objects. And because the resulting object is partially the original object and partially a test double, we commonly refer to this technique as *partial mocking and stubbing*.

Partial Stubbing

Consider a case in Ruby on Rails where we want to disconnect the system we are working on from the database. We can use real objects but stub the find() and save() methods that we expect to be invoked.

Given, When, Then with Test Spies

Libraries like RR and the ironically named not-a-mock use the Test Spy pattern to provide a means of expressing message expectations in the past tense, thereby maintaining the flow of expectations at the end of an example.* As of this writing, RSpec::Mocks does not support test spies, but, luckily, both not-a-mock and RR plug right into RSpec and can be used instead of RSpec::Mocks if spies are what you're after.

Here's what our statement, customer, logger example might look like using not-a-mock:[†]

```
describe Statement do
  it "logs a message when on generate()" do
    customer = stub('customer')
    customer.stub(:name)
    logger   = mock('logger')
    logger.stub(:log)
    statement = Statement.new(customer, logger)

    statement.generate

    logger.should have_received(:log)
  end
end
```

And here it is with RR:[‡]

```
describe Statement do
  it "logs a message when on generate()" do
    customer = Object.new
    stub(customer).name
    logger   = Object.new
    stub(logger).log
    statement = Statement.new(customer, logger)

    statement.generate

    logger.should have_received.log
  end
end
```

---

* http://xunitpatterns.com/Test%20Spy.html
† http://github.com/notahat/not_a_mock
‡ http://github.com/btakita/rr

Here's an example:

```
describe WidgetsController do
  describe "PUT update with valid attributes"
    it "redirects to the list of widgets"
      widget = Widget.new()
      Widget.stub(:find).and_return(widget)
      widget.stub(:update_attributes).and_return(true)
      put :update, :id => 37
      response.should redirect_to(widgets_path)
    end
  end
end
```

There are a few things going on in this example:

- We stub the class-level find() method to return a known value, in this case, the Widget object created on the previous line.

- We stub the update_attributes() method of the widget object, programming it to return true.

- We invoke the put() method from the Rails functional testing API.[3]

- We set an expectation that the response object should redirect to the list of widgets.

This example specifies exactly what the description suggests: Widgets-Controller PUT update with valid attributes redirects to the list of widgets. That the attributes are valid is a given in this example, and we don't really need to know what constitutes *valid attributes* in order to specify the controller's behavior in response to them. We just program the Widget to pretend it has valid attributes.

This means that changes to the Widget's validation rules will not have any impact on this example. As long as the controller's responsibility does not change, this example won't need to change, nor will the controller itself.

There is also no dependency on the database in this example—well, no explicit dependency. Rails will try to load up the schema for the widgets table the first time it loads widget.rb, but that is the only database interaction. There are no additional database interactions as a result of

---

3. As you'll learn about in Chapter 24, *Rails Controllers*, on page 341, the rspec-rails library provides rspec-flavored wrappers around Rails' built-in testing facilities.

this example. If we use a Rails plug-in like NullDB,[4] we can completely disconnect from the database, and this example will still run.

Partial Mocking

In the WidgetsController example, it is possible to get it to pass without ever actually finding a widget or updating its attributes. As long as the controller method redirects to the widgets_path, that example passes. For this reason and for the purposes of documentation, we may want separate examples that specify these details. For these examples, we can set message expectations on the Widget class and instance instead of method stubs. This is called *partial mocking.*

Here's what this might look like:

```
describe WidgetsController do
  describe "PUT update with valid attributes"
    it "finds the widget"
      widget = Widget.new()
      widget.stub(:update_attributes).and_return(true)

      Widget.should_receive(:find).with("37").and_return(widget)

      put :update, :id => 37
    end

    it "updates the widget's attributes" do
      widget = Widget.new()
      Widget.stub(:find).and_return(widget)

      widget.should_receive(:update_attributes).and_return(true)

      put :update, :id => 37
    end
  end
end
```

Note how we mix method stubs and message expectations in these examples. The first example specifies that the WidgetsController finds the widget, so we set an expectation that the Widget class should receive the find() method. We need to program the widget to return true for update_attributes(), but we're not specifying that it is called in this example, so we just use a method stub.

Message expectations on the real model objects allow us to specify how the controller interacts with them, rather than a specific outcome.

---

4. http://avdi.org/projects/nulldb/

These two examples, combined with the redirect example in which we used only method stubs on the model objects, produce the following output:

```
WidgetsController
  PUT update with valid attributes
    finds the widget
    updates the widget's attributes
    redirects to the list of widgets
```

As you can see just from the output, these techniques help us specify what the WidgetsController *does*. And by using different techniques in different examples, we are able to keep each example focused on a specific granular facet of the behavior.

Partial stubbing/mocking isn't risk free. We must take care not to replace too much of the real objects with stub/mock methods. This is especially important for the subject of the example, because we end up not working with the object we thought we were. So, keep partial mocking to an absolute minimum.

14.5 More on Method Stubs

The examples we saw before only touch the surface of the API for test doubles. In this section and the next, we'll take a deeper look at the utilities supported by RSpec::Mocks.

One-Line Shortcut

Most of the time that we use method stubs, we simply return a stubbed value. For these cases, RSpec offers a simple shortcut:

```
customer = double('customer', :name => 'Bryan')
```

The double(), mock(), and stub() methods each accept a hash after the optional name. Each key/value pair in the hash is converted to a stub using the key as the method name and the value as the return value. The previous example is a shortcut for this:

```
customer = double('customer')
customer.stub(:name).and_return('Bryan')
```

The hash can be of any length, so if we have more than one method we want to stub, we just add key/value pairs for each method:

```
customer = double('customer',
  :name => 'Bryan',
  :open_source_projects => ['Webrat','Rack::Test']
)
```

Implementation Injection

From time to time we might stub a method that ends up getting called more than once in an example and we want to supply different return values for it based on the arguments. One way to handle this is to supply a block to the stub() method, like this:

```
ages = double('ages')
ages.stub(:age_for) do |what|
  if what == 'drinking'
    21
  elsif what == 'voting'
    18
  end
end
```

This is essentially what Meszaros calls the Fake pattern, in which a real method is replaced by a lightweight implementation. We're just injecting the implementation with a block, rather than defining a method directly on the object.

This is especially useful in cases in which we want to define the stub in a before() block and use it in several examples. The downside of this is that we separate the data and calculation from the example, so we recommend using that approach only for cases in which the returned value (21, 18, or nil in this case) is not part of what's being specified in the examples.

Stub Chain

Let's say we're building an educational website with Ruby on Rails, and we need a database query that finds all the published articles written in the last week by a particular author. Using a custom DSL built on ActiveRecord named scopes, we can express that query like so:

```
Article.recent.published.authored_by(params[:author_id])
```

Now let's say that we want to stub the return value of authored_by() for an example. Using standard stubbing, we might come up with something like this:

```
recent       = double()
published    = double()
authored_by  = double()
article      = double()
Article.stub(:recent).and_return(recent)
recent.stub(:published).and_return(published)
published.stub(:authored_by).and_return(article)
```

That's a *lot* of stubs! Instead of revealing intent, it does a great job of hiding it. It's complex, it's confusing, and if we should ever decide to change any part of the chain, we're in for some pain changing this. For these reasons, many people simply avoid writing stubs when they'd otherwise want to. Those people don't know about RSpec's stub_chain() method, which allows us to write this:

```
article = double()
Article.stub_chain(:recent, :published, :authored_by).and_return(article)
```

Much nicer! Now this is still quite coupled to the implementation, but it's also quite a bit easier to see what's going on and map this to any changes we might make in the implementation.

14.6 More on Message Expectations

Message expectations tend to be more tightly bound to implementation details of the method in development than method stubs. In the logger example, if the customer fails to log a message, the example fails. Had we only stubbed the log() method, we would not get a failure.

RSpec offers a number of utilities we can use to specify more focused aspects of implementation. Keep in mind that all of these utilities we're about to discuss increase the coupling between the spec and the object in development, which increases the likelihood that subsequent changes to the object in development will force changes in the specs. We recommend, therefore, that these only be used to express specific requirements.

Counts

Test doubles often stand in for objects with expensive operations like database and network calls. When we're optimizing, we may want to specify that a given message is not sent to the double any more times than is necessary for the operation. By default, should_receive() sets an expectation that a message should be received once, and only once. We can set this expectation explicitly like this:

```
mock_account.should_receive(:withdraw).exactly(1).times
```

Using the same syntax, we can specify any number:

```
mock_account.should_receive(:withdraw).exactly(5).times
```

Sometimes we may want to make sure that an operation is repeated no more than some number of times. Consider a double that is standing in for a collaborator that establishes network connections. If it can't get a connection, we want it to retry it five times, but no more. In this case, we can set an upper bound:

```
network_double.should_receive(:open_connection).at_most(5).times
```

Similarly, we can set a lower bound for a situation in which we want to specify that a call is made at least some number of times:

```
network_double.should_receive(:open_connection).at_least(2).times
```

RSpec includes a couple of convenience methods to handle the cases where the count is one or two. These are recommended, because they read a bit better than exactly(1).times:

```
account_double.should_receive(:withdraw).once
account_double.should_receive(:deposit).twice
```

Negative Expectation

Sometimes we want to specify that a specific message is *never* received during an example. Imagine a requirement that we only try to make connections after pinging a server. Here's one way we can express that requirement:

```
network_double.stub(:ping).and_return(false)
network_double.should_not_receive(:open_connection)
```

If the network_double receives open_connection(), the example will fail. Here are two more ways to express that a message should not be received:

```
network_double.should_receive(:open_connection).never
network_double.should_receive(:open_connection).exactly(0).times
```

These both work fine, but should_not_receive() is the most commonly used.

Specifying Expected Arguments

In cases in which we expect specific arguments, we can use the with method to constrain the expectation. For literal values, we can just pass them directly to the with() method:

```
account_double.should_receive(:withdraw).with(50)
```

If the account_double receives the withdraw() method with any value besides 50, it will raise an error saying it was expecting 50 but got the other value instead. We can pass any number of arguments to with(), and it will fail if any of the received arguments fail to match the expectation arguments:

```
checking_account.should_receive(:transfer).with(50, savings_account)
```

This example will pass only if the checking_account receives transfer() with arguments matching 50 and savings_account in the correct order. The arguments are evaluated using ==(), so in this example they have to ==(50) and ==(savings_account).

Argument Matchers

Sometimes we don't care about the specific values of all the arguments. When specifying a transfer operation as in the previous example, we might have separate examples for the two different arguments. In the example focused on the account, we need the second argument in the example, or the double would raise an error saying it got only one argument. But we don't care what that argument is, since this example is focused on the first argument.

instance_of()

We can address this using an *argument matcher*: a method that returns an object that can match against the real arguments received during the example. In this case, we want the second argument to be an instance of Fixnum, but we don't care what it is. We can use the instance_of() argument matcher to address this:

```
Line 1  describe Transfer do
   -      it "passes the target account to the source account" do
   -        source_account = double()
   -        target_account = double()
   5        transfer = Transfer.new(
   -          :source_account => source_account,
   -          :target_account => target_account,
   -          :amount         => 50
   -        )
   10       source_account.should_receive(:transfer).
   -          with(target_account, instance_of(Fixnum))
   -        transfer.execute()
   -      end
   -    end
```

On line 11, we specify that the first argument should ==(target_account) and that the second argument can be any Fixnum. Of course, we know it's going to be 50, because that is what is supplied on line 8, but we don't *care* about that in this example.

When we do this, we're coupling the example to a specific type, which is usually *not* recommended. Remember, these facilities are available, but we want to use them only when they help express the intent of the example.

anything()

When we want to specify that an argument is received but we really don't care what it is, we can use the anything() matcher, like this:

```
describe Transfer do
  it "passes the submitted amount to the source account" do
    source_account = stub()
    target_account = stub()
    transfer = Transfer.new(
      :source_account => source_account,
      :target_account => target_account,
      :amount         => 50
    )
    source_account.should_receive(:transfer).
      with(anything(), 50)
    transfer.execute()
  end
end
```

any_args()

As mentioned earlier, a message expectation without the with() method will accept any arguments. If you want, you can use the any_args() method to explicitly specify that any arguments are acceptable:

```
source_account.should_receive(:transfer).
  with(any_args())
```

no_args()

Now imagine we have an API that can accept zero or more arguments, and we want to specify that under certain conditions it should receive a message with no arguments. We can do that too, using the no_args() argument matcher:

```
collaborator.should_receive(:message).
  with(no_args())
```

hash_including()

If the expected argument is a Hash, we can specify the expected key/value pairs like this:

```
mock_account.should_receive(:add_payment_accounts).
        with(hash_including('Electric' => '123', 'Gas' => '234'))
```

The hash argument in this example is expected to include keys for 'Electric' and 'Gas' with the corresponding values 123 and 234, respectively.

hash_not_including()

We can also specify that those values should *not* be in the hash like this:

```
mock_account.should_receive(:add_payment_accounts).
            with(hash_not_including('Electric' => '123', 'Gas' => '234'))
```

In this case, an acceptable argument value would be a hash that does not have the specified key-value pairs.

Regular Expressions

For String arguments, we can expect just a part of the string using a Regexp that will be matched against it, like this:

```
mock_atm.should_receive(:login).with(/.* User/)
```

As you can see, RSpec comes with a range of useful argument matchers built in, but sometimes we need to express more specific constraints. In these cases, it's easy to extend RSpec with our own.

Custom Argument Matchers

Let's say we want to be able to expect a Fixnum argument that is greater than three. With a custom argument matcher, we can express this expectation like this:

```
calculator.should_receive(:add).with(greater_than_3)
```

An argument matcher is simply an object supporting a specific interface. The only method that is required is ==(actual), which acts as a match operation (not equality). It should return true if the actual argument matches (or conforms to) the matcher.

```
class GreaterThanThreeMatcher
  def ==(actual)
    actual > 3
  end
end
```

We can return an instance of GreaterThanThreeMatcher from a greater_than_3() method, like this:

```
def greater_than_3
  GreaterThanThreeMatcher.new
end
```

Using an argument matcher like this, the should_receive() method will give you failure messages like this:

```
Mock 'calculator' expected :add with (#<RSpec::Mocks::ArgumentMatchers::
  GreaterThanThreeMatcher:0x5e7af4>) but received it with (3)
```

We can improve on that message by adding a description method to the matcher:

```
def description
  "a number greater than 3"
end
```

Now, the message will be as follows:

```
Mock 'calculator' expected :add with (a number greater than 3)
  but received it with (3)
```

We can generalize this a bit by parameterizing the method and the matcher object like this:

```
class GreaterThanMatcher

  def initialize(expected)
    @expected = expected
  end

  def description
    "a number greater than #{@expected}"
  end

  def ==(actual)
    actual > @expected
  end
end

def greater_than(floor)
  GreaterThanMatcher.new(floor)
end
```

Now we can use this matcher for any situation in which we expect a number greater than some other number:

```
calculator.should_receive(:add).with(greater_than(37))
```

Returning Consecutive Values

Sometimes we want the subject to send the same message to the collaborator more than once, and we want to set up different return values each time in order to trigger a particular behavior in the subject.

Consider a gateway_client, which depends on a network object to connect to the real gateway. We want to specify that the gateway client will ask the network to try to open a connection up to three times before it gives up. Here are a few examples we might write to specify this:

```
Line 1   describe GatewayClient, "#connect" do
    -      before(:each) do
    -        @network = stub()
    -        @gateway_client = GatewayClient.new(@network)
    5      end

    -      it "returns true if network returns connection on first attempt" do
    -        @network.should_receive(:open_connection).
    -          and_return(Connection.new)
    10       @gateway_client.connect.should be_true
    -      end

    -      it "returns true if network returns connection on third attempt" do
    -        @network.should_receive(:open_connection).
    15         and_return(nil, nil, Connection.new)
    -        @gateway_client.connect.should be_true
    -      end

    -      it "returns false if network fails to return connection in 3 attempts" do
    20       @network.should_receive(:open_connection).
    -          and_return(nil, nil, nil)
    -        @gateway_client.connect.should be_false
    -      end

    25  end
```

On line 9 in the first example, we program the @network to return a Connection the first time open_connection() is called. This is how we normally set return values for a method stub or message expectation.

The second example is a bit different. On line 15, we program the @network to expect open_connection(), returning nil the first two times and a Connection the third. We do so by passing nil, nil, and Connection.new to the and_return() method. With three arguments passed to and_return(), we're implicitly telling the @network to expect open_connection() three times.

The third example programs open_connection() to return nil three times in a row. We're implicitly telling @network to expect open_connection() three times. We could get the same behavior by explictly telling the @network to expect open_connection() three times and return nil:

```
Line 1   it "returns false if network fails to return connection in 3 attempts" do
    2      @network.should_receive(:open_connection).
    3        exactly(3).times.
    4        and_return(nil)
    5      @gateway_client.connect.should be_false
    6    end
```

In that variation, we only pass nil (once) to and_return() because we're already telling the @network to expect open_connection() three times on line 3. The @network in each of these variations behaves in exactly the same way.

Throwing or Raising

To specify an object's behavior in response to errors, we want to have our collaborator throw a symbol or raise an error in response to a specific message. RSpec::Mocks provides several ways to do this. The most common approach is to simply raise an exception:

```
account_double.should_receive(:withdraw).and_raise
```

With no arguments, the and_raise() method tells the account_double to raise an instance of Exception when it receives the withdraw() message. To raise a specific type of exception, we can pass and_raise an exception class, like this:

```
account_double.should_receive(:withdraw).and_raise(InsufficientFunds)
```

RSpec will create an instance of InsufficientFunds by calling Insufficient-Funds.new. If the exception class we need requires any arguments to its constructor, we can create an instance in the example and pass that instead:

```
the_exception = InsufficientFunds.new(:reason => :on_hold)
account_double.should_receive(:withdraw).and_raise(the_exception)
```

We can also throw symbols instead of raising errors. As you might expect, this is done with the and_throw() method instead of and_raise:

```
account_double.should_receive(:withdraw).and_throw(:insufficient_funds)
```

Ordering

When specifying interactions with a test double, the order of the calls is rarely important. In fact, the ideal situation is to specify only a single call. But sometimes, we need to specify that messages are sent in a specific order.

Consider an implementation of a database-backed class roster in which we want the roster to ask the database for the count of students registered for a given class before adding any new students for that class. We can specify this using the ordered() method and specifying the message expectations in the order in which we expect them:

```
describe Roster do
  it "asks database for count before adding" do
    database = double()
```

```
    student  = double()
    database.should_receive(:count).with('Roster', :course_id => 37).ordered
    database.should_receive(:add).with(student).ordered

    roster = Roster.new(37, database)
    roster.register(student)
  end
end
```

This example will pass only if the count() and add() messages are sent with the correct arguments and *in the same order*. Here is a possible implementation:

mocking/ordering.rb

```
class Roster
  def initialize(id, database)
    @id = id
    @database = database
  end

  def register(student)
    @database.count('Roster', :course_id => @id)
    @database.add(student)
  end

end
```

Note that ordering has an effect only within the context of a single object. You can specify ordering of expectations for multiple objects in an example, but the order is *not enforced across objects*.

Also note that ordering ignores any messages besides the ones assigned as ordered. For example, the following implementation would still pass the previous example, provided that we told the database double to act as_null_object().

mocking/ordering.rb

```
def register(student)
  @database.count('Roster', :course_id => @id)
  @database.begin
  @database.add(student)
  @database.commit
end
```

The fact that the database receives begin() and commit() is ignored by the ordering mechanism. As long as the ordered messages are received in the correct order, the example will pass.

Overriding Method Stubs

In the statement examples earlier this chapter, we looked at examples specifying that the statement uses the customer's name in the header and that it logs a message on generate(). We never really looked at those together at the point that the statement supports both. Here's what that looks like without any refactoring:

```
describe Statement do
  it "uses the customer's name in the header" do
    customer = double('customer')
    customer.stub(:name).and_return('Aslak')
    logger   = double('logger')
    logger.stub(:log)
    statement = Statement.new(customer, logger)

    statement.generate.should =~ /^Statement for Aslak/
  end

  it "logs a message on generate()" do
    customer = stub('customer')
    customer.stub(:name).and_return('Aslak')
    logger   = mock('logger')
    statement = Statement.new(customer, logger)

    logger.should_receive(:log).with(/Statement generated for Aslak/)

    statement.generate
  end
end
```

As you can see, there is a lot of noise and a lot of duplication. We can reduce this significantly by exploiting the fact that message expectations can override stubs:

```
describe Statement do
  before(:each) do
    @customer = double('customer')
    @logger   = double('log', :log => nil)
    @statement = Statement.new(@customer, @logger)
  end

  it "uses the customer's name in the header" do
    @customer.should_receive(:name).and_return('Aslak')
    @statement.generate.should =~ /^Statement for Aslak/
  end

  it "logs a message on generate()" do
    @customer.stub(:name).and_return('Aslak')
    @logger.should_receive(:log).with(/Statement generated for Aslak/)
    @statement.generate
  end
end
```

Now the code in each example is very well aligned with their docstrings, with no unnecessary noise. By setting the log() stub on the @logger double in the before() block, we don't need to set that stub in the first example. In the second example, we override that stub with the expectation. Once the expectation is met, any subsequent calls to log() are caught by the stub and essentially ignored.

14.7 When to Use Test Doubles and Test-Specific Extensions

Now that we know how to use test doubles and test-specific extensions, the next question is *when* to use them! There are a lot of opinions about this, and we're not going to be able to cover every topic (this could easily fill an entire book), but let's look at some guidelines that can help you navigate your way.

Isolation from Dependencies

Even the most highly decoupled code has some dependencies. Sometimes they are on objects that are cheap and easy to construct and have no complex state. These generally don't present a problem, so there is no need to create stubs for them.

The problematic dependencies are the ones that are expensive to construct, involve external systems (network, servers, even the file system), have dependencies on other expensive objects, or function slowly. We want to isolate our examples from these dependencies because they complicate setup, slow down runtimes, and increase potential points of failure.

Consider the system depicted in Figure 14.1, on the next page, with dependencies on a database and a network connection. We can replace the dependencies with test doubles, as shown in Figure 14.2, on the following page, thereby removing the real dependencies from the process. Now we are free of any side effects arising from external systems.

Isolation from Nondeterminism

Depending on external systems can also be a source of nondeterminism. When we depend on components with nondeterministic characteristics, we may find that files get corrupted, disks fail, networks time out, and servers go down in the middle of running specs. Because these are things that we have no control over, they can lead to inconsistent and surprising results when we run our specs.

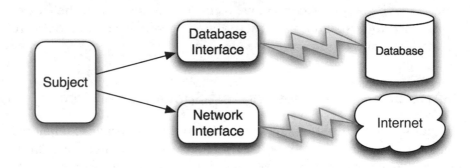

Figure 14.1: EXTERNAL DEPENDENCIES

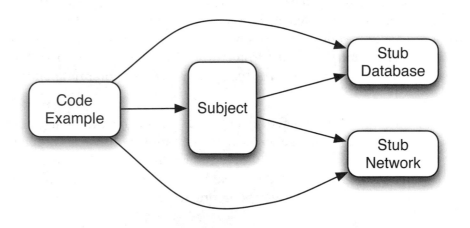

Figure 14.2: STUBBED DEPENDENCIES

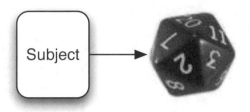

Figure 14.3: DEPENDENCY ON A RANDOM GENERATOR

Doubles can disconnect our examples from real implementations of these dependencies, allowing us to specify things in a controlled environment. They help us focus on the behavior of one object at a time without fear that another might behave differently from run to run.

Nondeterminism can also be local. A random generator may well be local but is clearly a source of nondeterminism. We would want to replace the real random generator with stable sequences to specify different responses from our code. Each example can have a pseudo-random sequence tailored for the behavior being specified.

Consider a system that uses a die, like the one shown Figure 14.3. Because a die is a random generator, there is no way to use it to write a deterministic example. Any specifications would have to be statistical in nature, and that can get quite complicated. Statistical specs are useful when we're specifying the random generators directly, but when we're specifying their clients, all that extra noise takes focus away from the behavior of the object we should be focused on.

If we replace the die with something that generates a repeatable sequence, as shown in Figure 14.4, on the following page, then we can write examples that illustrate the system's behavior based on that sequence. A stub is perfect for this, because each example can specify a different sequence.

Making Progress Without Implemented Dependencies

Sometimes we are specifying an object whose collaborators haven't been implemented yet. Even if we've already designed their APIs, they might be on another team's task list and just haven't gotten to it yet.

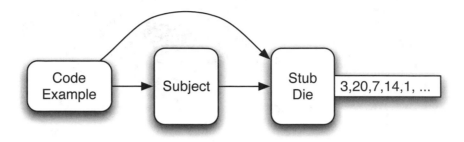

Figure 14.4: DEPENDENCY ON A REPEATABLE SEQUENCE

Rather than break focus on the object we're specifying to implement that dependency, we can use a test double to make the example work. Not only does this keep us focused on the task at hand, but it also provides an opportunity to explore that dependency and possible alternative APIs before it is committed to code.

Interface Discovery

When we're implementing the behavior of one object, we often discover that it needs some service from another object that may not yet exist. Sometimes it's an existing interface with existing implementations, but it's missing the method that the object we're specifying really wants to use. Other times, the interface doesn't even exist at all yet. This process is known as *interface discovery* and is the cornerstone of mock objects.

In cases like these, we can introduce a mock object, which we can program to behave as the object we are currently specifying expects. This is a very powerful approach to writing object-oriented software, because it allows us to design new interfaces as they are needed, making decisions about them as late as possible, when we have the most information about how they will be used.

Focus on Role

In 2004, Steve Freeman, Nat Pryce, Tim Mackinnon, and Joe Walnes presented a paper entitled "Mock Roles, not Objects."[5] The basic premise is that we should think of *roles* rather than specific objects when we're using mocks to discover interfaces.

---

5. http://mockobjects.com/files/mockrolesnotobjects.pdf

In the logging example in Section 14.3, *Mixing Method Stubs and Message Expectations*, on page 184, the logger could be called a logger, a messenger, a recorder, a reporter, and so on. What the object is doesn't matter in that example. The only thing that matters is that it represents an object that will act out the *role* of a logger at runtime. Based on that example, in order to act like a logger, the object has to respond to the log() method.

Focusing on roles rather than objects frees us up to assign roles to different objects as they come into existence. Not only does this allow for very loose coupling between objects at runtime, but it provides loose coupling between concepts as well.

Focus on Interaction Rather Than State

Object-oriented systems are all about interfaces and interactions. An object's internal state is an implementation detail and not part of its observable behavior. As such, it is more subject to change than the object's interface. We can therefore keep specs more flexible and less brittle by avoiding reference to the internal state of an object.

Even if we already have a well-designed API up front, mocks still provide value because they focus on interactions between objects rather than side-effects on the internal state of any individual object.

This may seem to contradict the idea that we want to avoid implementation detail in code examples. Isn't that what we're doing when we specify what messages an object sends? In some cases, this is a perfectly valid observation. Consider this example with a method stub:

```
describe Statement do
  it "uses the customer's name in the header (with a stub)" do
    customer = stub("customer", :name => "Dave Astels")
    statement = Statement.new(customer)
    statement.header.should == "Statement for Dave Astels"
  end
end
```

Now compare that with the same example using a message expectation instead:

```
describe Statement do
  it "uses the customer's name in the header (with a mock)" do
    customer = mock("customer")
    customer.should_receive(:name).and_return("Dave Astels")
    statement = Statement.new(customer)
    statement.header.should == "Statement for Dave Astels"
  end
end
```

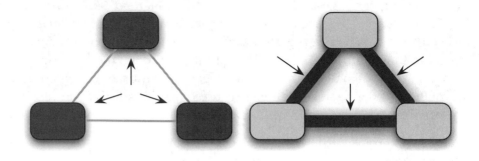

Figure 14.5: FOCUS ON STATE VS. INTERACTION

In this case, there is not much value added by using a message expectation in the second example instead of the method stub in the first example. The code in the second example is more verbose and more tightly bound to the underlying implementation of the header() method. Fair enough. But consider the logger example earlier this chapter. That is a perfect case for a message expectation, because we're specifying an interaction with a collaborator, not an outcome.

A nice way to visualize this is to compare the left and right diagrams in Figure 14.5. When we focus on state, we design objects. When we focus on interaction, we design behavior. There is a time and place for each approach, but when we choose the latter, mock objects make it much easier to achieve.

14.8 Risks and Trade-Offs

In this section, we'll look at some of the common pitfalls related to test doubles, things that we should avoid, and things that can alert us to design problems.

Over-specification

Mock objects should make it easy to set up the context for our examples. If we need a bunch of mocks in one example, we end up with a long and confusing setup.

Specify only what is absolutely necessary for the current example. If that turns out to be a lot, it's time to reevaluate the design; it may be more coupled than previously thought.

Nested Doubles

Doubles should not only be simple to set up; they should be shallow as well. Although not all methods that we specify on doubles need to return values, many do. When they do, it's generally best if the return value is a simple value, such as a language primitive or a value object.

One exception to this guideline is when we want to introduce a double through a query, as we demonstrated in Section 14.4, *Test-Specific Extensions*, on page 185. In this case, we can stub the query method to return the double.

When we do find it necessary to nest doubles, it's quite often a sign that we're working with a preexisting design that may have some coupling problems. A general rule of thumb is that if the code is hard to use in examples, it's going to be hard to use everywhere else.

Absence of Coverage

One goal of BDD (and TDD) is to develop confidence in the system by taking small, verifiable steps and building up a suite of regression tests as we go. When we're using mock objects in dynamic languages like Ruby, it is possible to change an object's API and forget to change the examples that mock that same API.

The result can be that all of our examples pass, yet when we start up the application, the wheels fall off right away because one object is sending the wrong message to another. There is little that can knock our confidence in our system more than finding such a gaping hole in our regression test suite.

One remedy for this situation is to have some higher level of automated testing in place. In BDD, we start with automated acceptance criteria before we even start developing objects, so this should not be an issue. Even if we forget to change the API on a mock, the automated scenarios should catch any problems we've introduced very shortly after we introduce them.

But, to the extent that we do *not* follow this practice, we also increase the risk of getting false-positive feedback from our specs.

Brittle Examples

The biggest pitfall of over-use of mocks is that examples can become brittle. The more we specify about interactions with dependencies in an example, the more likely that example will be impacted by changes to other code in the system. This is the same impact that any highly coupled code has on a system.

This brittleness is more likely to emerge when back-filling examples onto existing code that is already highly coupled. Mocks can be helpful in this situation if we listen to them. If mocks are painful to set up, it's a red flag that the design might be too highly coupled.

When we're using mocks as intended, to discover new roles and APIs, there is a natural tendency for them to be simple and usable because we're working from the client perspective. This becomes somewhat of a self-fulfilling prophecy. We want our mocks to be simple to set up, and so they are. And when they are simple to set up, the resulting code is generally more highly decoupled.

14.9 Choosing Other Test Double Frameworks

In RSpec's early days, we felt that including a test double framework was crucial. There were other frameworks we could have used, but they were all still young, and we wanted to experiment with our own ideas.

Fast-forward four years, and the landscape has changed. As RSpec's user base grew, so did the range of preferences. The existing test double frameworks matured, and new ones appeared, and their maintainers were all willing to support RSpec's runner as well as that of Test::Unit.

Built-in Support

RSpec uses its own test double framework unless we tell it otherwise. We can, however, choose any other framework provided that it has an adapter for RSpec's runner. RSpec ships with adapters for Mocha, Flexmock, and RR, three of the most popular Ruby test double frameworks. To select one of those frameworks, we just add a little bit of configuration.

```
RSpec::configure do |config|
  config.mock_with <framework id>
end
```

The framework id is one of :rspec, :mocha, :flexmock, or :rr. RSpec's own framework is used unless you specify something else, but you can set it explicitly if you choose.

Custom Adapters

To use a mock framework that doesn't have built-in support, we need to write a custom adapter. Assuming that the framework has the necessary extension points, this is a trivial exercise. As an example, here is the built-in adapter we use for Flexmock:

```
Line 1    require 'flexmock/rspec'
    -
    -     module RSpec
    -       module Core
    5         module MockFrameworkAdapter
    -           include FlexMock::MockContainer
    -           def setup_mocks_for_rspec
    -             # No setup required
    -           end
    10          def verify_mocks_for_rspec
    -             flexmock_verify
    -           end
    -           def teardown_mocks_for_rspec
    -             flexmock_close
    15          end
    -         end
    -       end
    -     end
```

The setup_mocks_for_rspec() method on line 7 is called before each example is run. Flexmock doesn't have anything to set up, so in this case it's a no-op. Other frameworks do things like attach behavior to Object to support transparent access to test-specific extensions or simply create a global storage area to record test double activity.

At the end of each example, RSpec calls verify_mocks_for_rspec() on line 10. In the Flexmock adapter, this delegates to flexmock_verify(), which verifies any message expectations.

The teardown_mocks_for_rspec() on line 13 is guaranteed to be called, even in the event of a failure or error. In this example, it delegates to Flexmock's flexmock_close() method, which removes test double extensions from any classes or other global objects, restoring them to their state before the example.

That's all there is to writing an adapter. Once we have one to use, we can pass its module name directly to the mock_with() method, like this:

```
RSpec::Runner.configure do |config|
  config.mock_with MyMockFrameworkAdapter
end
```

We encourage you to explore the other frameworks. The concepts that we've discussed in this chapter can generally be applied to any test double framework, each of which has its own personality and, in some cases, offers additional behavior that RSpec::Mocks does not support, like test spies in RR.

One at a Time

The one caveat for using the other frameworks is that you can use only one framework in a suite of examples. We enforce this to avoid collisions. RSpec and Mocha both expose the mock() and stub() methods to each example. Also, both frameworks add behavior to Object, and even with RSpec enforcing one test-double framework per suite, we have seen cases in which RSpec::Mocks was being used, but failure messages were coming from Mocha because another library involved was implicitly using Mocha if it happened to be loaded.

This *is* something we plan to improve in the future. For the time being, however, you can still get a lot of flexibility by using different test double frameworks in different suites.

14.10 What We've Learned

In this chapter, we explored method stubs and message expectations on test doubles and test-specific extensions of real objects. We learned that there are a lot of different names for test doubles, but we can usually use the same kind of object to enact several different patterns.

We took a look at some of the risks involved with method stubs and message expectations and some pitfalls that we can keep our eyes out for. We also looked at some of the underlying motivations for method stubs and message expectations, including the following:

- Focusing on roles

- Focusing on interaction

- Interface discovery

- Making progress without implemented dependencies

- Isolation from dependencies

- Isolation from nondeterminism

We've now covered the different libraries that are part of RSpec. In the remaining chapters in this section, we'll explore the RSpec ecosystem including peripheral tooling and techniques for extending RSpec.

## Chapter 15

Tools and Integration

In the Codebreaker tutorial in Part I, we used the rspec command to run specs from a command-line shell. In this chapter, we'll show you a number of command-line options that you may not have tried yet, as well as how RSpec integrates with other command-line tools such as Rake and Autotest and GUI editors like TextMate.

15.1 The rspec Command

The rspec command is installed when you install the rspec-core gem; it provides a number of options that let you customize how RSpec works. You can print a list of these options by asking for help:

```
rspec --help
```

Most of the options have a long form using two dashes and a shorthand form using one dash. The help option, for example, can be invoked with --help or -h. We recommend using the long form if you put it in a script such as a Rakefile (for clarity) and the short form when you run it directly from the command line (for brevity).

Run One Spec File

Running a single file is a snap. To try it, enter the following into simple_math_spec.rb:

```ruby
describe "simple math" do
  it "provides a sum of two numbers" do
    (1 + 2).should == 3
  end
end
```

Now run that file with the rspec command:

```
rspec simple_math_spec.rb
```

You should see output like this:

```
.

Finished in 0.00064 seconds
1 example, 0 failures
```

This is RSpec's default output format, the *progress bar* format. It prints out a dot for every example that is executed and passes (only one in this case). If an example fails, it prints an F. If an example is pending, it prints an *. These dots, F's, and *'s are printed after each example is run, so when you have many examples, you can actually see the progress of the run, which is why it's called a "progress" bar.

After the progress bar, it prints out the time it took to run and then a summary of what was run. In this case, we ran one example, and it passed, so there are no failures.

Run Several Specs at Once

Running individual files directly is handy for some cases, but in most cases you really want to run many of them in one go. To do this, just pass the directory containing your spec files to the rspec command. So, if your spec files are in the spec directory (they are, aren't they?), you can just do this:

```
rspec spec
```

...or if you're in a Rails project, you can do this:

```
bundle exec rspec spec
```

In either case, the rspec command will load all the spec files in the spec directory and its subdirectories. By default, the rspec command only loads files ending with _spec.rb. Although this is the convention, you can configure RSpec to load files based on any pattern you choose. We'll explore that later in this chapter.

Executing files is only the tip of the iceberg. The rspec command offers several options, so let's take a closer look at them.

Modify the Output with --format

By default, RSpec reports the results to the console's standard output by printing something like ...F.....F.... followed by a backtrace for each failure. This is fine most of the time, but sometimes we want a more expressive form of output. RSpec has several built-in formatters that provide different output formats.

TestDox

In 2003, Chris Stevenson, who was working with Aslak in Thought-Works at the time, created a little Java tool called TestDox (http://agiledox.sourceforge.net/). What it did was simple: it scanned Java source code with JUnit tests and produced textual documentation from it. The following Java source code:

```
public class AccountDepositTest extends TestCase {
    public void testAddsTheDepositedAmountToTheBalance() { ... }
}
```

would produce the following text:

```
Account Deposit
- adds the deposited amount to the balance
```

It was a simplistic tool, but it had a profound effect on the teams that were introduced to it. They started publishing the TestDox reports for everyone to see, encouraging the programmers to write real sentences in their tests, lest the TestDox report look like gibberish.

Having real sentences in their tests, the programmers started to think about behavior and what the code should do, and the BDD snowball started to roll.

The documentation formatter, for example, can be used to print out the results in a documentation format inspired by TestDox (see the sidebar on this page). You activate it simply by telling the rspec command the following:

```
rspec path/to/my/specs --format documentation
```

The output will look something like the following:

```
Stack (empty)
  should be empty
  should not be full
  should add to the top when sent #push
  should complain when sent #peek
  should complain when sent #pop

Stack (with one item)
  should not be empty
  should return the top item when sent #peek
  should NOT remove the top item when sent #peek
  should return the top item when sent #pop
  should remove the top item when sent #pop
  should not be full
  should add to the top when sent #push
```

Several Formatters?

RSpec lets you specify several formatters simultaneously by using several --format options on the command line. Now why would anyone want to do that? Maybe you're using a continuous integration (CI) environment to build your code on every check-in. If both you and the CI use the same rake tasks to run RSpec, it can be convenient to have one progress formatter that goes to standard output and one HTML formatter that goes to a file.

This way, you can see the CI RSpec result in HTML and your own in your console—and share the rake task to run your specs.

If you use nested example groups, like this:

```
describe Stack do
  context "when empty" do
    it "should be empty" do
```

then the output will look like this:

```
Stack
  when empty
    should be empty
    should not be full
    should add to the top when sent #push
    should complain when sent #peek
    should complain when sent #pop
  with one item
    should not be empty
    should return the top item when sent #peek
    should NOT remove the top item when sent #peek
    should return the top item when sent #pop
    should remove the top item when sent #pop
    should not be full
    should add to the top when sent #push
```

RSpec also bundles a formatter that can output the results as HTML. You probably don't want to look at the HTML in a console, so you should tell RSpec to output the HTML to a file:

```
rspec path/to/my/specs --format html:path/to/my/report.html
```

RSpec treats whatever comes after the colon as a file and writes the output there. Of course, you can omit the colon and the path and redirect

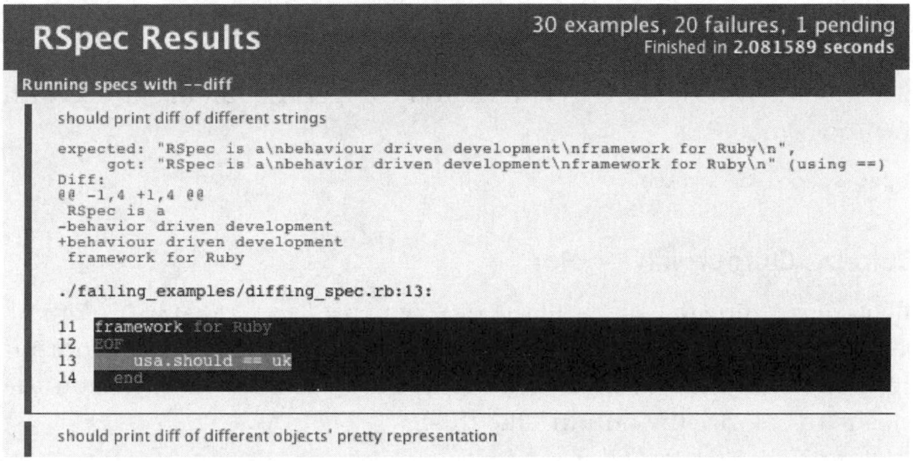

RSpec Results

30 examples, 20 failures, 1 pending
Finished in **2.081589 seconds**

Running specs with --diff

should print diff of different strings

```
expected: "RSpec is a\nbehaviour driven development\nframework for Ruby\n",
     got: "RSpec is a\nbehavior driven development\nframework for Ruby\n" (using ==)
Diff:
@@ -1,4 +1,4 @@
 RSpec is a
-behavior driven development
+behaviour driven development
 framework for Ruby

./failing_examples/diffing_spec.rb:13:
```

```
11  framework for Ruby
12  EOF
13      usa.should == uk
14  end
```

should print diff of different objects' pretty representation

Figure 15.1: HTML REPORT

the output to a file with >, but using the --format flag supports output of multiple formats simultaneously to multiple files, like this:

```
rspec path/to/my/specs --format progress \
                    --format nested:path/to/my/report.txt \
                    --format html:path/to/my/report.html
```

After you've done this and opened the resulting HTML file in a browser, you should see something like Figure 15.1.

You can see a full list of all the built-in formatters with RSpec's --help option.

Load Extensions with --require

If you're developing your own extensions to RSpec, such as a custom --formatter, you must use the --require option to load the code containing your extension.

The reason you can't do this in the spec files themselves is that when they get loaded, it's already too late to hook in an RSpec plug-in, because RSpec is already running.

Get the Noise Back with --backtrace

Most of the time, most of the backtrace is just noise. By default, RSpec shows you only the frames from *your* code. The entire backtrace can, however, be useful from time to time, such as when you think you may have found a bug in RSpec or when you just want to see the whole picture of why something is failing. You can get the full backtrace with the --backtrace flag:

```
rspec spec --backtrace
```

Colorize Output with --color

If you're running the specs all the time (you are, aren't you?), it requires some focus to notice the difference between the command-line output from one run and the next. One thing that can make it easier on the eyes is to colorize the output, like this:

```
rspec spec --color
```

With this option, passing examples are indicated by a green dot (.), failing examples by a red F, and pending examples by a yellow asterisk (*). Error reports for any failing examples are red.

The summary line is green if there are no pending examples and all examples pass. If there are any failures, it is red. If there are no failures, but there are pending examples, it is yellow. This makes it much easier to see what's going on by just looking at the summary.

Store Options in .rspec

Commonly used options can be stored in either of two files: ~/.rspec (in the current user's home directory) and ./.rspec (in the project root directory). You can list as many options as you want, with one or more words per line. As long as there is a space, tab, or newline between each word, they will all be parsed and invoked. Here's an example:

```
--color
--format documentation
```

Options that are stored in ./.rspec take precedence over options stored in ~/.rspec, and any options declared directly on the command line will take precedence over those in either file.

15.2 TextMate

The RSpec development team maintains a TextMate bundle that provides a number of useful commands and snippets. The bundle has been relatively stable for some time now, but when we add new features to

RSpec, they are sometimes accompanied with an addition or a change to the TextMate bundle.

See http://github.com/rspec/rspec-tmbundle for installation details.

15.3 Autotest

Autotest monitors changes to files in your project. Based on a set of internal mappings, each time you save a test file, Autotest will run that test file. And every time you save a library file, Autotest will run the corresponding test file.

RSpec provides an Autotest extension with mappings that make sense in an RSpec project. To tell Autotest to load this extension, create an autotest directory in the project root directory, and then create a discover.rb file in the autotest directory with the following content:

```
Autotest.add_discovery { "rspec2" }
```

To try this, add that file to the codebreaker directory that you created in Chapter 4, *Automating Features with Cucumber*, on page 35. If you use command-line editors such as Vim or Emacs, open a second shell to the same directory; otherwise, open the project in your favorite text editor.

In the first shell, type the autotest command. You should see it start up and execute a command that loads up some number of spec files and runs them. Now, go to one of the spec files and change one of the code examples so it will fail and save the file. When you do, Autotest will execute just that file and report the failure to you. Note that it only runs *that* file, not all of the code example files.

Now reverse the change you just made so the example will pass, and save the file again. What Autotest does now is quite clever. First it runs the one file, which is the one with failures from the last run and sees that all the examples pass. Once it sees that the previous failures are now passing, it loads up the entire suite and runs all of the examples again.

15.4 Rake

Rake is a great automation tool for Ruby, and RSpec ships with custom tasks that let you use RSpec from Rake. You can use this to define one or several ways of running your examples. For example, rspec-rails ships with several different tasks:

```
rake spec           # Run all specs in spec directory
rake spec:controllers # Run the code examples in spec/controllers
rake spec:helpers   # Run the code examples in spec/helpers
rake spec:models    # Run the code examples in spec/models
rake spec:requests  # Run the code examples in spec/requests
rake spec:routing   # Run the code examples in spec/routing
rake spec:views     # Run the code examples in spec/views
```

This is only a partial list. To see the full list, cd into the root directory of any Rails project you have using RSpec, and type rake -T spec. All of these tasks are defined using the RSpec::Core::RakeTask.

RSpec::Core::RakeTask

The RSpec::Core::RakeTask class can be used in your Rakefile to define a task that lets you run your specs using Rake.[1] The simplest way to use it is to put the following code in your Rakefile:

```
require 'rspec/core/rake_task'

RSpec::Core::RakeTask.new
```

This creates a task named spec that runs all the specs in the spec directory (relative to the directory Rake is run from—typically the directory where Rakefile lives). To run the task from a command window, just type this:

```
rake spec
```

Simple, no? And that's only the beginning. The RakeTask exposes a collection of useful configuration options that let you customize the way the command runs.

To begin with, you can declare any of the command-line options. If you want to have the SpecTask colorize the output, for example, you would do this:

```
RSpec::Core::RakeTask.new do |t|
  t.rspec_opts = ["--color"]
end
```

---

1. Spec::Rake::SpecTask in RSpec-1.

> ### About Code Coverage
>
> Code coverage is a very useful metric, but be careful, because it can be misleading. It is possible to have a suite of specs that execute 100 percent of your code base without ever setting any expectations. Without expectations, you'll know that the code will probably run, but you won't have any way of knowing whether it behaves the way you expect it to behave.
>
> So, although low code coverage is a clear indicator that your specs need some work, high coverage does not necessarily indicate that everything is hunky-dory.

spec_opts takes an array of strings, so if you also wanted to format the output with the specdoc format, you could do this:

```
RSpec::Core::RakeTask.new do |t|
  t.rspec_opts = ["--color", "--format", "specdoc"]
end
```

Check RDoc for RSpec::Core::RakeTask to see the full list of configuration options.

15.5 RCov

RCov is a code coverage tool. The idea is that you run your specs, and RCov observes what code in your application is executed and what is not. It then provides a report listing all the lines of code that were never executed when you ran your specs and a summary identifying the percentage of your code base that is covered by specs.

There is no command-line option to invoke RCov with RSpec, so you have to set up a rake task to do it. Here's an example (this would go in Rakefile):

```
require 'rake'
require 'rspec/core/rake_task'

namespace :spec do
  desc "Run specs with RCov"
  RSpec::Core::RakeTask.new('rcov') do |t|
    t.spec_files = FileList['spec/**/*_spec.rb']
    t.rcov = true
    t.rcov_opts = ['--exclude', '\/Library\/Ruby']
  end
end
```

This is then invoked with rake spec:rcov and produces a report that excludes any file with /Library/Ruby as part of its path. This is useful if your library depends on other gems, because you don't want to include the code in those gems in the coverage report. See RCov's documentation for more information on the options it supports.

15.6 What We've Learned

In this chapter, we learned how to use the rspec command to run specs in a single file or a directory. We also discussed many of the command-line options we can use to further tailor a spec run.

We also talked about a few of the many tools that are supported by RSpec or that support RSpec:

- Autotest monitors changes we make in spec and implementation files and runs the appropriate specs when we make them.

- RCov observes implementation code that gets executed during a spec run and reports on any lines that were not executed and therefore may need our attention.

- RSpec's RakeTask allows us to configure any number of Rake tasks targeted at different subsets of a suite.

- RSpec's TextMate bundle lets TextMate users run their specs right from their favorite editor.

As we've been writing this, support for RSpec has also emerged in other editors such as Vim and Emacs, as well as IDEs such as Aptana and RubyMine.

Now that we've seen some of the tools that are available out of the box, in the next chapter we'll look at tools and techniques we can use to extend the behavior of RSpec.

Extending RSpec

RSpec provides a wealth of generic functionality out of the box, but sometimes we want to express things in more domain-specific ways or modify the output format to better serve as documentation for a specific audience. In this chapter, we'll explore the extension points and utilities that RSpec provides to satisfy these needs.

16.1 Metadata

Every example group and each example within has rich metadata associated with it. To see what this metadata looks like, type the following into a file named metadata.rb:

```
describe "something" do
  it "does something" do
    p example.metadata
  end
end
```

Now run that file with the rspec command:

```
rspec metadata.rb
```

The output contains the contents of a hash with keys such as:example_ group, :description,:location,:caller, and so on. RSpec uses this metadata internally for things such as reporting and filtering. Additionally, we can add arbitrary metadata by passing a Ruby hash to the describe() and it() methods like this:

```
describe "something", :a => "A" do
  it "does something", :b => "B" do
    puts example.metadata[:a]
    puts example.metadata[:b]
  end
end
```

Run that with rspec, and you'll see A and B printed in the output. OK, great! But now you must be wondering what we can actually *do* with this ability. We'll get to that soon, but first we need to introduce another concept: configuration.

16.2 Configuration

RSpec exposes a configuration object that supports the definition of global before, after, and around hooks, as well as hooks to include modules in examples or extend example group classes. We can access it like this:

```
# rspec-2
RSpec.configure {|config| ... }

# rspec-1
Spec::Runner.configure {|config| ... }
```

The config block argument is the configuration object, and it exposes several methods we use to filter which examples are run and extend their behavior in a variety of ways. Let's start by talking about filtering.

16.3 Filtering

Sometimes we want to run just one or two examples, or perhaps a group, that relate to the work in process. We can accomplish this using methods provided to us by the Configuration class, combined with metadata we add to the examples or groups we're interested in.

Inclusion

To see this in action, type the following into a file, focused_example.rb:

extending_rspec/focused_example.rb

```
RSpec.configure do |c|
  c.filter = { :focus => true }
end

describe "group" do
  it "example 1", :focus => true do
  end

  it "example 2" do
  end
end
```

Now run that with rspec focused_example.rb, and you should see output like this:

```
Run filtered using {:focus=>true}

group
  example 1

Finished in 0.00066 seconds
1 example, 0 failures
```

As you can see, the example with :focus => true in the metadata passed to it() gets run, but the other example does not. Now try it with a group. Type the following into focused_group.rb:

extending_rspec/focused_group.rb

```ruby
RSpec.configure do |c|
  c.filter = { :focus => true }
end

describe "group 1", :focus => true do
  it "example 1" do
  end

  it "example 2" do
  end
end

describe "group 2" do
  it "example 3" do
  end

  it "example 4" do
  end
end
```

Run that with rspec group_example.rb, and you should see this:

```
Run filtered using {:focus=>true}

group 1
  example 1
  example 2

group 2

Finished in 0.00092 seconds
2 examples, 0 failures
```

Both group names are reported, but only the examples in the group with :focus => true are run (2 examples, 0 failures). We see the name of the second group because RSpec reports the group name before it looks to see whether it has any examples to run. In this case, it does not find any in the second group, so it continues and finishes up the run.

Exclusion

When there are one or two examples that run very slowly, we tend to try to disable them so we can run rest of the suite faster while we're working in other areas. We can use an exclusion filter combined with metadata to accomplish this:

`extending_rspec/exclusion_filter.rb`

```
RSpec.configure do |c|
  c.exclusion_filter = { :slow => true }
end

describe "group" do
  it "example 1", :slow => true do
  end

  it "example 2" do
  end
end
```

Run that with rspec exclusion_filter.rb, and you should see this:

`extending_rspec/exclusion_filter.out`

```
group
  example 2

Finished in 0.00067 seconds
1 example, 0 failures
```

This time, the example we added metadata to was *excluded* from the run, while the other example was run as expected.

Lambdas

Inclusion and exclusion filters can accept lambdas with arbitrarily complex code for more sophisticated filtering. This gives us much more power than primitive values give us.

Imagine an app that connects to an external service. Most of the examples stub out the service, but there is one example that really talks to the service as a sanity check. The problem is that this example can run only when the computer is connected to a network, and we don't want to have to worry about disabling it when there is no network available.

We can use an exclusion filter with a lambda for this, like so:

```
extending_rspec/network.rb
require 'ping'

RSpec.configure do |c|
  c.exclusion_filter = {
    :if => lambda {|what|
      case what
      when :network_available
        !Ping.pingecho "example.com", 10, 80
      end
    }
  }
end

describe "network group" do
  it "example 1", :if => :network_available do
  end
  it "example 2" do
  end
end
```

Try running this example with your computer connected to a network and then again while not connected. You should see that the first example runs only when you're connected.

16.4 Extension Modules

In addition to the filter methods, the Configuration object exposes two methods we can use to extend the behavior of individual example groups. Both of these accept options, which are matched against metadata in each group in order to filter the groups to which the extension applies.

include(*modules, options={}) Includes the submitted module or modules in selected example groups, making their methods available to the examples in each group.

extend(*modules, options={}) Extends selected example groups with the submitted module or modules. This is the recommended way to make macros (see Section 16.8, *Macros*, on page 233) available to example groups.

16.5 Global Hooks

The Configuration object also has hooks you can use to add blocks that are evaluated before, after, or around examples:

before(scope = :each, options={}, &block) Adds the submitted block to the end of a list of blocks that get evaluated before examples that match the submitted scope and options. scope can be any of :each,:all, or :suite. If :each, the block is run before each matching example. If :all, the block is run once per group, before any matching examples have been run. If :suite, the block is run once before any example groups have run.

after(scope = :each, options={}, &block) Adds the submitted block to the beginning of the list of after blocks that get run by every example group. See before(), earlier, for notes about scope and filtering.

around(options={}, &block) Allows you to wrap behavior around examples by passing the example to the supplied block. This is especially useful when working with a library that exposes facilities through methods that accept a block. The most obvious example is database transactions. Here's an example using the Sequel library with Rails 3:

```
RSpec.configure do |config|
  config.around { |example| DB.transaction &example }
end
```

Every example is passed to this block, which executes the example in the context of a Sequel transaction. This leaves Sequel responsible for managing the details of the transaction and keeps the configuration nice and clean.

16.6 Mock Framework

RSpec uses its own mocking framework by default. You can, however, configure RSpec to use virtually any framework:

```
RSpec.configure do |c|
  c.mock_with(:rr)
end
```

The mock_with() method can accept a Symbol or a module reference. If it's a symbol, it can be any of :rspec (default), :mocha,:flexmock, and :rr. These are all reference adapters that ship with RSpec.

If you use a different mock framework or perhaps you've written your own, you can write an adapter module for it and then pass that module to mock_with(). See Chapter 14, *RSpec::Mocks*, on page 179 for more information about writing your own adapter.

16.7 Custom Matchers

RSpec's built-in matchers support most of the expectations we'd like to write in our examples out of the box. There are cases, however, in which a subtle change would allow us to express exactly what we want to say rather than *almost* exactly what we want to say. For those situations, we can easily write our own custom matchers.

You're already using some of these if you're using the rspec-rails gem. render_template(), for example, is a Rails-domain-specific matcher for expecting that a specific template gets rendered by a controller action. Without that matcher, we'd write expectations such as this:

```
response.rendered_template.should == "accounts/index"
```

With this custom matcher, we are able to write examples using language closer to the domain:

```
response.should render_template("accounts/index")
```

All of RSpec's built-in matchers follow a simple protocol, which we use to write our own custom matchers from scratch. We'll go over the protocol in a bit, but first let's take a look at RSpec's Matcher DSL for defining custom matchers in just a few lines of code.

Matcher DSL

RSpec's Matcher DSL makes defining custom matchers a snap.[1] Let's say we're working on a personnel application, and we want to specify that joe.should report_to(beatrice).

To get there, we would probably start off with something like joe.reports_to?(beatrice).should be_true. That's a good start, but it presents a couple of problems. If it fails, the failure message says expected true, got false. That's accurate but not very helpful.

Another problem is that it just doesn't read as well as it could. We really want to say joe.should report_to(beatrice). And if it fails, we want

---

1. The Matcher DSL is based on suggestions from Yehuda Katz.

the message to tell us we were expecting an employee who reports to Beatrice.

We can solve the readability and feedback problems using RSpec's Matcher DSL to generate a report_to() method, like this:

```
RSpec::Matchers.define :report_to do |boss|
  match do |employee|
    employee.reports_to?(boss)
  end
end
```

The define() method on RSpec::Matchers defines a report_to() method that accepts a single argument.[2] We can then call report_to(beatrice) to create an instance of RSpec::Matchers::Matcher configured with beatrice as the boss, and the match declaration stored for later evaluation.

Now when we say that joe.should report_to(beatrice), the report_to() method creates an instance of RSpec::Matchers::Matcher that will call the block with joe.

The match block should return a boolean value. True indicates a match, which will pass if we use should() and fail if we use should_not(). False indicates no match, which will do the reverse: fail if we use should() and pass if we use should_not().

In the event of a failure, the matcher generates a message from its name and the expected and actual values. In this example, the message would be something like this:

```
expected <Employee: Joe> to report to <Employee: Beatrice>
```

The representation of the employee objects depends on how to_s() is implemented on the Employee class, but the matcher gleans "report to" from the Symbol passed to define().

In the event of a failure using should_not(), the generated message would read like this:

```
expected <Employee: Joe> not to report to <Employee: Beatrice>
```

These default messages generally work well, but sometimes we'll want a bit of control over the failure messages. We can get that by overriding them, and the description, with blocks that return the messages we want.

---

2. Spec::Matchers in RSpec-1

```
RSpec::Matchers.define :report_to do |boss|
  match do |employee|
    employee.reports_to?(boss)
  end

  failure_message_for_should do |employee|
    "expected the team run by #{boss} to include #{employee}"
  end

  failure_message_for_should_not do |employee|
    "expected the team run by #{boss} to exclude #{employee}"
  end

  description do
    "expected a member of the team run by #{boss}"
  end
end
```

The block passed to failure_message_for_should() will be called, and the result will be displayed in the event of a should() failure. The block passed to failure_message_for_should_not() will be called, and the result will be displayed in the event of a should_not() failure. The description() will be displayed when this matcher is used to generate its own description.

As with the stock matchers, RSpec's Matcher DSL will probably cover 80 percent of the remaining 20 percent. Still, there are cases where you'll want even more control over certain types of things. As of this writing, for example, there is no support for passing a block to the matcher itself. RSpec's built-in change() matcher needs that ability to express expectations like this:

```
account = Account.new
lambda do
  account.deposit(Money.new(50, :USD))
end.should change{ account.balance }.by(Money.new(50, :USD))
```

We can't easily define a matcher that accepts a block with the DSL because Ruby won't let us pass one block to another without first packaging it as a Proc object. We probably could do it with some gymnastics, but in cases like this, it is often simpler to just write some clear code using RSpec's Matcher protocol.

Matcher Protocol

A matcher in RSpec is any object that responds to a specific set of messages. The simplest matchers only need to respond to these two:

matches? The should() and should_not() methods use this to decide whether the expectation passes or fails. Return true for a passing expection or false for a failure.

failure_message_for_should The failure message to be used when you use should() and the matches?() method returns false.

Here's the report_to() matcher we used in Section 16.7, *Matcher DSL*, on page 229, written using these two methods:

```
class ReportTo
  def initialize(manager)
    @manager = manager
  end

  def matches?(employee)
    @employee = employee
    employee.reports_to?(@manager)
  end

  def failure_message_for_should
    "expected #{@employee} to report to #{@manager}"
  end
end

def report_to(manager)
  ReportTo.new(manager)
end
```

This is clearly more verbose than the Matcher DSL, because we have to define a class *and* a method. We also have to store state in order to generate the failure message, which is not necessary in the DSL because it delivers the actual and expected objects to the match and message declaration blocks. Still, if writing a matcher this way is more expressive than using the DSL in a given circumstance, then a custom matcher from scratch is the way to go.

The following methods are also part of the protocol, supported by the should() and should_not() methods, but they're completely optional:

failure_message_for_should_not Optional. The failure message to be used when you use should_not() and the matches?() method returns true.

description Optional. The description to be displayed when you don't provide one for the example (in other words, it { ... } instead of it "should ... " do ... end).

does_not_match? Optional. On rare occasions it can be useful for the matcher to know if it's being called by should() or should_not(). In these cases, we can implement a does_not_match?() method on the matcher.

The should_not() method will call does_not_match?() if it is implemented. When it does, it considers a response of true to be a success and false to be a failure.

If the matcher does not respond to does_not_match?(), should_not() will call matches?() and consider a response of false to be a success and true to be a failure.

With just these few methods and the expressive support of the Ruby language, we can create some sophisticated matchers. While we recommend using the Matcher DSL first, this simple protocol offers a robust backup plan.

16.8 Macros

Custom matchers can help us build up domain-specific DSLs for specifying our code, but they still require a bit of repetitive ceremony. In rspec-rails, for example, it is quite common to see examples like this:

```
describe Widget do
  it "requires a name" do
    widget = Widget.new
    widget.valid?
    widget.should have(1).error_on(:name)
  end
end
```

With a custom matcher, we can clean that up a bit:

```
describe Widget do
  it "requires a name" do
    widget = Widget.new
    widget.should require_attribute(:name)
  end
end
```

We can even get more terse by taking advantage of the implicit subject, which you read about in Section 13.8, *Implicit Subject*, on page 176, like this:

```
describe Widget do
  it { should require_attribute(:name) }
end
```

Now that is terse, expressive, and complete all at the same time. But for the truly common cases like this, we can do even better. In 2006, the shoulda library emerged as an alternative to RSpec for writing more expressive tests.[3] One of the innovations that came from shoulda was *macros* to express the common, redundant things we want to express in tests. Here's the widget example with a shoulda macro instead of a custom matcher:

```
class WidgetTest < Test::Unit::TestCase
  should_require_attributes :name
end
```

In late 2007, Rick Olsen introduced his own rspec-rails extension library named rspec_on_rails_on_crack,[4] which added macros to rspec-rails. In rspec_on_rails_on_crack, the widget example looks like this:

```
describe Widget do
  it_validates_presence_of Widget, :name
end
```

Macros like this are great for the things that are ubiquitous in our applications, like Rails' model validations. They're a little bit like shared example groups, which you read about in Section 12.5, *Shared Examples*, on page 151, but they are more expressive because they have unique names, and unlike shared examples, they can accept arguments.

Macros are also quite easy to add to RSpec. Let's explore a simple example. Here is some code that you might find in a typical controller spec:

```
describe ProjectsController do
  context "handling GET index" do
    it "should render the index template" do
      get :index
      controller.should render_template("index")
    end
```

---

3. http://www.thoughtbot.com/projects/shoulda
4. http://github.com/technoweenie/rspec_on_rails_on_crack

```
    it "should assign @projects => Project.all" do
      Project.should_receive(:all).and_return(['this array'])
      get :index
      assigns[:projects].should == ['this array']
    end
  end
end
```

This would produce output like this:

```
ProjectsController handling GET index
  should render the index template
  should assign @projects => Project.all
```

Using macros inspired by rspec_on_rails_on_crack and shoulda, we can express the same thing at a higher level and get the same output like this:

> extending_rspec/macro_example/spec/controllers/projects_controller_spec.rb

```
describe ProjectsController do
  get :index do
    should_render "index"
    should_assign :projects => [Project, :all]
  end
end
```

The underlying code is quite simple for the experienced Rubyist:

> extending_rspec/macro_example/spec/spec_helper.rb

```
module ControllerMacros
  def should_render(template)
    it "should render the #{template} template" do
      do_request
      response.should render_template(template)
    end
  end

  def should_assign(hash)
    variable_name = hash.keys.first
    model, method = hash[variable_name]
    model_access_method = [model, method].join('.')
    it "should assign @#{variable_name} => #{model_access_method}" do
      expected = "the value returned by #{model_access_method}"
      model.should_receive(method).and_return(expected)
      do_request
      assigns[variable_name].should == expected
    end
  end
```

```
    def get(action)
      define_method :do_request do
        get action
      end
      yield
    end
  end

RSpec.configure do |config|
  config.use_transactional_fixtures = true
  config.use_instantiated_fixtures  = false
  config.fixture_path = RAILS_ROOT + '/spec/fixtures/'
  config.extend(ControllerMacros, :type => :controller)
end
```

The get() method defines a method that is used internally within the macros named do_request() and yields to the block that contains the other macros, giving them access to the do_request() method.

The should_assign() method seems a bit complex, but it goes out of its way to provide you with nice feedback so when you're writing the examples first (as I trust you are), you'll get a failure message like this:

```
expected: "the value returned by Project.all",
     got: nil (using ==)
```

We exposed these macros to controller specs by extending all controller example groups with the ControllerMacros module in the last line of the configuration. If we didn't want them in all controller specs, we could also explicitly extend individual groups inline, like this:

```
describe ProjectsController do
  extend ControllerMacros
  ...
```

At this point, we've explored a number of ways to make RSpec code examples more expressive, but all these techniques apply only to the *input*: the code we write and read in our examples. This is great if you're a developer, but part of RSpec's value-add is its ability to customize output for different audiences. We'll explore how RSpec does this and how we can customize it in the next section.

16.9 Custom Formatters

RSpec uses message formatters to generate the output you see when running a suite of specs. These formatters receive notification of events, such as when an example group is about to be run or an individual example fails.

RSpec ships with a number of built-in formatters designed to generate plain-text output, an all-purpose HTML formatter, and a TextMate-specific HTML formatter as well. You're probably already familiar with the progress bar formatter, which is the default formatter when you run the rspec command with no options. Run rspec --help to see a full listing of all the built-in formatters.

If none of the built-in formatters satisfies your specific reporting needs, you can easily create a *custom formatter*. This can be very useful for building out custom spec reports for co-workers or a client. And if you happen to be an IDE developer, custom formatters are definitely your friend.

In this section, we'll review the APIs for the various parts of the puzzle that RSpec uses to write all of its built-in formatters and anybody can use to write a custom formatter.

Formatter API

The simplest way to write a custom formatter is to subclass RSpec::Core::Formatters::BaseFormatter, which implements all the required methods as no-ops. This allows us to implement only the methods we care about and reduces the risk that changes in future versions of RSpec will impact the formatter.

Here is a list of all the required methods as of this writing, but be sure to look at the documentation for RSpec::Core::Formatters::BaseFormatter to ensure that you have the latest information:

initialize(output) The output is STDOUT by default but can be overridden on the command line to be a filename, in which case a File object is passed to initialize().

To handle either possibility, RSpec's built-in formatters write to the output object with output << "text", which works for any IO object.

start(example_count) This is the first method that is called. example_count is the total count of examples that will be run, allowing the formatter to keep track of progress (how many examples have run compared to how many there are altogether).

example_group_started(example_group) Called as an example group is started. The example_group includes metadata that can be used for reporting, including its description, location, and so on.

example_started(example) Called as an example is started. The example includes an execution_result in its metadata.

example_passed(example) Called when an example passes. The example is the same object that was passed to example_started().

example_pending(example) Called when an example is declared pending. The example is the same object that was passed to example_started().

example_failed(example) Called when an example fails. The example is the same object that was passed to example_started().

start_dump() Called after all of the code examples have been executed.

def dump_summary(duration, example_count, failure_count, pending_count) duration is the total time it took to run the suite. example_count is the total number of examples that were run. failure_count is the number of examples that failed. pending_count is the number of examples that are pending.

dump_failures() Trigger to output messages about failures. It is up to the formatter to collect information about failed examples and generate the appropriate output.

dump_pending() Trigger to output messages about pending examples. It is up to the formatter to collect information about pending examples and generate the appropriate output.

close() Called once at the very end of the run, signaling the formatter to clean up any resources it still has open.

Invoking a Custom Formatter

Once we've put in all of the energy to write a formatter using the APIs we've discussed, we'll probably want to start using it! Invoking a custom formatter couldn't be much simpler. We just need to require the file in which it is defined and then add its class to the command line.

Let's say we have a PDF formatter that generates a PDF document that we can easily ship around to colleagues. Here is the command we'd use, assuming that it is named PdfFormatter and defined in formatters/pdf_formatter.rb:

```
rspec spec --require formatters/pdf_formatter --format PdfFormatter:report.pdf
```

The structure of the --format argument is FORMAT[:WHERE]. FORMAT can be any of the built-in formatters or the name of the class of a custom formatter. WHERE is STDOUT by default or a filename. Either way, that's what gets submitted to the initialize() method of the formatter.

16.10 What We've Learned

In this chapter, we explored the utilities and extension points that RSpec provides to support extending RSpec to meet your specific needs. These include the following:

- Metadata associated with every group and example is used internally by RSpec for reporting. It can also be extended with arbitrary key/value pairs passed to the describe() and it() methods. This can then be used to filter examples to run.

- Global configuration lets us assign before and after blocks to every example group. We can also use it to add methods to example groups by *extending* them with custom modules, and we can add methods to individual examples by *including* custom modules.

- We can use custom matchers to build up a DSL for expressing code examples.

- Macros also support DSLs but with a different flavor than the custom matchers. Because they generate code themselves, we can also use them to express groups of expectations in a single command.

- Custom formatters let us control the output that RSpec provides so we can produce different spec reports for different purposes and audiences.

In practice, we find that the global configuration, custom matchers defined with the Matcher DSL, and macros tend to be the most common ways that we extend RSpec. There are already numerous matcher and macro libraries for RSpec that are targeted at Rails development. Custom formatters tend to be the domain of IDEs that support RSpec, such as NetBeans and RubyMine.

Part IV

Cucumber

## Chapter 17

Intro to Cucumber

A common understanding of *done* is crucial to the success of any project. How do we know when we're done if we can't agree on what *done* means? Such agreement is pretty easy to find in many kinds of projects. A cake is done when it reaches the right consistency. A building is done when the city inspector says it meets code. If we apply the right tests and they pass, we'll know when we're done. But with software, there's a catch.

We use software because we long ago recognized that requirements for computer programs evolve and that changing programs with a soldering iron to meet changing requirements is not very pragmatic.

The notion of evolving requirements is central to the very existence of software.

That brings up a very interesting question: if software requirements are evolving, how can we know what the right tests are? How can we know when we're done?

Enter Cucumber.

Cucumber supports collaboration and communication between stakeholders and the delivery team. It uses a simple language for describing scenarios that can be written and read with ease by both technical and nontechnical people. These scenarios represent *customer acceptance tests* and are used to automate the system we're developing.

Thanks to the simple format, Cucumber scenarios are very easy to modify as we learn more about the needs of the software throughout the development cycle. And thanks to Cucumber's tagging feature, which you'll read about later in Section 17.11, *Tags*, on page 256, we can easily build workflows around scenarios, identifying them as works in progress, regression tests, or both (scenarios that we're revisiting because of changes in requirements).

17.1 From 20,000 Feet

At a high level, there are three parts to Cucumber: features, the cucumber command, and step definitions.

We write features in a simple language called Gherkin. A feature has a title, a free-form narrative, and an arbitrary number of scenarios, each of which contains an arbitrary number of steps.

We write step definitions in the language of the system that we're developing. In our case that's Ruby, but there are helper libraries that support step definitions in other languages as well.[1]

When we run the cucumber command, Cucumber parses the steps in each scenario and tries to map them to one of the step definitions we've written in Ruby. If it finds one, it executes it, at which point our step definition takes over in automating our application through its APIs.

In this chapter, we'll look at the role that Cucumber plays in a BDD project. We'll examine the Gherkin syntax we use in Cucumber's feature files and explore some higher-level concepts such as style and organization.

In the next chapter, we'll learn how to hook them up to the code we're writing and explore some of the options we have to configure and execute features.

17.2 Features

In Cucumber, a *feature* is a high-level requirement expressed from the perspective of a person or another computer using the system. Features play a role similar to that of user stories in XP, but we take things a step further.

Like user stories, Cucumber features have a title and a brief narrative. In addition, Cucumber features include automated scenarios that serve as acceptance criteria.

---

1. See the Cucumber wiki at http://wiki.github.com/aslakhellesoy/cucumber/ for more about support for Cucumber in different programming languages.

Feature Title

The title of a Cucumber feature is typically just a few words that represent an activity for which a user might engage the system. Here are a few examples:

- Stock clerk adds inventory item

- Anonymous visitor adds blog comment

- Code-breaker submits guess

When putting together an initial list of features, keeping them terse like this makes it easy to assemble a big picture quickly without getting mired down with too much detail. Sooner or later, we'll need more detail if we're going to understand what we're developing. But even after we've written the detail, the title provides us a clear and simple way to refer to the stories in written and verbal communication.

We will be adding two levels of detail: a brief narrative and detailed scenarios. Let's start with the narrative.

Narrative

We use a short narrative to provide context for the executable scenarios we'll be writing. These narratives are just like the narratives we write in user stories. In *Extreme Programming Installed* [JAH02], which was published in 2001, Ron Jeffries provides some example user stories that vary slightly in size and detail but are generally small and simple, like "When the code-breaker submits a guess, the game displays a mark that indicates how close the guess is to the secret code."

From that single sentence, we can glean the role of the user (the code-breaker), the action the user takes (submit a guess), and the expected response to the action (display a mark).

It also exposes a wealth of questions. How does one submit a guess? How does the system present the mark? What are the rules about marking a guess? This is a good thing, since a user story is a *token for a conversation*.

It also leaves out one important question: what is the goal? Why is the code-breaker submitting a guess? What value does the system provide by marking the guess?

In recent years, there has been a lot of exploration into standardized formats or templates that focus on three properties of every story: the

---

The Connextra Format

In 2000, Peter Marks and John Nolan at Connextra hired Tim Mackinnon to help them with Agile. They hit upon the story card format for user stories shown in Figure 17.1, on the next page.

It didn't use the terms *role*, *feature*, and *business value*, but the intent was very much the same. They noticed that matching the "requirement" with the "reason" fostered more discussion with the users and a deeper understanding of the requirement.

When Tim joined ThoughtWorks, this format caught on with Dan North, Chris Matts, and Liz Keogh. From there it became the "official" narrative format in BDD stories and was the most commonly used format for Cucumber features.

More recently, Liz Keogh has been exploring similar templates that reorder the points of focus and solve problems related to expressing business value. For example, when a narrative suggests "As a visitor to the site, I want to log in," it's unlikely that a real visitor actually *wants* to log in. It's the security manager who wants the visitor to log in, so that's the role that provides context for business value, even though the visitor is the active role in the narrative. See Liz's blog for more on this.*

---

*. http://lizkeogh.com

---

role of the user, the action that user takes, and, most importantly, the value provided *to the business* in return for investing in writing code to support this action.

The Connextra Format

The format that is probably the most well known one originated in an Agile project at Connextra and is featured in Mike Cohn's *User Stories Applied* [Coh04]:

```
As a <role>
I want <feature>
So that <business value>
```

This template helps us focus on the answers to those three very important questions: Who is using the system? What is he/she doing? Why does he/she care? Almost all expressions of user stories express the

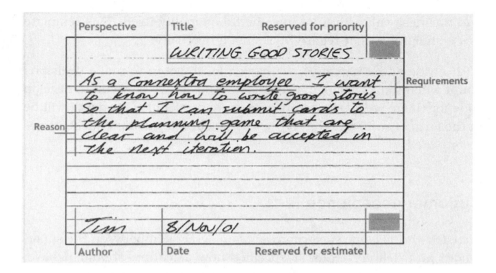

Figure 17.1: CONNEXTRA CARD

what, but adding the *who* and the *why* can provide context for a lot of very important discussion.

Let's take an example from a photo-editing system. A professional photographer is going to want much more detail and complexity from a photo-editing system than the casual red-eye remover/cropper sort of user. Being clear about the target user for a feature is going to impact the decisions you make about user interaction with the system.

The *why* is about business value and really gets to the heart of any Agile development process. We want to minimize waste by keeping focus on features that will provide some meaningful benefit and will therefore actually be used. We say that BDD is about writing software that matters—this focus on features that will be used is directly related to that.

Although this template is recommended, it is certainly not a requirement of BDD or of Cucumber. The narrative of a feature can be expressed in completely free form with virtually no restrictions.[2] The important thing is that we have a conversation that covers the role

---

2. The only restriction is that a narrative cannot include a line that begins with a Gherkin keyword.

and business value and not just the functionality itself. This template can be helpful in that regard but is not a necessity.

With a title and a narrative, we have a lot to go on to make decisions about when to tackle which features, but before we move on to develop code for them, we're going to need even more detail. This detail will be in the form of scenarios that represent executable customer acceptance tests.

17.3 Customer Acceptance Tests

A *customer acceptance test* represents an agreement between the stakeholder and delivery team. It specifies how a feature should behave. When the developers deliver code that passes the test, the stakeholder accepts that feature as done.

We consider acceptance in the context of the current iteration. If a new idea emerges mid-iteration, we can talk about it without changing the acceptance criteria for features for the current iteration and add new stories to the backlog for future consideration. The work that was done in the iteration is still valued and accepted as meeting the agreed-upon criteria. This is good for morale, as well as tracking.

The new stories can be prioritized intelligently, without the gravity of *unfinished* work getting more weight than it may deserve. Maybe it makes sense to add a story for the next iteration, but maybe it makes more sense to add the story to the backlog and not introduce it right away.

Considering acceptance to be contextual is not without its costs. Sometimes an idea is sufficiently game-changing as to render any further work on a related story a complete waste of time. Just beware that the disruption of changing a story mid-stream is often a bigger waste of time than simply finishing the story and keeping things moving.

17.4 Gherkin

Cucumber is an interpreter. Just like the ruby executable interprets Ruby code in .rb files, the Cucumber executable interprets Gherkin code in .feature files.

Internationalization

The Gherkin keywords are translated into thirty-five different languages. This means you can write features in your own native language. All you need to do is to have a header in your .feature file with the language you're using. For example, if you want to use Portuguese, the first two lines might look like this:

```
# language: pt
Ele é português
```

Or in English:

```
# language: en
Feature: Addition
```

If you don't provide a language header, Cucumber will default to English.

To see what languages are available, just run this:

```
cucumber --i18n help
```

To see the translations for a particular language, specify the language code. Here's an example:

```
cucumber --i18n fr
```

The Gherkin grammar consists of a few keywords that you must use when you write a feature file:

- Feature
- Background
- Scenario
- Scenario outline
- Scenarios (or examples)
- Given
- When
- Then
- And (or but)
- | (which is used to define tables)
- """ (which is used to define multiline strings)
- # (which is used for comments)

You can write whatever you want after a keyword. The keywords Given, When, Then, And, and But indicate steps in a scenario, which we use to build up a domain-specific language for a project.

Every feature file must start with the Feature keyword, followed by a colon and a description. The description can be on several lines, and the most common pattern is to have a short name followed by a brief narrative on the next few lines, like this:

```
# language: en
Feature: Compute distance
  In order to calculate fuel consumption
  As a driver
  I want to see the total distance of a trip
```

It is important to point out that Cucumber does not care what you write here. It will simply ignore everything from the top of the file until it sees one of the keywords Background, Scenario, or Scenario Outline. The only reason we write this text is for communication purposes.

Now that we have seen how to start a feature, let's dive into the interesting parts. We'll start with scenarios and cover the other keywords later.

17.5 Scenarios

Scenarios are concrete examples of how we want the software to behave. They are more explicit than some traditional ways to describe requirements and help us raise and answer questions that we might miss otherwise. Consider this requirement: it shouldn't be possible to book a room if the hotel is full.

This leaves a lot of open questions. If the hotel is full, is it still possible to try to book and get an error if we try? Is the booking option disabled? Or is it hidden? What do we display?

Scenarios allow us to answer these questions by describing exactly what should happen under what circumstances. The first part of a scenario is the Scenario keyword, followed by a colon and then a name that describes the scenario in one sentence. Here is the beginning of a feature, with a title, a narrative, and the introductory line of a scenario:

```
Feature: Traveler books room
  In order to reduce staff
  As a hotel owner
  I want travelers to book rooms on the web

  Scenario: Successful booking
```

Each scenario is made up of steps that appear below the Scenario keyword and are typically indented two spaces. We'll talk about steps in the next section.

When you start writing a new feature, it's generally easiest to start with a scenario that describes the most common "happy path." Once you are done with that, you can add more scenarios that describe different edge cases:

```
Feature: Traveler books room
  In order to reduce staff
  As a hotel owner
  I want travelers to book rooms on the web

  Scenario: Successful booking

  Scenario: Hotel is full

  Scenario: Visitor forgets to enter email
```

Let's take a closer look at the first scenario, Successful booking. What does a successful booking look like? We have to fill in some steps to make this a concrete example.

17.6 Steps

Scenarios each use an arbitrary number of steps to describe everything that happens within a scenario. A step is generally a single line of text that starts with one of the step keywords: Given, When, Then, And, and But.

Let's write some steps for the Successful booking scenario. First, create the directories hotel/features/ in an empty directory, and open a command prompt in the hotel directory. Now, create features/booking.feature, and paste the following code:

cucumber/01/features/book_room.feature

```
# language:en
Feature: Traveler books room
  In order to reduce staff
  As a hotel owner
  I want travelers to book rooms on the web

  Scenario: Successful booking
    Given a hotel with "5" rooms and "0" bookings
```

17.7 The cucumber Command

Once we have a file with a feature in it, we can run it with the cucumber command:[3]

```
cucumber
```

The cucumber command runs all the *.feature files below the features directory. In our case, we have only one, so Cucumber runs it and prints out the following:

```
# language:en
Feature: Traveler books room
  In order to reduce staff
  As a hotel owner
  I want travelers to book rooms on the web

  Scenario: Successful booking                  # features/book_room.feature:7
    Given a hotel with "5" rooms and "0" bookings # features/book_room.feature:8

1 scenario (1 undefined)
1 step (1 undefined)
0m0.001s
```

You can implement step definitions for undefined steps with these snippets:

```
Given /^a hotel with "([^"]*)" rooms and "([^"]*)" bookings$/ do |arg1, arg2|
  pending # express the regexp above with the code you wish you had
end
```

The output is very similar to the text in features/booking.feature, with some extra information. The first thing we notice is that the Scenario and Step lines each have comments at the end of the line, which display the location of the scenario as a filename and line number. This is particularly useful if you want to execute a single scenario. Copy the location and try running it again:

```
cucumber features/book_room.feature:7
```

You should see exactly the same output as before. You'll find yourself using this technique often as you write more features and scenarios—if you run all of the features and only a few of them fail, you only want to run the failing ones while you are working yourself back to green.

The next thing we notice is a couple of lines summarizing how many scenarios and steps we have and the result of running them. Cucumber reports that we had an undefined step. This is Cucumber's way of

---

3. Run gem install cucumber if you haven't already.

telling us that it recognizes a step, but it doesn't know what to do with it. We need a *step definition* to move on.

Cucumber always tries to be helpful and tell you the next thing to do, so it will suggest how you can implement a step definition whenever it encounters an undefined step. We'll talk about step definitions in Section 18.1, *Step Definitions*, on page 261, but, for now, let's talk about the step keywords.

17.8 Given/When/Then

"*Given* I have $100 in my checking account, *When* I withdraw $70, *Then* I should have $30 left." That's how anybody might describe a real-life scenario in conversation. This is why we use Given, When, and Then in BDD, whether we're talking about application behavior or object-level behavior. *It's all behavior!*

This is also why Cucumber uses Given, When, and Then as keywords in scenarios. We can also use And and But as synonyms for whichever of Given, When, or Then appeared before. If we say "Given x, And y," then And means Given. If we say "Then x, But not y," then But means Then.

Given indicates something that we accept to be true in a scenario: Given I have $20 in my checking account; Given the world is round; Given today is a holiday; and so on. These statements provide context for the events and outcomes that we talk about later in the scenario.

Given is often misconstrued to mean preconditions, but that is a different concept. Preconditions are part of a contract that indicates we can go no further unless a precondition is met. Givens are not bound by precondition contracts and can explicitly violate them in order to specify how an app should behave under conditions it should, in theory, never be in (Given the world is flat).

When indicates the event in a scenario: When I withdraw $15; When I fly in a perfectly straight line perpendicular to the earth's axis; and so on. We generally prefer to have a single event in any scenario, because this makes it easier to understand the intent of each scenario and what may have gone wrong when it fails.

Then indicates an expected outcome: Then I should have $5 remaining; Then I should be at a higher altitude than when I started; and so on. It's OK to have more than one outcome in a scenario (hence And and But), but we want to make sure they are cohesive.

Consider a scenario in which we transfer money from one account to another, and we have two outcomes: Then I should have $20 in checking, And I should have $30 in savings. If we add, Then I should earn $0.04 interest in my savings account, while that may be a legitimate outcome of the scenario, it is not related to the other outcomes and becomes a source of confusion. Better to put that in a separate scenario.

17.9 Declarative and Imperative Scenario Styles

Although there are many different approaches to writing steps and scenarios, we can talk about two general approaches that offer different costs and benefits: declarative and imperative.

To illustrate the difference between these two styles, consider the following two scenarios:

```
Scenario: transfer money (declarative)
  Given I have $100 in checking
  And I have $20 in savings
  When I transfer $15 from checking to savings
  Then I should have $85 in checking
  And I should have $35 in savings

Scenario: transfer money (imperative)
  Given I have $100 in checking
  And I have $20 in savings
  When I go to the transfer form
  And I select "Checking" from "Source Account"
  And I select "Savings" from "Target Account"
  And I fill in "Amount" with "15"
  And I press "Execute Transfer"
  Then I should see that I have $85 in checking
  And I should see that I have $35 in savings
```

These two scenarios tell the same story but at different levels of abstraction. The imperative scenario has five When steps that go step-by-step through filling in and submitting a form, whereas the declarative scenario wraps all that activity up into a single step. These two approaches impact different parts of the process in different ways.

Imperative steps are more composable, which means we can generally support more scenarios with fewer step definitions. This means we spend more time in the early iterations building generic step definitions, and more of the long-term maintenance burden is borne by the plain-text features.

Conversely, declarative steps tend to be more customized to each scenario, which means that the work of writing step definitions spreads out more throughout the development of an app. It also means that more of the maintenance burden is borne by the step definitions, in Ruby.

If you're on a larger team with dedicated business analysts who can manage the plain-text scenarios, then the imperative style puts more power in their hands and makes it easy for them to compose new scenarios with little developer involvement. If you're on a smaller team in which the developers are responsible for business analysis and testing tasks as well as development tasks, then the declarative style might make more sense.

We also need to consider the communication value of the scenarios and the needs of the customer team. Imperative scenarios are more verbose, which makes some customers very happy, while it makes the eyes of others glaze over because there is so much more to read. We want to specify business value, but those words mean different things to different people and in different contexts.

Many people report that the right answer is a balance of imperative and declarative scenarios in the same project. In our money transfer example, we could have a single scenario with the imperative approach and then a series of declarative scenarios to cover common alternative paths.

17.10 Organizing Features

When you run the cucumber command with no options, Cucumber will look for all of the .rb and .feature files below the ./features directory, load all of the .rb files, and then run all of the .feature files. For very small projects, the simplest way to organize the feature files is to keep them in the root of the ./features directory. If you want to run subsets of features, you can easily manage that with tags (see Section 17.11, *Tags*, on the next page) and profiles (see Section 18.9, *Configuration*, on page 272).

For larger projects or for features with lots of scenarios, we can create subdirectories for each feature, with multiple files in each subdirectory and with cohesive subsets of scenarios in each file. One good way to determine that a group of scenarios is cohesive is if they share a background, as described in Section 18.5, *Background*, on page 267.

We can also go to a higher level of abstraction with feature sets, or themes, each in its own subdirectory of ./features. Consider an HR benefits management application that has general functional areas like insurance and personal time off (PTO). This might result in a directory structure like this:

```
features
  insurance
    medical
    dental
    life
    disability
  pto
    accrual
    usage
```

With a structure like this, we can easily choose what to run when using the directory/feature argument to the cucumber command. Given a directory, Cucumber runs all the features in that directory and its subdirectories. In the HR example, we could run all features with cucumber features, all insurance-related features with cucumber features/insurance, or only medical insurance features with cucumber features/insurance/medical.

Now we could get similar groupings using tags, but we suggest using tags for workflow (@wip,@current,@passing,@iteration_12,@in_browser, and so on) and use directories for organization.

17.11 Tags

Once we get a scenario passing, any subsequent failure is considered a regression. We want to fix it quickly, ideally before committing code. The life cycle before a scenario passes the first time, however, is a different matter.

The Life of a Scenario

Before work commences on a feature, each scenario may go through an approval process in which developers and customers collaborate to write a scenario that expresses the right requirements at the right level of abstraction, and so on. During this time, a scenario might be considered to be pending approval, for example.

Once all parties agree and we're ready to commence work, the feature becomes a work in progress. Even after we have one scenario passing, we might have other scenarios in the same feature that are still works in progress or pending approval to start work.

We therefore want to run controlled subsets of a full suite. When we're working on a scenario, we might want to run only that scenario until we get it passing. Our continuous integration build might run only scenarios that should be passing and ignore all of the works in progress or scenarios pending approval.

Cucumber supports running selected subsets of features and scenarios with tags.

Tags to the Rescue

A tag in Cucumber looks like an instance variable in Ruby. It starts with an @ symbol followed by an alpha character or an underscore, followed by an arbitrary number of alphanumeric characters and underscores. Examples include @wip (work in progress), @iteration_12, @approved, and so on.

Any number of tags can be applied to any feature or scenario by typing them on the line before the Feature or Scenario keyword:

```
@approved @iteration_12
Feature: patient requests appointment

  @wip
  Scenario: patient selects available time
```

A Scenario inherits tags specified on the Feature, so in the previous example, the Scenario will have the tags @approved @iteration_12 @wip.

With scenarios tagged, we can now run all of the scenarios tagged with a specific tag with the --tags command-line argument. For example, this command would run all of the scenarios tagged with @wip:

```
cucumber --tags @wip
```

The --tags option can accept a complex *tag expression*, including conditional AND, OR, and NOT expressions. Here are some examples:

```
cucumber --tags @foo,@bar
# @foo || @bar
# runs all of the scenarios tagged with @foo OR @bar
```

```
cucumber --tags @foo --tags @bar
# @foo && @bar
# runs all of the scenarios tagged with @foo AND @bar

cucumber --tags ~@dev
# !@dev
# runs all of the scenarios NOT tagged with @dev

cucumber --tags @foo,~@bar --tags @baz
# (@foo || !@bar) && @baz
# runs all of the scenarios (tagged with @foo OR NOT tagged with @bar) AND
# tagged with @baz
```

Type cucumber --help for more information about tags.

Other Uses for Tags

In addition to using tags to manage the life cycle of a scenario, we can also use tags to do the following:

- Identify scenarios only to be run in a certain environment

- Identify scenarios that represent different sorts of testing, like workflow vs. business rules

- Run only scenarios that run fast

- Run scenarios related to a feature set or theme

17.12 What We've Learned

Cucumber provides a standard format for expressing requirements in the form of features and scenarios that we can use to automate the systems we write. The Gherkin language provides a common basic structure and a variety of tools for describing features.

A Cucumber feature is made up of a title, a narrative, and an arbitrary number of scenarios. Scenarios are composed of steps beginning with Given, When, or Then. We use Given steps to create context, When steps to describe an event that occurs within that context, and Then steps to describe the expected outcomes.

We can also use And or But, each of which take on the quality of the previous step. An And step preceded by a When step is considered another When step.

We use two common styles for composing steps into scenarios: declarative and imperative. Declarative scenarios tend to be shorter and more specific, putting the maintenance burden in the step definitions that are written in Ruby. Imperative scenarios tend to be longer and more detailed, but with more generic steps. This pushes the maintenance burden more toward the plain-text scenarios themselves.

We typically group features in subdirectories of the features directory named for the each feature.

We can choose which features to run under given conditions using tags in the feature files themselves and referencing those tags from the command line.

In the next chapter, we'll look more closely at the Ruby code we use to connect the plain-text scenarios to the code we're driving out.

Chapter 18

Cucumber Detail

In the previous chapter, we learned about Cucumber's Gherkin language for expressing features and scenarios in plain text. In this chapter, we'll take a look at the Ruby code we write to connect the plain-text scenarios to the code we're writing.

We'll also take a look at some more advanced techniques we can use in the scenarios to manage complexity as our suite of scenarios grows. But before we can get into that, we'll begin with the basic bit of glue that we use to connect scenario steps to code: step definitions.

18.1 Step Definitions

Step definitions are Cucumber's equivalent of method definitions or function declarations in a conventional programming language. We define them in Ruby,[1] and they are invoked when Cucumber parses steps in the plain-text features.

We wrote a scenario with a single step earlier in Section 17.6, *Steps*, on page 251. Open a command prompt to the hotel directory again, and type the cucumber command. Here's the output:

```
# language:en
Feature: Traveler books room
  In order to reduce staff
  As a hotel owner
  I want travelers to book rooms on the web

  Scenario: Successful booking                 # features/book_room.feature:7
    Given a hotel with "5" rooms and "0" bookings # features/book_room.feature:8
```

---

1. The Cuke4Duke project at http://wiki.github.com/aslakhellesoy/cuke4duke also lets you define step definitions in other programming languages such as Java, Groovy, and Scala.

```
1 scenario (1 undefined)
1 step (1 undefined)
0m0.001s
```

You can implement step definitions for undefined steps with these snippets:

```
Given /^a hotel with "([^"]*)" rooms and "([^"]*)" bookings$/ do |arg1, arg2|
  pending # express the regexp above with the code you wish you had
end
```

Cucumber-Provided Code Snippets

The last part of the output is a snippet of code we can use to build a step definition. Create a step_definitions subdirectory in features, and add a file named hotel_steps.rb. Copy the snippet into that file, and modify it as follows:

```
cucumber/02/features/step_definitions/room_steps.rb
```

```
Given /^a hotel with "([^"]*)" rooms and "([^"]*)" bookings$/ do
  |room_count, booking_count|
end
```

The code that hooks up to the application code goes in the block passed to the Given() method. For demo purposes, we're leaving the block empty. Run your feature again as before, and look at the output. Everything should be passing in nice green color:

```
# language:en
Feature: Book room
  In order to attract more people
  Travelers should be able to book on the web

  Scenario: Successful booking
          # features/book_room.feature:6
    Given a hotel with "5" rooms and "0" bookings
          # features/step_definitions/hotel_steps.rb:1

1 scenario (1 passed)
1 step (1 passed)
0m0.002s
```

Several things changed when we added the step definition. First, the scenario and step are no longer pending, but passing. This means that for each of our steps, Cucumber found a matching step definition. Each step definition consists of a regular expression and a block. Whenever Cucumber executes a step, it will look for a step definition with a matching regular expression, and if it finds one, it will execute the block.

Arguments

If a step definition's regular expression contains one or more *capture groups*, it will treat them as arguments to the step definition's block. The step definition has the regular expression /^a hotel with "([^\"]*)" rooms and "([^\"]*)" bookings$/, and when that is matched with the plain-text step a hotel with "5" rooms and "0" bookings, it extracts the strings 5 and 0 and passes them as arguments to the block.

Note that arguments are always passed as Strings, so if we want to treat an argument as a different type, we have to manage that explicitly. More about that in a little while.

18.2 World

Every scenario runs in the context of a new instance of an object that we call World. By default, World is just an instance of Object that Cucumber instantiates before each scenario. All of the step definitions for a scenario will execute their blocks in the context of this same instance.

In some cases, it can be handy to invoke helper methods from step definitions. To make such methods available, we can customize World using the World() method, which takes one or more Ruby modules as arguments:

```
module MyHelper
  def some_helper
    ...
  end
end
```

```
World(MyHelper)
```

This makes the some_helper method available from our step definitions. We can configure World in any Ruby file in features or its subdirectories, but we recommend doing it in a file called features/support/world.rb, because this makes it easier to remember where the code lives.

In addition to mixing Ruby modules into the World object (which by default is an instance of Object), we can also change the default behavior so that the World is an instance of some other class. This is done with the same World() method, passing a block:

```
class MyWorld
  def some_helper
    ...
  end
end
```

```
World do
  MyWorld.new
end
```

These techniques for altering World can also be used by Cucumber "plug-ins" such as cucumber-rails, which configures World to be an instance of ActionController::IntegrationTest. It also mixes in various modules from RSpec and Webrat so that those libraries' helper methods are available from within your step definitions.

18.3 Calling Steps Within Step Definitions

We often find ourselves repeating a series of steps across scenarios. One approach to reducing this duplication is to define a higher-level step that encapsulates several steps.

Consider the following scenario steps for transferring money from one account to another:

```
When I select checking as the source account
And I select savings as the target account
And I set $20.00 as the amount
And I click transfer
```

That's fine if it appears in one scenario, but if it appears in several, we might want to condense these four steps into one, like this:

```
When I transfer $20.00 from checking to savings
```

Cucumber makes it easy for us to do this, by allowing us to invoke steps from within step definitions. Assuming that we already have the four-step definitions for the four-step version earlier, we can write a step definition for the one-step version like this:

```
When /I transfer (.*) from (.*) to (.*)/ do |amount, source, target|
  When "I select #{source} as the source account"
  When "I select #{target} as the target account"
  When "I set #{amount} as the amount"
  When "I click transfer"
end
```

This can also be expressed like this, using some additional sugar provided by Cucumber:

```
When /I transfer (.*) from (.*) to (.*)/ do |amount, source, target|
  steps %Q{
    When I select #{source} as the source account
    And I select #{target} as the target account
    And I set #{amount} as the amount
    And I click transfer
  }
end
```

> ### Joe Asks...
> #### When Should I Quote Arguments?
>
> There are two common styles for steps that take arguments. First is the implicit style, where you can't *see* where the argument is:
>
> ```
> When I select checking as the source account
> ```
>
> The second is explicit:
>
> ```
> When I select "checking" as the source account
> ```
>
> There are a couple of benefits to using the explicit style. First, the double quotes give us a hint that this might be an argument, which might make it easier to reuse a step definition. The second benefit is that Cucumber will be extra helpful when generating snippets for undefined steps that use quotes and suggest the capture groups for you. This doesn't mean you should always use the explicit style; it also adds "noise." Discuss the pros and cons with your team.

Both approaches have the same result, so pick the one that you find easiest to read, write, and maintain.

Calling steps from step definitions can help keep things DRY, but they add additional layers of indirection. If we're calling steps that call steps that call steps, it can become difficult to understand failures.

This technique also results in different levels of abstraction across step definitions: some with simple Ruby statements, and some with calls to other steps, which we typically do from within the feature files.

We recommend that you experiment with the different approaches and decide for yourself which work better based on the balance of readability and maintainability.

18.4 Hooks

For most nontrivial applications, it becomes necessary to perform common operations before and after each scenario. For example, cucumber-rails starts a database transaction before each scenario and rolls it back when it has finished, ensuring that the database is in a pristine state for each scenario.

In Cucumber, we do this with *hooks*. Here is a simple example of a Before hook:

```
Before do
  puts "This will run before each scenario"
end
```

Cucumber supports three different kinds of hooks:

- Before: Executed before every scenario

- After: Executed after every scenario

- AfterStep: Executed after every step

We can configure hooks in any of the Ruby files below features/, but we recommend doing it in a file called features/support/hooks.rb, because this makes it easier to remember where the code lives.

Hooks can be defined any number of times. If there are ten different things we need to do before each scenario, we can define ten Before hooks. They'll be run in the order in which they are defined.

When we do have multiple hooks, we sometimes find that we don't need to run all of them for every single scenario. When we do, we can use *tagged hooks*.

Tagged Hooks

A tagged hook behaves just like a regular hook, but it runs only for certain scenarios. When we declare a hook, we can also pass one or more tag expressions. Consider this example:

```
Before("@foo") do
  puts "This will run before each scenario tagged with @foo"
end
```

For more fine-grained control, we can use more complex tag expressions, just like we can do on the command line with --tags, as described in Section 17.11, *Tags*, on page 256.

```
Before("@foo,~@bar", "@zap") do
  puts "This will run before each scenario tagged with @foo or not @bar AND @zap"
end
```

Visibility

Although hooks can be practical for common operations that need to happen before and after a scenario, they do have one drawback. They cannot be read by nontechnical people on your team. Hooks are defined in Ruby code, and you will never see any evidence of their existence (unless you have a failure, in which case the backtrace will show it).

Sometimes it's OK that nontechnical people can't see it. Take the case with Ruby on Rails, where Cucumber starts a transaction in a Before hook and rolls it back in an After hook. This is low-level technical stuff that nontechnical people don't care about (and shouldn't have to care about).

In other situations, there might be some common setup that also provides *important context* in order for a scenario to make logical sense. For those situations, we can use a Background.

18.5 Background

Backgrounds let us write steps once that will be invoked before every scenario in a given feature. We use them instead of Before hooks when we want the steps to be visible in the feature file because they create logical context for each scenario.

Consider the act of logging in to a website. Many websites offer a limited set of functionality to users who are not logged in and more functionality for those who are.

When writing features for such a system, we often find it necessary to start every scenario with either Given I am logged in or Given I am logged out (or some variants of this). For cases like this, Cucumber allows us to define common steps in a Background:

```
Feature: invite friends

  Background: Logged in
    Given I am logged in as "Aslak"
    And the following people exist:
      | name   | friend? |
      | David  | yes     |
      | Vidkun | no      |

  Scenario: Invite someone who is already a friend

  Scenario: Invite someone who is not a friend

  Scenario: Invite someone who doesn't have an account
```

A Background will run before each of our scenarios, just like a Before hook in code. If there are any Before hooks, they will run before the Background.

When we have a common setup, we usually have a choice whether to use Before or Background. Which one to use boils down to whether it is valuable to be explicit about it in the feature.

18.6 Multiline Text

For software that uses text files as either input or output, Cucumber lets us embed their content right into features with multiline text. RSpec, for example, reads text files. In RSpec's own Cucumber scenarios, we see examples that look like this:

```
Scenario: pending implementation
  Given a file named "example_without_block_spec.rb" with:
    """
    describe "an example" do
      it "has not yet been implemented"
    end
    """
  When I run "spec example_without_block_spec.rb"
  Then the exit code should be 0
  And the stdout should include
    """
    Pending:

    an example has not yet been implemented \(Not Yet Implemented\)
    .\/example_without_block_spec.rb:2

    Finished in ([\d\.]*) seconds

    1 example, 0 failures, 1 pending
    """
```

In this scenario, the Given and And (Then) steps take Python-style multiline strings as their arguments. This gives us a lot of flexibility because we can represent input and output data (almost) exactly as it would appear in a file. The margin is determined by the position of the first double quote, so the words *describe* and *end* are left aligned, and the word *it* on the second line is indented only two spaces.

The regular expression in the step definition does not need to capture this text. It should end on the last character of the step's sentence. Here are the step definitions for the steps in the previous example:

```
Given /^a file named "([^\"]*)" with:$/ do |filename, text|
  # ...
end

Then /^the stdout should include$/ do |text|
  # ...
end
```

Cucumber delivers the text to the step definition as the last block argument. In the previous Given step definition, the filename block argument contains the value of the regular expression capture, and the text variable holds the multiline text. The Then step definition has no capture groups defined, so the one and only block argument contains the multiline text.

The step definition behind the And step compiles a regexp and compares it to the expected output, which is why we see a group with a character class and the parentheses around "Not Yet Implemented" are escaped.

18.7 Tables in Steps

Sentences that begin with Given, When, and Then are great for expressing activities and interactions that users have with a software system. They are not, however, very useful for tabular data. It turns out that the best thing for tables is... tables! Cucumber supports tabular data in steps with a wiki-style table format that is well suited for both Given and Then steps.

Imagine we're writing a poker hand evaluator. Here's how we might describe the cards in the hand using tables:

```
Scenario: three of a kind beats two pair
  Given a hand with the following cards:
    | rank | suit |
    | 2    | H    |
    | 2    | S    |
    | 2    | C    |
    | 4    | D    |
    | A    | H    |
  And another hand with the following cards:
    | rank | suit |
    | 2    | H    |
    | 2    | S    |
    | 4    | C    |
    | 4    | D    |
    | A    | H    |
  Then the first hand should beat the second hand
```

When Cucumber sees a | at the beginning of a line following a line with a Step keyword, it parses that and all subsequent lines beginning with | and stores the cell values in a Cucumber::Ast::Table object, which exposes the data as an array of hashes via a hashes() method.

Each hash in the array uses the column headers in the first row as keys, like this:

```
[
  { :rank => '2', :suit => 'H' },
  { :rank => '2', :suit => 'S' },
  { :rank => '4', :suit => 'C' },
  { :rank => '4', :suit => 'D' },
  { :rank => 'A', :suit => 'H' }
]
```

Cucumber delivers the Cucumber::Ast::Table to the block as the last (and only, in this case) block argument. The step definition for the first step might look like this:

```
Given /^a hand with the following cards:$/ do |cards_table|
  hands << Hand.new do |hand|
    cards_table.hashes.each {|hash| hand << Card.new(hash)}
  end
end
```

The step definition guides us to write the initialize method on Card such that it can set its internal state from a hash with the keys :rank, and :suit.

The Cucumber::Ast::Table offers several other utilities. See the RDoc for more information.[2]

18.8   Scenario Outlines

For cases that involve several similar cases, Cucumber gives us scenario outlines. We saw this in the Codebreaker tutorial in Part I of the book, where we had several scenarios that involved the same three steps with different values each time.

```
Given the secret code is 1234
When I guess 1234
Then the mark should be bbbb

Given the secret code is 1234
When I guess 1235
Then the mark should be bbb

# etc, etc
```

After about three or four scenarios like that, they become very hard to scan through and get a sense of the relationship between them and the rules that they are trying to express.

---

2.   http://wiki.github.com/aslakhellesoy/cucumber/rdoc

Scenario outlines solve this problem by letting us define an outline for a scenario once, with placeholders for the values that might change from scenario to scenario. Then we can express the values in a tabular format that is very easy to scan and get the whole picture:

```
Scenario Outline: submit guess
  Given the secret code is "<code>"
  When I guess "<guess>"
  Then the mark should be "<mark>"

Scenarios: all numbers correct
  | code | guess | mark |
  | 1234 | 1234  | ++++ |
  | 1234 | 1243  | ++-- |
  | 1234 | 1423  | +--- |
  | 1234 | 4321  | ---- |
```

The Scenarios keyword identifies a table of input data for the outline.[3] See how the column headers in the table match up to the placeholders in the outline? Cucumber processes the outlined scenario once for each row in the table after the first row with the column headers. In this case, we get four scenarios.

The substitutions in scenario outlines also work with multiline text and tabular input. Here's an example:

```
Scenario Outline:
  Given a discount of <discount>
  When I order the following book:
    | title                        | price   |
    | Healthy eating for programmers | <price> |
  Then the statement should read:
    """

    Statement for David
    Total due:    <total>
    """

  Scenarios:
    | discount | price   | total   |
    | 10%      | $29.99  | $26.99  |
    | 15%      | $29.99  | $25.49  |
```

---

3. Cucumber supports Scenarios and Examples keywords to identify tabular data for a scenario outline. Some users prefer to use Scenarios to avoid using words we use in RSpec, but many people like to use Examples in order to better differentiate from the Scenario keyword. Both do exactly the same thing, so the choice is a subjective one and yours to make.

In the first scenario, <discount> is replaced with 10%, <price> in the table in the When step becomes $29.99, and <total> in the multiline text in the Then step becomes $26.99.

18.9 Configuration

Cucumber offers a wide array of command-line switches and options, but nobody wants to type all those options every time we run cucumber. To that end, Cucumber offers us a simple configuration mechanism in the form of profiles defined in a cucumber.yml or config/cucumber.yml file.

The most common use for profiles is selecting sets of scenarios to run based on associated tags. For example, it is conventional to tag the scenarios that we're currently working with @wip for *work in progress*. We can add the following line to cucumber.yml in the project root directory:

```
wip: --tags @wip features
```

The wip: at the beginning of the line identifies the name of the profile. The --tags @wip is the command-line option we learned about in the previous section and it tells Cucumber to run the scenarios tagged with @wip. With that profile defined, we can type the following command to invoke it:

```
cucumber -p wip
```

We can set up as many profiles as we want, which gives us tremendous flexibility in our ability to manage what to run when. We can have profiles we use locally in our minute-to-minute development. We can set up profiles to run on our build servers. We can set up profiles we want to use temporarily because we're working on a specific area of the application.

We can also use this to create custom workflows and life cycles for scenarios. Consider a scenario that's been passing, but we're about to make it obsolete with a new feature we're working on now. We can identify that scenario as ready to be phased out but keep running it until we're ready to actually remove it.

18.10 What We've Learned

In this chapter, we learned how to write step definitions to connect plain-text steps to the Ruby code we are developing. Each scenario is run in its own World, allowing us to share state between step definitions without leaking state across scenarios.

We learned that we can call steps from inside step definitions. This can help keep things DRY but also introduces a different level of abstraction within step definitions. Some like this, some don't. The choice is yours.

There are three kinds of hooks: Before and After hooks are run before and after each scenario, and AfterStep hooks are run after each step. We can limit which scenarios and steps these hooks apply to by adding tags to their declarations.

When several scenarios involve the same series of steps with different data, scenario outlines allow us to express the steps once and feed in data using a succinct tabular format.

We also learned about multiline text and tables in steps. These offer us clean ways to express more complicated data in our plain-text scenarios.

This brings us to the end of our journey through the finer details of RSpec and Cucumber. In the next part of the book, we'll show you how we approach BDD for Ruby on Rails projects. We'll build on the material we've covered so far and add some new ideas and tools like Webrat and Selenium to the mix.

Part V

Behaviour-Driven Rails

## Chapter 19

BDD in Rails

Ruby on Rails lit the web development world on fire by putting developer happiness and productivity front and center. Concepts such as convention over configuration, REST, declarative software, and the Don't Repeat Yourself principle are first-class citizens in Rails and have had a profound impact on the Ruby community and the wider web development community.

In the context of this book, the single most important concept expressed directly in Rails is that automated testing is a crucial component in the development of web applications. Rails was the first web development framework to ship with an integrated full-stack testing framework. This lowered the barrier to entry for those new to testing and, in doing so, raised the bar for the rest of us.

RSpec's extension library for Rails, rspec-rails, extends the Rails testing framework by offering separate classes for spec'ing Rails models, views, controllers, and even helpers, in complete isolation from one another.[1] All of that isolation can be risky if not accompanied by automated end-to-end functional testing to make sure all the pieces work together. For that we use Cucumber and supporting tools such as Webrat and Selenium.

Although these tools are great additions to any web developer's arsenal of testing tools, in the end, tools are tools. RSpec and Cucumber are

---

1. Early versions of the rspec-rails plug-in were built on ZenTest (http://www.zenspider. com/ZSS/Products/ZenTest/), which offered support for testing models, views, controllers, and helpers separately. We later decided that we wanted more runtime component isolation than ZenTest provided, so we rolled our own, but we owe a debt of gratitude to ZenTest's author, Ryan Davis, for paving the way.

optimized for BDD, but using them doesn't automatically mean you're *doing* BDD, nor does using other tools mean you are not!

In the chapters that follow, we'll show you how to use rspec-rails in conjunction with tools such as Cucumber, Webrat, and Selenium, to drive application development from the outside in with a powerful tool set.

19.1 Outside-In Rails Development

Outside-in Rails development means starting with views and working our way in toward the models. This approach lets customer-defined acceptance criteria drive development and puts us in a position to discover objects and interfaces earlier on in the process and make design decisions based on real need.

The BDD cycle with Rails is the same outside-in process we use with any other framework (or no framework), web, desktop, command line, or even an API. The cycle (depicted in Figure 19.1, on the facing page) is the same cycle depicted in Figure 1.1, on page 10; however, we've added some detail to help map it to Rails.

1. Start with a scenario. Make sure you have a clear understanding of the scenario and the expected outcomes, including how the UI should support a user interacting with the app.

2. Run the scenario with Cucumber. This reveals which steps are undefined, or pending. Most, if not all, of the steps will be pending at first.

3. Write a step definition for the first step. Run the scenario with Cucumber, and watch it fail.

4. Drive out the view implementation using the red/green/refactor cycle with RSpec. You'll discover assigned instance variables, controllers, controller actions, and models that the view will need in order to do its job.

5. Drive out the controller with RSpec, ensuring that the instance variables are properly assigned. With the controller in place, you'll know what models it needs to do its job.

6. Drive out those objects with RSpec, ensuring that they provide the methods needed by the view and the controller. This typically leads to generating the required migrations for fields in the database.

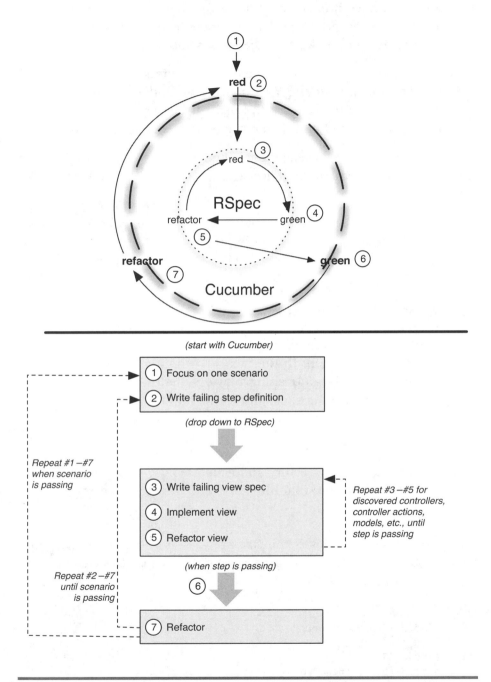

Figure 19.1: THE BDD CYCLE IN RAILS

7. Once you have implemented all of the objects and methods that you have discovered are needed, execute the scenario with Cucumber again to make sure the step is satisfied.

Once the step is passing, move on to the next unimplemented step, and continue working outside in. When a scenario is done, move on to the next scenario or, better yet, ask the nearest customer to validate that it's working as expected and *then* move on to the next scenario.

This is outside-in Rails development—implementing a scenario from its outermost-point down and building what we discover is needed to make it work.

Now that you have a high-level view of the outside-in process in Rails, let's get started by setting up a Rails project with the necessary tools. This will let us explore ground zero in the following chapters.

19.2 Setting Up a Rails 3 Project

Rails 3 makes configuring an application for use with RSpec and Cucumber a trivial operation. In the next few chapters, we'll be working with an application for publishing movie schedules, which we'll call Showtime. Let's set up the skeleton for this app now. Start by generating a new Rails app:

```
$ rails new showtime
```

This creates a showtime directory and generates the skeleton for a Rails app inside it. Now cd into that directory, and take a look around:

```
$ cd showtime
```

One of the generated files is the Gemfile we use to configure the gems we want bundled with our app using Bundler. Open the Gemfile, and modify it as follows:

rails_bdd/01/Gemfile

```
source 'http://rubygems.org'

gem 'rails', '3.0.0'
gem 'sqlite3-ruby', :require => 'sqlite3'
► group :development, :test do
►   gem "rspec-rails", ">= 2.0.0"
►   gem "cucumber-rails", ">= 0.3.2"
►   gem "webrat", ">= 0.7.2"
► end
```

We add these to the :development group so that their generators and rake tasks are available without having to type RAILS_ENV=test. We add them to the :test group to make sure that their code is available when running in the test environment.

Now we'll use Bundler to install those gems and all of their dependencies:

```
$ bundle install
```

Now we'll use the rspec:install generator to install a few files we'll need in the app:

```
$ script/rails generate rspec:install
      create   .rspec
      create   spec
      create   spec/spec_helper.rb
      create   autotest
      create   autotest/discover.rb
```

Here's a description of each file and directory that was generated:

- spec: The directory where you place specs for your Rails app.

- .rspec: Add options to this file that you want rspec to utilize when running any of the rake spec tasks.

- spec/spec_helper.rb: This file is used to load and configure rspec. It is also where you would require and configure any additional helpers or tools that your project utilizes when running specs.

- autotest/discover.rb: Used by Autotest to discover what type of Autotest class to load.

Now we'll use the cucumber:install generator to install files Cucumber needs:

```
$ script/rails generate cucumber:install
      create   config/cucumber.yml
      create   script/cucumber
       chmod   script/cucumber
      create   features/step_definitions
      create   features/step_definitions/web_steps.rb
      create   features/support
      create   features/support/env.rb
      create   features/support/paths.rb
       exist   lib/tasks
      create   lib/tasks/cucumber.rake
        gsub   config/database.yml
        gsub   config/database.yml
       force   config/database.yml
```

Cucumber adds a few more files than RSpec does. Let's take a look at each one:

- config/cucumber.yml: Used to store profiles that provide control over what features and scenarios to run. See Section 18.9, *Configuration*, on page 272.

- script/cucumber: The command-line feature runner.

- features/step_definitions: All of your step definitions will go in this directory.

- features/step_definitions/web_steps.rb: Contains step definitions that are commonly used with web apps. We'll learn more about this file in Chapter 21, *Simulating the Browser with Webrat*, on page 293.

- features/support: This directory holds any Ruby code that needs to be loaded to run your scenarios that are *not* step definitions, like helper methods shared between step definitions.

- features/support/env.rb: Bootstraps and configures the Cucumber runner environment.

- features/support/paths.rb: Support for mapping descriptive page names used in scenario steps to their URLs.

- lib/tasks/cucumber.rake: Adds the rake cucumber task, which prepares the test database and runs all of your application's features.

And that's it! To make sure everything is wired up correctly, run these commands:

```
$ rake db:migrate
$ rake db:test:prepare
$ rake spec
$ rake cucumber
```

You should see output like this when you run rake spec:[2]

```
No examples matching ./spec/**/*_spec.rb could be found
```

And you should see output like this when you run rake cucumber:

```
0 scenarios
0 steps
```

---

2. Later versions of rspec may say 0 examples, 0 failures.

19.3 Setting Up a Rails 2 Project

To set up a Rails 2 project, we need to first install all of the gems we need:

```
$ [sudo] gem install rails --version 2.3.10
$ [sudo] gem install rspec-rails --version 1.3.3
$ [sudo] gem install cucumber-rails --version 0.3.2
$ [sudo] gem install database_cleaner --version 0.5.0
$ [sudo] gem install webrat --version 0.7.1
$ [sudo] gem install selenium-client --version 1.2.18
$ [sudo] gem install sqlite3-ruby --version 1.3.1
```

Now run the following commands:

```
$ rails showtime
$ cd showtime
$ script/generate rspec
$ script/generate cucumber --webrat --rspec
$ rake db:migrate
$ rake db:test:prepare
```

At this point, you can run the rake spec and rake cucumber commands, and you should see output similar to that which we saw previously in the Rails 3 app.

19.4 What We've Learned

So far, we explored the concepts of BDD in Rails at a high level and set up a project with the recommended tools. In the next chapter, we'll take a look at how Cucumber and Rails work together to help us drive application development from the outside in. Turn the page, and let's begin.

## Chapter 20

Cucumber with Rails

Cucumber supports collaboration between project stakeholders and application developers, with the goal of developing a common understanding of requirements and providing a backdrop for discussion. The result of that collaboration is a set of plain-text descriptions of features and automated scenarios that application code must pass to be considered *done*. Once passing, the scenarios serve as regression tests as development continues.

As with any BDD project, we use Cucumber in a Rails project to describe application-level behavior. In this chapter, we'll look at how Cucumber integrates with Rails, exploring a variety of approaches to setting up context, triggering events, and specifying expected outcomes as we describe the features of our web application.

20.1 Step Definition Styles

Step definitions connect the natural-language steps in a plain-text feature file to Ruby code that interacts directly with the application. Since Cucumber helps us describe behavior in business terms, the steps shouldn't express technical details. Given I'm logged in as an administrator could apply to a CLI, client-side GUI, or web-based application. It's within the step *definitions* that the rubber meets the road and code is created to interact with the application.

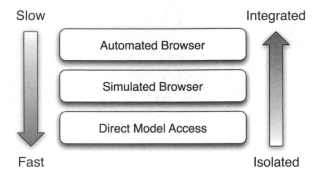

Figure 20.1: COMPARING STEP DEFINITION STYLES

When building step definitions for a Rails application, we typically deal with three step definition styles for interacting with a web-based system in order to specify its behavior:

- *Automated Browser*: Access the entire Rails MVC stack in a real web browser by driving interactions with the Webrat API and its support for piggybacking on Selenium. This style is fully integrated but is the slowest to run and can be challenging to maintain.

- *Simulated Browser*: Access the entire MVC stack using Webrat, a DSL for interacting with web applications. This style provides a reliable level of integration while remaining fast enough for general use, but it doesn't exercise JavaScript.

- *Direct Model Access*: Access ActiveRecord models directly, bypassing routing, controllers, and views. This is the fastest but least integrated style.

When writing Cucumber scenarios, integration and speed are opposing forces, as illustrated in Figure 20.1. Fast is better than slow, of course, but integrated is better than isolated when we're looking for confidence that an app will work in the hands of users once it is shipped. So, what's the best approach to take?

Recommendations

We recommend using Simulated Browser with Webrat for Whens and Thens. This helps drive out the pieces that a user will interact with, providing confidence that the component parts are working well together but still produces a suite that can be executed relatively quickly and without depending on a real web browser.

We generally recommend using direct model access in Givens, but there are a few exceptions. For anything that needs to set up browser session state, such as logging in, you should use Simulated Browser.

If there is any JavaScript or Ajax, add scenarios that use the Automated Browser approach in their Whens and Thens for the *happy path* and critical less common paths. The added value we get from doing this is exercising client-side code, so when no client code is necessary, there is no reason to use the browser.

Edge Cases

For features that produce many edge cases, it can be useful to drive a few through the Rails stack and the rest using just Direct Model Access for everything. This may seem more like a unit test, but keep in mind that scenarios are about communication. We want to make sure that we're writing the right code. If the customer asks for specific error messages depending on a variety of error conditions, then it's OK to go right to the model if that's the source of the message, as long as the relevant slice of the full stack is getting sufficient coverage from other scenarios.

In this chapter, we'll start with the simplest style, Direct Model Access, and walk through implementing a feature. Then we'll explore using Webrat for the Simulated Browser style in Chapter 21, *Simulating the Browser with Webrat*, on page 293 and Automated Browser in Chapter 22, *Automating the Browser with Webrat and Selenium*, on page 315.

20.2 Direct Model Access

Direct Model Access (DMA) step definitions execute quickly, but that speed and isolation comes at a price. They don't provide much assurance that the application works, and they are unlikely to catch bugs beyond those that should be caught by granular RSpec code examples that we'll be writing in a few chapters.

They do, however, facilitate conversation between the customer and developers and will catch regressions if the logic inside the models is broken in the future. In this way, DMA step definitions are useful for exercising fine-grained behaviors of a system, when driving all of them through the full stack would be too cumbersome.

To see this in action, let's look at some scenarios for a movie box office system we'll call Showtime. Start by bootstrapping a Rails app as we did in Section 19.2, *Setting Up a Rails 3 Project*, on page 280.

The customer wants the structured movie schedule data to be distilled into a human-readable one-line showtime description for display on a website. Create a feature file named showtime_descriptions.feature in the features directory, and add the following text to it:

cucumber_rails/01/features/showtime_descriptions.feature

```
Feature: Showtime Descriptions

  So that I can find movies that fit my schedule
  As a movie goer
  I want to see accurate and concise showtimes

  @wip
  Scenario: Show minutes for times not ending with 00
    Given a movie
    When I set the showtime to "2007-10-10" at "2:15pm"
    Then the showtime description should be "October 10, 2007 (2:15pm)"

  Scenario: Hide minutes for times ending with 00
    Given a movie
    When I set the showtime to "2007-10-10" at "2:00pm"
    Then the showtime description should be "October 10, 2007 (2pm)"
```

Now run the feature with one of the rake tasks that Cucumber installed when we ran the cucumber:install generator:

```
rake cucumber:wip
```

This task runs all the scenarios with the @wip tag. Right now we have just two scenarios and only one tagged with @wip, so that is the only scenario that gets run. You should see that all of the steps are undefined and that Cucumber has provided code snippets for the missing step definitions:

```
1 scenario (1 undefined)
3 steps (3 undefined)
0m0.317s
```

```
You can implement step definitions for undefined steps with these snippets:

Given /^a movie$/ do
  pending # express the regexp above with the code you wish you had
end

When /^I set the showtime to "([^"]*)" at "([^"]*)"$/ do |arg1, arg2|
  pending # express the regexp above with the code you wish you had
end
```

```
Then /^the showtime description should be "([^"]*)"$/ do |arg1|
  pending # express the regexp above with the code you wish you had
end
```

Getting the First Scenario to Pass

We'll implement the step definitions for the first scenario using the Direct Model Access style. Create a file named showtime_steps.rb in the features/step_definitions directory, copy in the snippets Cucumber supplied, and modify them as follows:

cucumber_rails/02/features/step_definitions/showtime_steps.rb

```
Given /^a movie$/ do
  @movie = Movie.create!
end

When /^I set the showtime to "([^"]*)" at "([^"]*)"$/ do |date, time|
  @movie.update_attribute(:showtime_date, Date.parse(date))
  @movie.update_attribute(:showtime_time, time)
end

Then /^the showtime description should be "([^"]*)"$/ do |showtime|
  @movie.showtime.should eq(showtime)
end
```

The step definitions are executed in the context of a Rails environment, so we can use any techniques that work in Rails unit tests or RSpec model specs, which you'll read about in Chapter 25, *Rails Models*, on page 361. This includes creating models in the database and using RSpec's Expectations API.

The steps are all run in the same object, so the @movie instance variable created in the Given() step is available to all subsequent steps.

Now run rake cucumber:wip, and you should see the following in the output:

```
@wip
Scenario: Show minutes for times not ending with 00
  Given a movie
    uninitialized constant Movie (NameError)
    ./features/step_definitions/showtime_steps.rb:2:in `/^a movie$/'
    features/showtime_descriptions.feature:9:in `Given a movie'
```

The first step is failing because it references a Movie object that we have yet to create. Go ahead and create that using the Rails model generator, and then run the migration for the development and test environments.

```
$ script/rails generate model movie showtime_date:date showtime_time:time
    invoke  active_record
    create    db/migrate/xxxxxxxxxxxxx_create_movies.rb
    create    app/models/movie.rb
    invoke    rspec
    create      spec/models/movie_spec.rb
$ rake db:migrate
$ rake db:test:prepare
```

The model generator creates a movie_spec.rb because RSpec registered itself as the test framework when we ran script/rails generate rspec:install.

Now run rake db:migrate and rake cucumber:wip, and you should see that the first and second steps are passing, but we get an undefined method 'showtime' for the third step. To get that to pass, go ahead and modify movie.rb as follows:

cucumber_rails/04/app/models/movie.rb

```ruby
class Movie < ActiveRecord::Base

  def showtime
    "#{formatted_date} (#{formatted_time})"
  end

  def formatted_date
    showtime_date.strftime("%B %d, %Y")
  end

  def formatted_time
    showtime_time.strftime("%l:%M%p").strip.downcase
  end

end
```

Now run rake cucumber:wip again, and the output should include the following:

```
1 scenario (1 passed)
3 steps (3 passed)
0m0.263s
```

That's looking much better, isn't it? This would probably be a good time to commit to a version control system. Working scenario by scenario like this, we get the benefit of ensuring we don't break previously passing scenarios as we continue to add behavior and refactor.

⟍⟋ Joe Asks...

Where Does RSpec Fit into This Picture?

In this example, we go straight from a Cucumber scenario to the Rails model code without any more granular code examples written in RSpec. This is really just to keep things simple and focused on Cucumber for this chapter.

We have yet to introduce you to the other styles of step definitions or the Rails-specific RSpec contexts provided by the rspec-rails library. As you learn about them in the coming chapters, you'll begin to get a feel for how all these puzzle pieces fit together and how to balance the different tools and approaches.

Completing the Feature

Now that we have the first scenario passing, let's see how we're doing on the second one. Run both scenarios with rake cucumber (without :wip), and you should see this in the output:

```
2 scenarios (2 passed)
6 steps (6 passed)
0m0.233s
```

Now we can go back to our Movie model and enhance the logic of the formatted_time() method.

cucumber_rails/05/app/models/movie.rb

```ruby
def formatted_time
  format_string = showtime_time.min.zero? ? "%l%p" : "%l:%M%p"
  showtime_time.strftime(format_string).strip.downcase
end
```

That should be enough to get us to green:

```
2 scenarios (2 passed)
6 steps (6 passed)
0m0.233s
```

Success! We've completed our work on the "Showtime Descriptions" feature. Our passing scenarios tell us that we've written the right code and that we're done. Before we leap into the next chapter, let's take a second to consider what we learned.

20.3 What We've Learned

Like most important development decisions, when choosing a step definition style, there are opposing forces on each side that need to be considered and balanced. Direct Model Access step definitions offer the speed and flexibility of model specs at the cost of reduced confidence that the application is working for its users.

For most situations, it makes more sense to create a more integrated set of step definitions that ensure the models, views, and controllers are working together correctly, even though they will execute a bit slower. Next we'll take a look at how we can use Webrat to implement either the Simulated Browser or Automated Browser style to do just that.

Chapter 21

Simulating the Browser with Webrat

Even though we call Rails an MVC framework, there are really more than three layers in a Rails app. In addition to the model, view, and controller, we also have a routing layer, a persistence layer (the class methods in Rails models), and a database, and we want to ensure that all of these layers work well together.

In the previous chapter, we introduced Direct Model Access step definitions and used them to implement Givens, Whens, and Thens. This approach can be useful to specify fine-grained model behaviors, but running those scenarios doesn't give us any confidence that the different layers of our application are working well together.

We rarely use DMA-only scenarios in practice, and when we do, it's to augment a strong backbone of coverage established by Simulated Browser scenarios exercising the full Rails stack. We covered DMA first because it's the simplest style, but the primary role of DMA step definitions is to help keep our Simulated and Automated Browser scenarios focused by quickly setting up repeated database state in Givens, as we'll see later in this chapter.

We consider the Simulated Browser style to be the default approach for implementing Whens and Thens for a Rails app because it strikes a good balance between speed and integration. We can count on the software to work correctly in the hands of our end users when we ship, and we can execute the scenarios quickly as the requirements and code evolve.

If you're building an application without much JavaScript, the Simulated Browser (combined with DMA for Givens) is likely all you'll need. It's a fast, dependable alternative to in-browser testing tools like Selenium and Watir. Even when JavaScript is important to the user experience, we like to start with a set of Simulated Browser scenarios and then add Automated Browser scenarios (which we'll cover in Chapter 22, *Automating the Browser with Webrat and Selenium*, on page 315) to drive client-side interactions.

If you've ever written a Rails integration test, you've probably used the Simulated Browser style of testing. In that context, methods such as get_via_redirect() and post_via_redirect() build confidence because they simulate requests that exercise the full stack, but they don't make it easy to express user behaviors clearly. In this chapter, we'll explore how Webrat builds on this approach to help us bridge the last mile between page loads and form submissions and the behavior our applications provide to the real people whose lives they touch.

21.1 Writing Simulated Browser Step Definitions

We're going to focus on Cucumber with Webrat and Selenium, so we're going to skip over some of the low-level details that we use RSpec for in practice. We'll cover all of that in Chapter 23, *Rails Views*, on page 327; Chapter 24, *Rails Controllers*, on page 341; and Chapter 25, *Rails Models*, on page 361. If you plan to follow along and run the examples, we recommend you download the code examples from http://pragprog.com/ titles/achbd/source_code, cd into the simulated_browser directory, and work in the numbered directories within. That way, you can type the parts we focus on here, but you don't have to worry about the parts we don't.

We'll be building on the web-based movie box-office system from the previous chapter, so you can, alternatively, continue to use the same code base. If you do, however, you'll be on your own a couple of times during this chapter. We'll let you know when we get there, and you can always choose to download the code later.

Now let's walk through implementing a few step definitions for a simple scenario using the Simulated Browser technique. The next requirement is that administrators should be able to assign a movie to a genre so that customers can later browse by genre. We start by creating a file named create_movie.feature in the features directory with the following content:

```
Feature: Create movie

  So that customers can browse movies by genre
  As a site administrator
  I want to create a movie in a specific genre

  Scenario: Create movie in genre
    Given a genre named Comedy
    When I create a movie Caddyshack in the Comedy genre
    Then Caddyshack should be in the Comedy genre
```

If you're following with the downloaded code, this is already created for you in simulated_browser/01/. As usual, we'll begin by running the feature with rake cucumber to show us the step definitions we need to implement:

```
You can implement step definitions for undefined steps with these snippets:

Given /^a genre named Comedy$/ do
  pending # express the regexp above with the code you wish you had
end

When /^I create a movie Caddyshack in the Comedy genre$/ do
  pending # express the regexp above with the code you wish you had
end

Then /^Caddyshack should be in the Comedy genre$/ do
  pending # express the regexp above with the code you wish you had
end
```

The Given a genre named Comedy step could be implemented using either DMA or the Simulated Browser style. Using a Simulated Browser would ensure that the views and controllers used to create genres are working with the models properly. DMA won't go through those layers of the stack, but it provides a bit more convenience, simplicity, and speed. So, which style should we use?

Choosing Between DMA and Simulated Browser

If we already have scenarios that thoroughly exercise the interface to manage genres using the Simulated Browser style, then we get no benefit from exercising those interfaces in this scenario. In that case, we can benefit from the DMA style without reducing our confidence in the application. If not, then we either want to use Simulated Browser here

Create a movie

Title   Caddyshack

Release year   1980 ⬍

Genres

☐ Action
☑ Comedy
☐ Drama

(Save)

Figure 21.1: CREATING A MOVIE WITH A FORM

or want to add separate scenarios specifically for managing genre in which we do.

As we add features throughout the evolution of an application, we see a pattern emerge in which we implement DMA Givens for a model that has its own Simulated Browser scenarios elsewhere in the Cucumber suite.

We'll imagine that those genre scenarios are already in place, but we're still going to have to create a Genre model and migration. Use the Rails model generator to do that, like this:

```
script/rails generate model genre name:string
rake db:migrate && rake db:test:prepare
```

Now we add a genre_steps.rb file in features/step_definitions/ with the following code (in simulated_browser/02/ in the code download):

```
simulated_browser/02/features/step_definitions/genre_steps.rb
Given /^a genre named Comedy$/ do
  @comedy = Genre.create!(:name => "Comedy")
end
```

Run the scenario, and you'll see this first step pass. All it needed was the Genre model and table that we just created. Now let's move on to the When step.

The wireframe for the Add Movie screen, shown in Figure 21.1, shows that a user will need to provide a movie's title, release year, and genres to add it to the system. Since our When step specifies the main *action* of the scenario, we'll use the Simulated Browser to drive this interaction through the full Rails stack.

Before we look at how Webrat can help us with this, let's see what Rails provides out of the box.

Rails Integration Testing

If you were to implement the When I create a movie Caddyshack in the Comedy genre step with the Rails integration testing API, you might end up with something like the following:

```
When /^I create a movie Caddyshack in the Comedy genre$/ do
  get_via_redirect movies_path
  assert_select "a[href=?]", new_movie_path, "Add Movie"

  get_via_redirect new_movie_path

  assert_select "form[action=?][method=post]", movies_path do
    assert_select "input[name=?][type=text]", "movie[title]"
    assert_select "select[name=?]", "movie[release_year]"
    assert_select "input[name=?][type=checkbox][value=?]", "genres[]", @comedy.id
  end

  post_via_redirect movies_path, :genres => [@comedy.id], :movie =>
    { :title => "Caddyshack", :release_year => "1980" }

  assert_response :success
end
```

This gets the job done, but a lot of implementation details such as HTTP methods, form input names, and URLs have crept up into our step definition. These sorts of details will change through the life span of an application, and that can make scenarios quite brittle. We could mitigate some of that risk by extracting helper methods for specifying forms and posts that might appear in multiple scenarios, but that still leaves a significant issue.

With the generated HTML being specified separately from the post, it is entirely possible to assert_select "input[name=?]", "movie[name]" and then post to movies_path, :movie => { :title => "Caddyshack"}. This specifies that the form display an input for movie[name], but then the step posts movie[title]. If the form is incorrectly displaying a movie[name] field, this step will pass, but the application will not work correctly.

Webrat

Like the Rails integration testing API, Webrat works like a fast, invisible browser. It builds on that functionality by providing a simple, expressive DSL for manipulating a web application. We can use Webrat to describe the same interaction at a high level, using language that is similar to how you might explain using the application to a nontechnical friend:

```
simulated_browser/04/features/step_definitions/movie_steps.rb
When /^I create a movie Caddyshack in the Comedy genre$/ do
  visit movies_path
  click_link "Add Movie"
  fill_in "Title", :with => "Caddyshack"
  select "1980", :from => "Release Year"
  check "Comedy"
  click_button "Save"
end
```

This is obviously more readable than the first version. Webrat lets us focus on exactly the details an end user would experience without concern for how it will be built. The only implementation detail remaining is using the movies_path() route as an entry point.

In addition to being more expressive, Webrat also catches regressions without the false positives described earlier. Don't worry about the details of how this works just yet. That will become clear throughout the rest of this chapter.

Run the scenario with Cucumber again (from simulated_browser/04/ in the code download), and it will show us what to implement first:

```
Scenario: Create movie in genre
  Given a genre named Comedy
  When I create a movie Caddyshack in the Comedy genre
    undefined local variable or method `movies_path' for
      #<Cucumber::Rails::World:0x81ac9a64> (NameError)
      ./features/step_definitions/movie_steps.rb:2:in
```

We need to make a number of changes and additions to get this first step passing, including new routes, controllers, views, models, and migrations. This is all done for you in the simulated_browser/05 directory of the code download. If you prefer to try it yourself, start with the code in the simulated_browser/04/ directory, run rake cucumber, and follow the failure messages until this step passes.

Once you have this step passing, rake cucumber tells us that we have one step remaining:

```
3 scenarios (1 undefined, 2 passed)
9 steps (1 undefined, 8 passed)
0m0.355s
```

To browse movies by genre, a site visitor would click over to the Comedy page, which displays one movie entitled Caddyshack. The Webrat step definition for our Then reflects this:

```
simulated_browser/06/features/step_definitions/movie_steps.rb
Then /^Caddyshack should be in the Comedy genre$/ do
  visit genres_path
  click_link "Comedy"
  response.should contain("1 movie")
  response.should contain("Caddyshack")
end
```

Once again, we'll learn later how to use RSpec to drive out the routes, controllers, views, models, and migrations that this Cucumber step needs to pass. You can either try this on your own, starting with the simulated_browser/05/ directory in the code download, or cd into simulated_browser/06/ and it's already done for you. In either case, when you're finished, run rake features, and everything should pass:

```
3 scenarios (3 passed)
9 steps (9 passed)
0m0.439s
```

Great. The passing scenario tells us that we're done. By leveraging the DMA style for Givens and combining it with the Simulated Browser style with Webrat for Whens and Thens, we've reached a good balance of expressive specification, speed, and coverage. We can read the scenario to understand what we should expect from the application at a high level, and we can be confident that it will work for our users when we ship it.

Throughout the rest of the chapter, we'll dive into the details of Webrat's features and how they work. Let's start by looking at how Webrat lets you navigate from page to page in your application.

21.2 Navigating to Pages

Just as a user can't click any links or submit any forms until he has typed a URL into his browser's address bar and requested a web page,

Webrat can't manipulate a page until you've given it a place to start. The visit() method lets you open a page of your application.

Inside each scenario, visit() must be called before any other Webrat methods. Usually you'll call it with a routing helper, like we did in our When step definition from the previous section:

```
When /^I create a movie Caddyshack in the Comedy genre$/ do
  visit movies_path
  # ...
end
```

Behind the scenes, Webrat leverages Rails' integration testing functionality to simulate GET requests and layers browser-like behavior on top. Like other Webrat methods that issue requests, it looks at the response code returned to figure out what to do next:

Successful (200–299) or Bad Request (400–499) Webrat stores the response so that subsequent methods can fill out forms, click links, or inspect its content.

Redirection (300–399) If the redirect is to a URL within the domain of the application, Webrat issues a new request for the destination specified by the redirect, preserving HTTP headers and including a proper Location header. If the redirect is external, Webrat saves it as the response for later inspection but won't follow it.

Server Error (500–599) Webrat raises a Webrat::PageLoadError. If you want to specify that making a request produces an error, you can use RSpec's raise_error() to catch it.

Clicking Links

Once you've opened a page of your application using visit(), you'll often want to navigate to other pages. Rather than using visit() to load each URL in succession, it's convenient to simulate clicking links to jump from page to page.

click_link() lets you identify a link by its text and follows it by making a request for the URL it points to. To navigate to the URL in the *href*, wherever that may be, of a Comedy link, we wrote this:

```
Then /^Caddyshack should be in the Comedy genre$/ do
  # ...
  click_link "Comedy"
  # ...
end
```

click_link() can lead to a more natural flow in your step definitions and has the advantage that your step definitions are less bound to your routing scheme. On the other hand, each page load takes a little bit of time, so to keep your scenarios running quickly, you'll want to avoid navigating through many pages of the site that aren't directly related to what you're testing. Instead, you could pick an entry point for visit() closer to the area of the application you're concerned with.

In addition to clicking links based on the text between the <a> tags, Webrat can locate links by their *id* and *title* values. For example, if we have the following HTML:

```
<a href="/" title="Example.com Home" id="home_link">
  Back to homepage
</a>
```

then the following step definitions would all be equivalent:

```
When /^I click to go back to the homepage$/ do
  # Clicking the link by its title
  click_link "Example.com Home"
end

When /^I click to go back to the homepage$/ do
  # Clicking the link by its id
  click_link "home_link"
end

When /^I click to go back to the homepage$/ do
  # Clicking the link by its text
  click_link "Back to homepage"
end
```

click_link() has rudimentary support for handling JavaScript links generated by Rails' link_to() for non-GET HTTP requests. Since it can't actually run any JavaScript, it relies on matching the *onclick* value with regular expressions. This functionality, though limited, can be useful when dealing with RESTful Rails applications that aren't implemented with unobtrusive JavaScript techniques.

Let's say the box-office application requires that a moderator approves movie listings before they are visible on the site. Here's how you might express that with Webrat:

```
When /^I approve the listing$/ do
  click_link "Approve"
end
```

---

web_steps.rb

You might be looking at the step definitions used throughout this chapter and wondering whether you'll be forced to write step definitions for every When and Then step in each of your app's scenarios. After all, maintaining separate step definitions for both When I click the Save button and When I click the Delete button (and more) would get tedious pretty quickly.

Fortunately, Cucumber has just the feature to help us out of this: parameterized step definitions. Instead of maintaining a step definition for each button, we can write one that's reusable by wrapping the Webrat API:

```
When /^I click the "(.+)" button$/ do |button_text|
  click_button button_text
end
```

In fact, Cucumber ships with a bunch of these sort of step definitions in a web_steps.rb file. It was added to your project's step_definitions directory when you ran the Cucumber generator.

Be sure to take a look at what's in there. It can save you quite a bit of time as you're implementing new scenarios.

And here's the likely implementation:

```
<%= link_to "Approve", approve_movie_path(movie), :method => :put %>
```

When clicked, the link would normally generate a PUT request to the approve_movie_path. You can disable this functionality by passing the :javascript => false option to click_link():

```
When /^I approve the listing$/ do
  click_link "Approve", :javascript => false
end
```

Instead of sending a PUT request, this tells Webrat to issue a GET request as if the JavaScript were not present. This can be useful when you want to specify the app works correctly for users without JavaScript enabled.

Now that we're comfortable navigating to pages within our application, we can take a look at how to use Webrat to submit forms.

21.3 Manipulating Forms

Once we've reached a page of interest, we'll want to trigger actions before we can specify outcomes. In the context of a web-based application, that usually translates to filling out and submitting forms. Let's take a look at Webrat's methods to do that. They'll serve as the bread and butter of most of our When step definitions.

fill_in()

You will use fill_in() to type text into *text* fields, *password* fields, and *<textarea>*s. We saw an example of this in the When step definition of our box-office example:

```
When /^I create a movie Caddyshack in the Comedy genre$/ do
  # ...
  fill_in "Title", :with => "Caddyshack"
  # ...
end
```

fill_in() supports referencing form fields by *id*, *name*, and *<label>* text. Therefore, if we have a conventional Rails form with proper label tags like this:

```
<dl>
  <dt>
    <label for="movie_title">Title</label>
  </dt>
  <dd>
    <input type="text" name="movie[title]" id="movie_title" />
  </dd>
</dl>
```

then all of the following would be functionally equivalent:

```
Line 1  When /^I fill in the movie title Caddyshack$/ do
          # using the field's label's text
          fill_in "Title", :with => "Caddyshack"
        end
5
        When /^I fill in the movie title Caddyshack$/ do
          # using the field's id
          fill_in "movie_title", :with => "Caddyshack"
        end
10
        When /^I fill in the movie title Caddyshack$/ do
          # using the field's name
          fill_in "movie[title]", :with => "Caddyshack"
        end
```

In practice, referencing fields by label text is preferred. That way, we can avoid coupling our step definitions to class and field names, which are more likely to change as we evolve the application. In the previous example, if we renamed the Movie class to Film, we'd have to change line 8, which uses the field *id*, and line 13, which uses the field *name*, but line 3 would continue to work just fine. Unless otherwise noted, Webrat's other form manipulation methods support targeting fields using these three strategies.

Beyond making your step definitions easier to write and maintain, providing active form field labels is a good habit to get into for accessibility and usability.

check() and uncheck()

check() lets you click a checkbox that was not selected by default or had been previously not selected. Here's an example:

```
When /^I create a movie Caddyshack in the Comedy genre$/ do
  # ...
  check "Comedy"
  # ...
end
```

To deselect a checkbox that was selected by default or has been previously selected, you'd write this:

```
When /^I uncheck Save as draft$/ do
  uncheck "Save as draft"
end
```

choose()

You'll use choose() to manipulate *radio* form fields. Just like a browser with a GUI, Webrat ensures only one radio button of a given group is checked at a time.

Let's say we wanted to select "Premium" from a list of plan levels on a signup page. You might write the following:

```
When /^I choose to create a Premium plan$/ do
  choose "Premium"
end
```

select()

You'll use select() to pick options from select drop-down boxes.

```
When /^I create a movie Caddyshack in the Comedy genre$/ do
  # ...
  select "1980"
  # ...
end
```

By default, Webrat will find the first option on the page that matches the text. This is usually fine. If you'd like to be more specific or you have multiple selects with overlapping options, you can provide the :from option. Then, Webrat will look for the option only inside selects matching the label, name, or ID. Here's an example:

```
When /^I create a movie Caddyshack in the Comedy genre$/ do
  # ...
  select "1980", :from => "Release Year"
  # ...
end
```

select_date(), select_time(), and select_datetime()

When rendering a form, Rails typically exposes date and time values as a series of <select> fields. Each individual select doesn't get its own <label>, so filling in a date using Webrat's select() method is a bit cumbersome:

```
When /^I select October 1, 1984 as my birthday$/ do
  select "October", :from => "birthday_2i"
  select "1", :from => "birthday_3i"
  select "1984", :from => "birthday_1i"
end
```

To ease this pain, Webrat now supports filling out conventional Rails date and time fields with the select_date(), select_time(), and select_datetime() methods. They act like a thin layer on top of select() to hide away the Rails-specific implementation details. Here's how you might use them:

```
When /^I select April 26, 1982$/ do
  # Select the month, day and year for the given date
  select_date Date.parse("April 26, 1982")
end
```

```
When /^I select 3:30pm$/ do
  # Select the hour and minute for the given time
  select_time Time.parse("3:30PM")
end
```

```
When /^I select January 23, 2004 10:30am$/ do
  # Select the month, day, year, hour and minute for the given time
  select_datetime Time.parse("January 23, 2004 10:30AM")
end
```

All three of the methods also support Strings instead of Date or Time objects, in which case they'll do the required parsing internally.

attach_file()

To simulate file uploads, Webrat provides the attach_file() method. Instead of passing a file field's value as a string, it stores an ActionController::TestUploadedFile in the params hash that acts like a Tempfile object a controller would normally receive during a multipart request.

When you use it, you'll want to save the fixture file to be uploaded somewhere in your app's source code. We usually put these in spec/fixtures. Here's how you could implement a step definition for uploading a photo:

```
When /^I attach my Vacation photo$/ do
  attach_file "Photo", "#{Rails.root}/spec/fixtures/vacation.jpg"
end
```

By default, Rails' TestUploadedFile uses the text/plain MIME type. When that's not right, you can pass in a specific MIME type as a third parameter to attach_file():

```
When /^I attach my Vacation photo$/ do
  attach_file "Photo",
              "#{Rails.root}/spec/fixtures/vacation.jpg",
              "image/jpeg"
end
```

set_hidden_field

Occasionally, it can be useful to manipulate the value of a hidden form field when using the Simulated Browser approach. The fill_in() method, like an app's real users, will never manipulate a hidden field, so Webrat provides a set_hidden_field() specifically for this purpose:

```
When /^I select Bob from the contact list dialog$/ do
  set_hidden_field "user_id", :to => @bob.id
end
```

Use this method with caution. It's interacting with the application in a different way than any end user actually would, so not all of the integration confidence normally associated with the Simulated Browser style applies, but it can help in a pinch.

click_button

After you've filled out your fields using the previous methods, you'll submit the form.

If there's only one submit button on the page, you can simply use this:

```
When /^I click the button$/ do
  click_button
end
```

If you'd like to be a bit more specific or there is more than one button on the page, click_button() supports specifying the button's *value*, *id*, or *name*. Let's say you have the following HTML on your page:

```
<input type="submit" id="save_button" name="save" value="Apply Changes" />
```

There are three ways you could click it using the Webrat API:

```
When /^I click the button$/ do
  # Clicking a button by id
  click_button "save_button"
end
```

```
When /^I click the button$/ do
  # Clicking a button by the name attribute
  click_button "save"
end
```

```
When /^I click the button$/ do
  # Clicking a button by its text (value attribute)
  click_button "Apply Changes"
end
```

Just like when navigating from page to page, when Webrat submits a form, it will automatically follow any redirects and ensure the final page did not return a server error. There's no need to check the response code of the request by hand. The returned page is stored, ready to be manipulated or inspected by subsequent Webrat methods.

submit_form()

Occasionally, you might need to submit a form that doesn't have a submit button. The most common example is a select field that is enhanced with JavaScript to autosubmit its containing form. Webrat provides the submit_form() method to help in these situations. To use it, you'll need to specify the <form>'s *id* value:

```
When /^I submit the quick navigation form$/ do
  submit_form "quick_nav"
end
```

reload

Real browsers provide a reload button to send another request for the current page to the server. Webrat provides the reload() method to simulate this action:

```
When /^I reload the page$/ do
  reload
end
```

You might find yourself using this if you want to ensure that refreshing a page after an important form submission behaves properly. Webrat will repeat the last request, resubmitting forms and their data.

21.4 Specifying Outcomes with View Matchers

Simply by navigating from page to page and manipulating forms in Whens, you've been implicitly verifying some behavior of your application. If a link breaks, a server error occurs, or a form field disappears, your scenario will fail. That's a lot of coverage against regressions for free. In Then steps, we're usually interested in explicitly specifying the contents of pages, and Webrat provides three custom RSpec matchers to help with this.

contain()

The simplest possible specification of a page is to ensure it displays the right words. Webrat's contain() takes a bit of text and ensures it's in the response's content:

```
Then /^I should see Thank you!$/ do
  response.should contain("Thank you!")
end
```

contain() also works with regular expressions instead of strings:

```
Then /^I should see Hello$/ do
  response.should contain(/Hello/i)
end
```

You will find that you can accommodate almost all of your day-to-day uses of the contain() matcher with a couple of reusable step definitions from Cucumber's generated web_steps.rb file described in the sidebar on page 302:

```
Then /^I should see "(.+)"$/ do |text|
  response.should contain(text)
end
```

```
Then /^I should not see "(.+)"$/ do |text|
  response.should_not contain(text)
end
```

contain() will match against the HTML-decoded text of the document, so if you want to ensure "Peanut butter & jelly" is on the page, you'd type just that in the string, not "Peanut butter & jelly".

have_selector()

Imagine you're building an online photo gallery. Specifying the text on the page probably isn't good enough if you're looking to make sure the photo a user uploaded is being rendered in the album view. In this case, it can be quite useful to ensure the existence of a CSS selector using Webrat's have_selector():

```
Then /^I should see the photo$/ do
  response.should have_selector("img.photo")
end
```

As you'd expect, that specifies there is at least one *<img>* element on the page with a class of *photo*. Webrat supports the full set of CSS3 selectors like the :nth-child pseudo-class, giving it lots of flexibility. The image's *src* is particularly important in this case, so we might want to check that too:

```
Then /^I should see the photo$/ do
  response.should have_selector("img.photo", :src => photo_path(@photo))
end
```

Webrat will take any keys and values specified in the options hash and translate them to requirements on the element's attributes. It's just a more readable way to do what you can do with CSS's img[src=...] syntax but saves you from having to worry about escaping strings.

Occasionally the number of elements matching a given selector is important. It's easy to imagine a scenario that describes uploading a couple photos and specifying the number of photos in the album view should increase. This is supported via the special :count option:

```
Then /^I should see the photo$/ do
  response.should have_selector("img.photo", :count => 5)
end
```

When we don't care where on the page a piece of text might be, contain() gets the job done, but in some cases the specific element the text is in may be important. A common example would be ensuring that the correct navigation tab is active. To help in these cases, Webrat provides the :content option. Here's how you use it:

```
Then /^the Messages tab should be active$/ do
  response.should have_selector("#nav li.selected", :content => "Messages")
end
```

This tells Webrat to make sure that at least one element matching the selector contains the specified string. Like contain(), the provided string is matched against the HTML decoded content, so there's no need to use HTML escaped entities.

Finally, for cases when you need to get fancy, have_selector() supports nesting. If you call it with a block, the block will be passed an object representing the elements matched by the selector, and within the block you can use any of Webrat's matchers. Here's how you might check that the third photo in an album is being rendered with the right image tag and caption:

```
Then /^the Vacation photo should be third in the album$/ do
  response.should have_selector("#album li:nth-child(3)") do |li|
    li.should have_selector("img", :src => photo_path(@vacation_photo))
    li.should contain("Vacation Photo")
  end
end
```

By combining the power of CSS3 selectors with a few extra features, Webrat's have_selector() should provide all you need to write expectations for the vast majority of your step definitions. For the rare cases where CSS won't cut it, let's take a look at the have_xpath() matcher, which lets you go further.

have_xpath

When CSS just isn't powerful enough, Webrat exposes have_xpath() as a matcher of last resort. It's infinitely powerful, but because of the nature of XPath, it's usually not the most expressive. Here's an example from a recent project:

```
Then /^the page should not be indexable by search engines$/ do
  response.should have_xpath(
    ".//meta[@name = 'robots' and @content = 'noindex, nofollow']"
  )
  response.should_not have_xpath(".//meta[@name = 'robots' and @content = 'all']")
end
```

Under the hood, have_selector() actually works by translating CSS selectors to XPath and using the have_xpath() implementation. That means all the have_selector() features we explored work with have_xpath() too.

This implementation strategy hints at an interesting rule about CSS and XPath: *all CSS selectors can be expressed as XPath, but not all XPath selectors can be expressed as CSS.* There are a lot of occasionally useful features XPath supports that CSS does not, such as traversing up the document tree (for example, give me all *<div>*s containing a *<p>*). Although an overview of XPath is outside the scope of this book, it's a good thing to get familiar with if you find yourself wanting more power than CSS selectors can provide.

21.5 Building on the Basics

Now that we've seen how to manipulate forms and specify page content with Webrat, we'll take a look at some of Webrat's more advanced, less commonly used features. You probably won't need them day to day, but it's helpful to have a rough idea of what's available so you can recognize cases when they might come in handy.

Working Within a Scope

Sometimes targeting fields by a label isn't accurate enough. Going back to our box-office example application, we might want a form where a user can add multiple genres at once. Each row of the form would have its own *<label>* for the genre name, but using Webrat's fill_in() method would always manipulate the input field in the first row.

For these cases, Webrat provides the within() method. By providing a CSS selector, you can scope all of the contained form manipulations to a subset of the page. Here's how you could fill out the second genre name field:

```
When /^I fill in Horror for the second genre name$/ do
  within "#genres li:nth-child(2)" do
    fill_in "Name", :with => "Horror"
  end
end
```

If no elements matching the CSS selector are found on the page, Webrat will immediately raise a Webrat::NotFoundError. Like most other Webrat methods, if multiple elements match, it will use the first one in the HTML source.

Locating Form Fields

When a form is rendered with prefilled values, you may want to check that the proper values are present when the page loads. To help with this, Webrat exposes methods that return objects representing fields on the page, which include accessors for their values. Here's a simple example based on field_labeled(), which looks up input fields based on their associated <label>s:

```
Then /^the email address should be pre-filled$/ do
  field_labeled("Email").value.should == "robert@example.com"
end
```

Checkboxes also provide a checked?() method for convenience:

```
Then /^the Terms of Service checkbox should not be checked$/ do
  field_labeled("I agree to the Terms of Service").should_not be_checked
end
```

When <label>-based lookups won't work, you can use field_named(), which matches against the field's *name* value, or field_with_id(), which matches against the field's *id*:

```
Then /^the email address should be pre-filled$/ do
  field_named("user[email]").value.should == "robert@example.com"
end
```

```
Then /^the email address should be pre-filled$/ do
  field_with_id("user_email").value.should == "robert@example.com"
end
```

Dropping Down to HTTP

To keep our scenarios as expressive and maintainable as possible, we generally try to avoid tying them to implementation details. For example, our users aren't concerned with the URL of the page they end up on, just that it's showing them the right information. Building our specifications of the app's behavior on page content rather than URLs aligns our executable specifications with our users' interactions.

For the rare cases where the lower-level operation of the application is important to the customers or it's the only available option for specifying a behavior, Webrat provides a few methods that expose these details. To check the current URL of the session after the last request (and following redirects), you can use the current_url() method:

```
Then /^the page URL should contain the album SEO keywords$/ do
  current_url.should =~ /vacation-photos/
end
```

If your application does some form of browser sniffing or you're building a REST API, you might be interested in specifying the behavior of an app in the presence of a specific HTTP header. You can set any request header for the duration of the test with Webrat's header() method:

```
Given /^I'm browsing the site using Safari$/ do
  header "User-Agent", "Mozilla/5.0 (Macintosh; U; Intel Mac OS X 10_5_6; en-us)"
end

When /^I request the users list using API version 2.0$/ do
  header "X-API-Version", "2.0"
  visit users_path
end
```

When the MIME type should affect the behavior of the application, you can use the http_accept() method as a shortcut to set the Accept header. It can be called with a small set of symbols that map to MIME types or a MIME type string:

```
Given /^my web browser accepts iCal content$/ do
  http_accept :ics
end

Given /^my user agent accepts MP3 content$/ do
  http_accept "audio/mpeg"
end
```

Finally, if you're going to use the HTTP protocol's built-in Basic authentication mechanism, Webrat includes a basic_auth() method for setting the HTTP_AUTHORIZATION header to the encoded combination of a username and password:

```
Given /^I am logged in as "robert" with the password "secret"$/ do
  basic_auth "robert", "secret"
end
```

When Things Go Wrong

Every once in awhile, you'll hit a point where you think a step should be passing, but it's failing. It might raise a Webrat::NotFoundError about a field that's not present or complain that an expected element is missing. Before diving into your test.log or the Ruby debugger, it's good to take a look at the page as Webrat is seeing it, to check whether it matches your understanding of what should be rendered.

You can use the save_and_open_page() method to capture the most recent response at any point in your scenario and open it up in a web browser as a static HTML file on your development machine.

Just drop it in before any line that seems to be misbehaving:

```
When /^I uncheck Save as draft$/ do
  save_and_open_page
  uncheck "Save as draft"
end
```

Now when you rerun the scenario, you'll be able to see the page response as Webrat captured it. If you're on Mac OS X, the file is opened automatically in your default browser. Otherwise, you can find it in the tmp directory below the project root.

21.6 What We've Learned

Before we move on to looking at how the Automated Browser style of step definitions can be used to exercise interactions that are dependent on JavaScript, let's take a moment to consider what we've learned.

- Webrat simulates a browser by building on the functionality of the Rails integration testing API, providing an expressive language to describe manipulating a web application.

- By specifying behavior at a high level and avoiding coupling our tests to implementation details, we can build expressive and robust step definitions that give us confidence that the full Rails stack stays working while avoiding brittle scenarios.

- Leveraging the DMA style for Givens can provide convenience, simplicity, and speed without reducing confidence. We use this approach when the actions required to get to a specific database state have already been exercised through the full Rails stack in their own Simulated Browser scenarios.

- Through the course of describing the actions in our scenarios in our When steps, Webrat implicitly ensures that requests are successful and the right links and form elements are on the page. In our Then steps, we specify the outcomes from our scenarios in terms of expected text and elements using Webrat's view matchers.

## Chapter 22

Automating the Browser with Webrat and Selenium

In the previous chapter, we explored how Webrat can simulate the core functionality of a web browser that you need when building a web application—navigating to pages, filling out forms, and submitting them to the server. This will allow you to specify 80 percent of the behavior for most applications without ever loading up Firefox.

This simulated approach doesn't help when you depend on rich client-side interactions built with JavaScript, however, and for that we look to Selenium.[1] Selenium is a software testing tool originally developed at ThoughtWorks that can automate most modern web browsers. Webrat supports a Selenium mode that translates the Webrat API calls to Selenium calls, allowing you to run the exact same Cucumber feature with and without running a real web browser.

By writing your step definitions with the Webrat API, you don't have to rewrite them as your application evolves to include more client-side enhancements. You can always use whichever execution mode is appropriate for a given scenario (or run the same scenario in both modes) without having to use different tools.

Before we get started, we need to install a couple of new gems. Add the database_cleaner and selenium_client gems to your Gemfile:

automated_browser/01/Gemfile

```
group :development, :test do
  gem "rspec-rails", ">= 2.0.0"
```

---

1. http://seleniumhq.org/

```
    gem "cucumber-rails", ">= 0.3.2"
    gem "webrat", ">= 0.7.2"
▶   gem "database_cleaner", ">= 0.5.2"
▶   gem "selenium-client", ">= 1.2.18"
  end
```

Now run bundle install, and we're all set to proceed.

22.1 Getting Started

To demonstrate just how easy it is to get started with Webrat's Selenium support, we'll walk through updating one of our Cucumber features from the previous chapter to use it. Here's what it says:

simulated_browser/06/features/create_movie.feature

```
Feature: Create movie

  So that customers can browse movies by genre
  As a site administrator
  I want to create a movie in a specific genre

  Scenario: Create movie in genre
    Given a genre named Comedy
    When I create a movie Caddyshack in the Comedy genre
    Then Caddyshack should be in the Comedy genre
```

And here are the three step definitions that make it executable:

simulated_browser/06/features/step_definitions/genre_steps.rb

```
Given /^a genre named Comedy$/ do
  @comedy = Genre.create!(:name => "Comedy")
end
```

simulated_browser/06/features/step_definitions/movie_steps.rb

```
When /^I create a movie Caddyshack in the Comedy genre$/ do
  visit movies_path
  click_link "Add Movie"
  fill_in "Title", :with => "Caddyshack"
  select "1980", :from => "Release Year"
  check "Comedy"
  click_button "Save"
end

Then /^Caddyshack should be in the Comedy genre$/ do
  visit genres_path
  click_link "Comedy"
  response.should contain("1 movie")
  response.should contain("Caddyshack")
end
```

And here's the env.rb file used by Cucumber to set up the environment (comments removed for brevity):

simulated_browser/06/features/support/env.rb

```
ENV["RAILS_ENV"] ||= "test"
require File.expand_path(File.dirname(__FILE__) + '/../../config/environment')

require 'cucumber/formatter/unicode'
require 'cucumber/rails/world'
require 'cucumber/rails/active_record'
require 'cucumber/web/tableish'

require 'webrat'
require 'webrat/core/matchers'

Webrat.configure do |config|
  config.mode = :rack
  config.open_error_files = false
end

World(Rack::Test::Methods)
World(Webrat::Methods)

ActionController::Base.allow_rescue = false

Cucumber::Rails::World.use_transactional_fixtures = true

if defined?(ActiveRecord::Base)
  begin
    require 'database_cleaner'
    DatabaseCleaner.strategy = :truncation
  rescue LoadError => ignore_if_database_cleaner_not_present
  end
end
```

To get this feature file to run through Selenium, we have to make three changes to env.rb. First, set use_transactional_fixtures to false:

automated_browser/01/features/support/env.rb

```
Cucumber::Rails::World.use_transactional_fixtures = false
```

When using Selenium, Cucumber runs in a separate process than the Rails application. This means they'll be using different database connections, and *that* means we can't wrap each of our scenarios with a transaction in our Cucumber process. If we did, the Rails process would never see the data we set up for it.

The downside of turning off transactions is we'll now be responsible for ensuring a "clean" database state is provided for each test on our own. We'll look at strategies for doing that a bit later in this chapter.

Next, we'll configure the Rails ActionController::Integration::Session#host() so that it generates URLs pointing to localhost:3001:

automated_browser/01/features/support/env.rb

```
class ActiveSupport::TestCase
  setup do |session|
    session.host! "localhost:3001"
  end
end
```

By default, if you use a routing helper like users_url() in a step definition, you'll get a URL in the form of http://test.host/.... With these lines, generated URLs will point to http://localhost:3001 instead, which is where Webrat will automatically boot an instance of your application.

Finally, we change Webrat's configuration as follows:

automated_browser/01/features/support/env.rb

```
Webrat.configure do |config|
▶   config.mode = :selenium # was :rack
▶   config.application_framework = :rack
    config.open_error_files = false
end
```

Let's give that a run and see what happens:

```
$ rake cucumber
..
==> Waiting for Selenium RC server on port 4444... Ready!
==> Waiting for rails application server on port 3001... Ready!
..
Finished in 11.679288 seconds.

2 tests, 2 assertions, 0 failures, 0 errors
```

While the previous output was appearing on your terminal, Firefox opened, loaded up your app, and ran through our Cucumber scenario like an invisible user following a script. As you accumulate more scenarios to run through Selenium, it can be pretty fun to watch.

Now that we've seen how to configure Webrat, Cucumber, and Rails to work with Selenium, we'll explore the nitty-gritty details of writing Selenium-driven scenarios to describe your application's behavior.

22.2 Writing Step Definitions for Selenium

Fortunately, most of the techniques for writing and maintaining step definitions for simulating the browser apply equally well when automating the browser with Selenium. There are a few things to watch out for and also some new tricks we can use.

Setting Up Database State in Givens

Just like when simulating the browser (as we saw in Section 21.1, *Writing Simulated Browser Step Definitions*, on page 294), it's useful to use Direct Model Access to set up models in the Given steps of a Selenium scenario. By specifying the behavior associated with creating those models in separate Cucumber features, we can do this to speed up our suite without sacrificing confidence in our coverage.

Unlike when simulating the browser, we have to turn off Rails' transactional fixture setting so the records we write to the database from our test process are visible to the application process. As a side effect, we have to worry about ensuring that each scenario starts off with a clean database state.

There are a couple ways to achieve that goal. The simplest is to manually destroy all the records in an After hook declared in features/support/env.rb:

```
After do
  Movie.destroy_all
  Genre.destroy_all
  # ...
end
```

As you might guess, this technique can get a bit cumbersome and error prone as the application grows. Eventually, you might want something that can quickly remove all the records in the database without needing to list all your model classes. Ben Mabey's database_cleaner[2] plug-in is a handy little library to give you just that. To install it, run the following command:

```
script/plugin install git://github.com/bmabey/database_cleaner.git
```

Now add the following lines to features/support/env.rb:

```
require 'database_cleaner'
require 'database_cleaner/cucumber'
DatabaseCleaner.strategy = :truncation
```

---

2. http://github.com/bmabey/database_cleaner

Setting DatabaseCleaner.strategy to :truncation tells the plug-in to run a TRUNCATE TABLE statement for each table in the database. TRUNCATE TABLE has the same effect as a DELETE statement that removes all rows, but it can be much faster.[3]

Manipulating the Application in Whens

Like Givens, Whens work mostly the same with Selenium as they do when simulating a browser, but there are a few key new concepts to explore.

Dropping Down to the selenium-client API

Occasionally, you might want to perform an action in your Selenium scenario that has no analog in a simulated, non-JavaScript environment. For example, you might want to drag and drop a photo in a gallery or double-click a *<div>* element. One of Webrat's goals is to ensure the programmer maintains the full power of its underlying tools, so it tries to make this as easy as possible.

Under the hood, Webrat's Selenium support is built on the selenium-client Ruby library maintained by Philippe Hanrigou. When you call a Webrat method such as fill_in(), it's translated to the appropriate call on an instance of Selenium::Client::Driver. Webrat exposes this instance through the selenium() method so you can easily leverage the full selenium-client API:

```
selenium.dragdrop("id=#{dom_id(@photo1)}", "+350, 0")
```

An explanation of the full selenium-client API is outside the scope of this chapter, but good documentation is available at http://selenium-client.rubyforge.org/.

Waiting

Each of the Webrat API methods covered in Chapter 21, *Simulating the Browser with Webrat*, on page 293, such as click_link() and fill_in(), work similarly in Selenium mode, but there's one additional concern intrinsic to the Selenium environment you need to watch out for: *waiting*.

When simulating a browser, everything happens in one Ruby process. A call to click_button() causes your scenario to pause while your application code processes the request before returning control to your step

---

3. You can read more about the minor differences between TRUNCATE TABLE and DELETE at http://dev.mysql.com/doc/refman/5.1/en/truncate.html.

definition to verify the response. When using Selenium, however, Cucumber and the Rails application server run in separate processes, so we have to worry about concurrency issues such as race conditions.

The typical solution to this involves instructing Selenium to wait for various conditions at points where the server or browser must do some work before the scenario can proceed. Webrat tries to make this seamless by *implicitly waiting* inside each action or expectation. Here's an example of how it works from Webrat::SeleniumSession:

```
def check(label_text)
  locator = "webrat=#{label_text}"
  selenium.wait_for_element locator, :timeout_in_seconds => 5
  selenium.click locator
end
```

Selenium uses various locators to find elements on the page. Webrat waits for the element to be available in the DOM before clicking it. In this way, Webrat's API means you don't have to think about concurrency very much. It doesn't do any waiting until your code interacts with the page, and then it waits for exactly what you're trying to manipulate.

So, with Webrat handling the waiting for you, why do you need to worry about it at all? There are three primary use cases:

- The Webrat's default timeout of five seconds is not long enough for the application code to finish. In this case, one option is to add your own explicit wait at that spot before the Webrat call:

  ```
  When /^I agree to the Terms of Service$/ do
    selenium.wait_for_element "id=tos_checkbox", :timeout_in_seconds => 10
    check "I agree to the Terms of Service"
  end
  ```

- You need to wait for something other than the element's presence. In this case, you can simply add an additional wait for whatever you need before the Webrat call:

  ```
  When /^I agree to the Terms of Service$/ d
    selenium.wait_for_condition "window.Effect.Queue.size() == 0", 10
    check "I agree to the Terms of Service"
  end
  ```

- You're not using the Webrat API. If you're using the technique described in Section 21.5, *Dropping Down to HTTP*, on page 312, you have to add your own waits. Webrat provides the wait_for() method to help in these situations.

It takes a block:

```
wait_for(:timeout => 3) do
  selenium.dragdrop("id=#{dom_id(@photo1)}", "+350, 0")
end
```

The wait_for() name will execute the block repeatedly until it runs without raising a Selenium, Webrat, or RSpec ExpectationNotMetError error, or it times out. In this way, it's a wait in the Cucumber process rather than the browser.

You can also take a look at selenium-client's API documentation to get an idea of the features it provides for waiting inside the web browser, which can be better for some situations.

Executing Arbitrary JavaScript

Sometimes, for maximum flexibility, you might find yourself wanting to execute a snippet of JavaScript in the browser during the scenario execution. For example, we've used this technique to replace a third-party Flash component with a fake in order to specify that our integration with it works properly.

The selenium-client library offers a get_eval() method for this:

```
When /^the Google API call returns no results$/ do
  selenium.get_eval(<<-JS)
    var currentWindow = selenium.browserbot.getCurrentWindow();
    currentWindow.onGoogleRequestComplete({});
  JS
end
```

JavaScript executed with get_eval() runs in the context of the Selenium window. To get access to the window where your application is open, we have to use the special selenium.browserbot.getCurrentWindow() call.

Specifying Outcomes in Thens

Webrat's three RSpec matchers are all available in Selenium mode: contain(), have_selector(), and have_xpath(). Like the methods for manipulating the application, they all implicitly wait for the expected content to appear (or disappear).

It's worth noting that in simulated mode Webrat uses the excellent libxml2 C library for XPath lookups, but in Selenium mode it leverages the browser's XPath implementation. This can vary a bit across browser versions (and, not surprisingly, is most error prone in Internet Explorer).

For situations where Webrat's API doesn't have what you're looking for, you can leverage the selenium-client API for more flexibility. It has about a dozen methods (prefixed with "is_") that check the state of the browser and return booleans:

```
Then /^the first photo should be first in the album$/ do
  wait_for do
    selenium.is_ordered(
      "id=#{dom_id(@photo1)}",
      "id=#{dom_id(@photo2)}"
    ).should be_true
  end
end
```

Finally, you can use the power to execute arbitrary code in the browser to craft Thens based on anything you can access from JavaScript. For example, if our site kept track of the number of Ajax requests fired by a page in ajax.requestCounter, we could write a step definition like this:

```
Then /^three AJAX requests should have executed$/ do
  ajax_requests = selenium.get_eval(<<-JS)
    var currentWindow = selenium.browserbot.getCurrentWindow();
    currentWindow.ajax.requestCounter;
  JS
  ajax_requests.to_i.should == 3
end
```

get_eval() returns strings, so in this example we have to call to_i() on ajax_requests if you want to compare it as an integer.

22.3 Debugging Selenium Issues

The highly integrated nature of Selenium-backed scenarios is a double-edged sword. On one hand, it gives us the power to work with our application in an environment very similar to how it will be deployed. On the other hand, with so many layers involved, from Selenium and Firefox all the way down to the database, there's a much bigger chance that problems in your test environment itself will lead to programmers tearing their hair out while debugging failures.

Before we wrap up, we'll take a look at a few general problems you might run into and some ways to approach solutions. With any luck, we'll be able to save some of *your* hair along the way.

Server Errors

When using a simulated browser, server errors are easy to spot. The exception bubbles up, and the scenario fails immediately with a message and a backtrace. When using Selenium, however, that's a luxury we don't get out of the box.

When investigating a Selenium failure, one of the first things you should always do is verify in the Rails log that no unexpected server errors (500s or 404s) occurred. If an Ajax request triggered an exception in your application, the information you get from the Rails log will be a lot more helpful to tracking down the root cause than the timeout exception printed to your console.

Isolation Issues

Isolation issues can cause problems with any sort of automated testing process but are particularly common in Selenium environments. They'll usually manifest themselves as scenarios that produce a different result when running on their own compared to when run as part of a suite.

Unfortunately, there's no catchall solution here. Be aware of any state that might carry from one scenario to the next, and isolate as much as you can. Use (or build) tools and abstractions that make keeping that isolation simple, such as database_cleaner. If you're using data stores beyond the database (like the file system or memcached), consider how they should be "cleaned" as well.

You'll also want to be careful to isolate your Selenium suite from external dependencies. If your scenarios fail when a third-party web service hiccups, it will erode your team's confidence in your build results.

One way we like to root out these sorts of issues is by running the Selenium suite with a computer that has its network connection turned off. If anything behaves differently, it's a pointer to an inadvertent external dependency that has crept in.

Timing Issues

The last class of Selenium trouble spots to keep an eye out for is timing issues. Because the Rails application server is running in a separate process, it's impossible for your Cucumber step definitions to know how long it will take for anything to complete. This leads to concurrency bugs such as race conditions that cause erratic results. When you run into a scenario that fails one out of ten times, this is probably the culprit.

Webrat does its best to combat this by using generous timeouts and waiting for the specific conditions it needs before continuing. If you tell Webrat to click a button, for example, it will first wait for the button to exist on the page. It's a simple technique, but Selenium does not handle it automatically, so you should consider using it whenever you access the selenium-client API directly.

Despite its best efforts, Webrat's waiting behavior is not perfect. Webrat can check only for the *existence* of an element before proceeding. While your page is loading, it might have a button in the DOM before all JavaScript events have been registered. In these cases, Webrat might see the button and proceed to click it too early. The fix will depend on the specifics of your situation but usually involves adding additional wait statements before you call the Webrat API.

22.4 What We've Learned

Automating a browser with Selenium is a deep topic, with a lot of tiny details. Let's take a second to review what we've just learned.

- Webrat allows you to migrate from simulated scenarios to Selenium when it becomes appropriate for your application. There's no need to worry that you'll have to rewrite all your existing step definitions if and when that day comes.

- Running in a Selenium environment involves multiple Ruby processes, so we need to turn off the per-scenario transactions that helped ensure the database state stayed isolated. Without this convenience, we have to take steps to ensure our scenarios clean up after themselves.

- The Webrat API works with Selenium, but we're not limited to it. It's easy to drop down to the selenium-client API as needed. For maximum flexibility, selenium-client allows executing arbitrary JavaScript inside the browser window.

- The fully integrated nature of Selenium-backed scenarios is a double-edged sword. With many moving parts, the chance of obscure bugs creeping in increases. Although there are no silver bullets to many of these issues, being aware of what you might run into will save you some trouble down the line.

## Chapter 23

Rails Views

The user interface is subject to more change than just about any other part of an application. These changes are driven by usability concerns, design aesthetics, and evolving requirements. Clearly, this makes producing simple, flexible views desirable and beneficial, but there is more.

We use views to display data provided by models that are, in turn, provided by controllers. As such, these views are clients of controllers and models. By focusing on views first, writing the code we wish we had, we are able to keep the views simple and lean on them to tell us what they need from the rest of the stack. This leads to controllers and models with targeted APIs that are well aligned with the application behavior.

23.1 Writing View Specs

A view spec is a collection of code examples for a particular view template. Unlike examples for plain old Ruby objects (POROs), view examples are inherently state-based. We provide data to the view and then set expectations about the rendered content.

In most cases, we're interested in the semantic content as it pertains to requirements of the application, as opposed to the syntactical correctness of the markup. The main exception to this is forms, in which case we do want to specify that form elements are rendered correctly within a form tag.

Now you may be thinking that we've already covered these same details with Cucumber and Webrat in the past couple of chapters, so why should we also have isolated view specs? This question is being asked quite a lot as we prepare to print this book, so you're not alone if you're asking it. We'll address this question at the end of the chapter, in Section 23.4, *When Should I Write View Specs?*, on page 339, but that will make more sense after you get a feel for how view specs work and the benefits they provide.

Getting Started

We need to generate a fresh Rails app and configure it to use rspec-rails: Start by generating the app:

```
rails new messages
cd messages
```

Next, copy the following to the Gemfile:

```
group :development, :test do
  gem "rspec-rails", ">= 2.0.0"
  gem "webrat", ">= 0.7.2"
end
```

Lastly, install the bundle and run the rspec:install generator:

```
bundle install
script/rails generate rspec:install
rake db:migrate
```

That's it! RSpec is ready to go.

We're going to build a view that displays a message, and we'll drive it out with a spec. Create a ./spec/views/messages/ directory, and add a show.html.erb_spec.rb file with the following content:

```
rails_views/messages/01/spec/views/messages/show.html.erb_spec.rb
```

```
require 'spec_helper'

describe "messages/show.html.erb" do
  it "displays the text attribute of the message" do
    render
    rendered.should contain("Hello world!")
  end
end
```

render(), rendered(), and contain()

Given no arguments, the render() method on the first line in the example renders the file passed to the outermost describe() block, "messages/show.html.erb" in this case. The rendered() method returns the rendered content, which is passed to the contain() matcher on the second line. If the rendered content contains the text "Hello world!" the example will pass. Note that this looks only at rendered text. If "Hello world!" is embedded in a comment or in a JavaScript document.write statement, for example, it would not be recognized by contain().

The rspec:install generator we ran earlier added some rake tasks we can use to run specs. Go ahead and run this:

```
rake spec
```

You should see the following failure:

```
Missing template messages/show.html.erb
```

The template doesn't exist yet, so add show.html.erb to the app/views/ messages/ directory (which you'll need to create), and run the spec again. Now we get this output:

```
expected the following element's content to include "Hello world!"
```

This time it failed because there's nothing in the show.html.erb template. Observing the practice of temporary sins to get to the green bar, add "Hello world!" to the show.html.erb file, run the spec again, and watch it pass. Now we know that the example is correctly wired up to the view implementation.

The sin was creating duplication between the spec and the implementation. Let's see what we can do about washing that away. The example says that messages/show.html.erb displays the text of the supplied message, but the implementation is simply hard-coded. Based on the example, here's the code we wish we had in show.html.erb:

> rails_views/messages/03/app/views/messages/show.html.erb

```
<%= @message.text %>
```

Add that to the file and run the example again, and now you should see undefined method `text' for nil:NilClass, referencing the line we just added. The view expects an @message variable to be set up for it. This will be the controller's responsibility once we get there, but in this case there *is no controller yet.* This puts the responsibility on the view spec itself.

assign()

View specs expose an assign method, which we use to provide data to the view. Modify the spec as follows:

> rails_views/messages/04/spec/views/messages/show.html.erb_spec.rb

```
describe "messages/show.html.erb" do
  it "displays the text attribute of the message" do
    assign(:message, double("Message", :text => "Hello world!"))
    render
    rendered.should contain("Hello world!")
  end
end
```

The new first line of the example creates a test double, which stubs the text() method with a return value of "Hello world!" and assigns it to an @message instance variable on the view.

Run rake spec again, and it should pass. And that's it for the first example. Pretty simple, right? Although this example didn't do justice to the intricacies views are often composed of, it did give us just enough to start us with a foundation on which to build.

In addition to understanding the basics of a view spec, here are a few more things we can glean from what we just did:

Directory organization The directory structure for view specs mimics the directory structure found in app/views/. For example, specs found in spec/views/messages/ will be for view templates found in app/views/messages/.

File naming View specs are named after the template they provide examples for, with an _spec.rb appended to the filename. For example, index.html.erb would have a corresponding spec named index.html.erb_spec.rb.

Always require spec_helper.rb Every view spec will need to require the spec_helper.rb file. Otherwise, you'll get errors about core rspec or rspec-rails methods not existing.

Describing view specs The outer describe() block in a view spec uses the path to the view minus the app/views/ portion. This is used by the render() method when it is called with no arguments, keeping things clean and DRY.

Now that you have the basics down, let's explore a little deeper.

23.2 Mocking Models

When working outside-in, we often discover the need for a model that doesn't exist yet. Rather than switch focus to the model, we can create a mock_model() and remain focused on the view we're working on.

Mock Example

Building on the messages example, we'll introduce the need for a model and continue driving the view. Following the convention we learned about earlier this chapter, add a spec named new.html.erb_spec.rb in the spec/views/messages/ directory with the content shown on the next page.

```
rails_views/messages/05/spec/views/messages/new.html.erb_spec.rb
require 'spec_helper'

describe "messages/new.html.erb" do
  it "renders a form to create a message" do
    assign(:message, double("Message"))
    render
    rendered.should have_selector("form",
      :method => "post",
      :action => messages_path
    ) do |form|
      form.should have_selector("input", :type => "submit")
    end
  end
end
```

Run the spec, and you should see a familiar Missing template error. Go ahead and create a new.html.erb template in app/views/messages with the following code:

```
rails_views/messages/05-1/app/views/messages/new.html.erb
<%= form_for @message do |f| %>
  <%= f.submit "Save" %>
<% end %>
```

Run the spec, and now the MissingTemplate error is gone, but the spec still fails with a new error:

```
undefined method `model_name' for RSpec::Mocks::Mock:Class
```

The form_for() method used in the view interacts with the object it's given as though it were an ActiveRecord model. We're using a stock test double, which doesn't know how to respond to the different messages it gets from form_for().

We can use the mock_model() method to provide a mock object that is configured to respond in this context as though it were an ActiveRecord model. Update the example to use mock_model() instead of double():

```
rails_views/messages/06/spec/views/messages/new.html.erb_spec.rb
it "renders a form to create a message" do
  assign(:message, mock_model("Message"))
  render
  rendered.should have_selector("form",
    :method => "post",
    :action => messages_path
  ) do |form|
    form.should have_selector("input", :type => "submit")
  end
end
```

Run the spec again, and you'll see this:

```
undefined method `message_path'
```

At this point, the example is failing because there are no routes set up for messages. But that's not all. Do you notice something odd about the route it's looking for?

By default, mock_model produces a mock that acts like an existing record (for example, persisted() returns true). When form_for gets an existing record, it produces a form that posts to the *update* action, which lives at message_path (singular) as opposed to messages_path (plural). We want a form that posts to the *create* action at messages_path. We can do this by telling the mocked model to act like a new record:

rails_views/messages/07/spec/views/messages/new.html.erb_spec.rb

```
it "renders a form to create a message" do
  assign(:message, mock_model("Message").as_new_record)
  render
  rendered.should have_selector("form",
    :method => "post",
    :action => messages_path
  ) do |form|
    form.should have_selector("input", :type => "submit")
  end
end
```

Now the spec fails with this:

```
undefined method `messages_path'
```

This is the failure message we're looking for, and we can resolve it by adding the appropriate declaration to config/routes.rb:

rails_views/messages/08/config/routes.rb

```
Messages::Application.routes.draw do
  resources :messages
end
```

After adding the route declaration, run the spec, and you should see one example and zero failures.

Now that we have the form working, let's add some input fields. We'll start with a text field for the message title:

rails_views/messages/09/spec/views/messages/new.html.erb_spec.rb

```
it "renders a text field for the message title" do
  assign(
    :message,
    mock_model("Message", :title => "the title").as_new_record
  )
```

```
    render
    rendered.should have_selector("form") do |form|
      form.should have_selector("input",
        :type => "text",
        :name => "message[title]",
        :value => "the title"
      )
    end
  end
end
```

Run that, watch it fail, and then implement the view to resolve that failure:

> rails_views/messages/10/app/views/messages/new.html.erb

```erb
<%= form_for @message do |f| %>
  <%= f.text_field :title %>
  <%= f.submit "Save" %>
<% end %>
```

Run the spec again, and this example passes, but now the first example is failing with the following:

```
Model Message does not respond to title
```

By default, an RSpec mock object will return false when asked if it responds to a method that it hasn't been told to expect. In this case, the text_field() helper in the view asks @message if it responds to title(). When the @message returns false, Rails raises the error shown earlier.

The first example doesn't care about the message title, so we don't want to have to tell the mock to expect title(). What we *can* do is tell the mocked message to ignore any messages it's not expecting by acting as a null object. This will let us write focused examples without introducing unnecessary verbosity in other examples. Go ahead and add as_null_object():

> rails_views/messages/11/spec/views/messages/new.html.erb_spec.rb

```ruby
it "renders a form to create a message" do
  assign(
    :message,
    mock_model("Message").as_new_record.as_null_object
  )
  render
  rendered.should have_selector("form",
    :method => "post",
    :action => messages_path
  ) do |form|
    form.should have_selector("input", :type => "submit")
  end
end
```

Run the spec, and you should see that it passes. We had red, and now we have green. Time to refactor. At this point, the view implementation is pretty clean, but we do have some duplication we can remove from the two examples. Modify new.html.erb_spec.rb as follows:

rails_views/messages/12/spec/views/messages/new.html.erb_spec.rb

```ruby
require 'spec_helper'

describe "messages/new.html.erb" do
  let(:message) do
    mock_model("Message").as_new_record.as_null_object
  end

  before do
    assign(:message, message)
  end

  it "renders a form to create a message" do
    render
    rendered.should have_selector("form",
      :method => "post",
      :action => messages_path
    ) do |form|
      form.should have_selector("input", :type => "submit")
    end
  end

  it "renders a text field for the message title" do
    message.stub(:title => "the title")
    render
    rendered.should have_selector("form") do |form|
      form.should have_selector("input",
        :type => "text",
        :name => "message[title]",
        :value => "the title"
      )
    end
  end
end
```

Run the specs again, and they should still be passing.

Now let's specify that the form has a text area for the text of the message. We can stub text() on message just as we stubbed title in the previous example:

rails_views/messages/13/spec/views/messages/new.html.erb_spec.rb

```ruby
it "renders a text area for the message text" do
  message.stub(:text => "the message")
  render
```

```
  rendered.should have_selector("form") do |form|
    form.should have_selector("textarea",
      :name => "message[text]",
      :content => "the message"
    )
  end
end
```

This should fail with this:

```
expected following output to contain a
  <textarea name='message[text]'>the message</textarea> tag;
```

Add <%= f.text_area :text %> to the view, and the example should pass. Note that adding a new field to the form doesn't cause other examples to fail this time. This is because we used as_null_object() in the before() block. This will hold true for any additional fields we describe in specs later, so this one-time refactoring will have benefits throughout the development of this view.

Mock models that act as_null_object keep view specs lean and simple, allowing each example to be explicit about only the things it cares about. They also save us from unwanted side effects being introduced in other examples. Now let's take a closer look at mock_model.

mock_model

The mock_model() method sets up an RSpec mock with common Active-Record methods stubbed out. In its most basic form, mock_model can be called with a single argument, which is the class you want to represent as an ActiveRecord model. The class must exist, but it doesn't have to be a subclass of ActiveRecord::Base. Here are the default stubs on a mocked model:

new_record? Returns false since mocked models represent existing records by default

id   Returns an autogenerated number to represent an existing record

to_param Returns a string version of the id

Just like standard mocks/stubs in RSpec, additional methods can be stubbed by passing in an additional Hash argument of method name/ value pairs. Here's an example:

```
user = mock_model(User,
  :login => "zdennis",
  :email => "zdennis@example.com"
)
```

When we don't want the mock to represent an existing record, we can tell it to be a new record by sending it the as_new_record() message:

```
new_user = mock_model(User).as_new_record
```

This will change the default values stubbed by mock_model to the following:

new_record? Will return true just like a new ActiveRecord object

id Will return nil just like a new ActiveRecord object

to_param Will return nil just like a new ActiveRecord object

Mock models are particularly useful when the model we need doesn't exist yet. The trade-off is that we have to use as_null_object() to keep them quiet. Once the model exists, however, rspec-rails offers us an alternative: stub_model().

stub_model

The stub_model() method is similar to mock_model() except that it creates an actual instance of the model. This requires that the model has a corresponding table in the database.

You create a stub_model just like a mock_model: the first argument is the model to instantiate, and the second argument is a Hash of method/ value pairs to stub.

```
user = stub_model(User)

user = stub_model(User,
  :login => "zdennis",
  :email => "zdennis@example.com"
)
```

Similar to mock_model, a stubbed model represents an existing record by default, and we can tell it to act like a new record with as_new_ record(). In fact, stub_model is a lot like mock_model, with just a couple of exceptions.

Because stub_model creates an ActiveRecord model instance, we don't need to tell it to act as_null_object() to keep it quiet when asked for its attributes. ActiveRecord will just return nil in those cases, as long as the attribute *is* defined in the schema.

The other difference is that stub_model() prohibits the model instance from accessing the database. If it receives any database-related messages, such as save() or update_attributes(), it will raise an error.

```
RSpec::Rails::IllegalDataAccessException: stubbed models are not allowed to \
access the database
```

This can be a good indicator that the view is doing something it should not be doing or that the method in question should really be stubbed out in the example.

Neither mock_model() nor stub_model() is restricted to view specs. As you'll see later this chapter and in the following chapter on controller specs, they can be very helpful throughout the spec suite.

23.3 Specifying Helpers

Rails helpers keep model transformations, markup generation, and other sorts of view logic cleanly separated from erb templates. This makes templates clean and maintainable and makes it easier to reuse little display nuggets that have a habit of reappearing throughout our applications.

Consider the common problem of displaying parts of a view only to administrators. One nice solution is to use a block helper, like this:

```
<%- display_for(:admin) do -%>
  Only admins should see this
<%- end -%>
```

The rspec-rails plug-in provides a specialized ExampleGroup for specifying helpers in isolation. To see this in action, create a spec/helpers/application_helper_spec.rb file. Assuming that views have access to a current_user() method, here's an example for the case in which the current_user is in the given role:

rails_views/roles/01/spec/helpers/application_helper_spec.rb

```ruby
require 'spec_helper'

describe ApplicationHelper do
  describe "#display_for(:role)" do
    context "when the current user has the role" do
      it "displays the content" do
        user = stub('User', :in_role? => true)
        helper.stub(:current_user).and_return(user)
        content = helper.display_for(:existing_role) {"content"}
        content.should == "content"
      end
    end
  end
end
```

The helper() method returns an object that includes the helper module passed to describe(). In this case, that's the ApplicationHelper. If you run that spec now, you should see it fail with this:

```
undefined method `display_for' for #<ActionView::Base:0x103367190>
```

Here's the implementation that gets this to pass:

rails_views/roles/02/app/helpers/application_helper.rb

```ruby
module ApplicationHelper
  def display_for(role)
    yield
  end
end
```

Now add another example for the negative case:

rails_views/roles/03/spec/helpers/application_helper_spec.rb

```ruby
context "when the current user does not have the role" do
  it "does not display the content" do
    user = stub('User', :in_role? => false)
    helper.stub(:current_user).and_return(user)
    content = helper.display_for(:existing_role) {"content"}
    content.should == nil
  end
end
```

That example fails with this:

```
expected: nil,
     got: "content" (using ==)
```

And here's the modified display_for() method that passes both examples:

rails_views/roles/04/app/helpers/application_helper.rb

```ruby
module ApplicationHelper
  def display_for(role)
    yield if current_user.in_role?(role)
  end
end
```

As you can see, helper specs make it easy to drive out presentation logic in granular, reusable chunks.

So now that we know how to write view and helper specs, let's explore the question we posed at the beginning of the chapter.

23.4 When Should I Write View Specs?

While we've been working on this book, the BDD tool set has been evolving at lightning speed. With the increasing capability of Cucumber + Webrat, the overlap between Cucumber step definitions and view specs increases as well, as the boundaries of what belongs where become more and more gray.

So, how can you know whether view specs make sense for you and your project? Here are a few questions you can ask yourself to help make that decision:

Am I using Cucumber and Webrat? If you're not using Cucumber and Webrat, then view specs are going to provide a lot of value you're probably not getting otherwise.

Will a Cucumber failure give me the right message? Sometimes the failure message we get from Cucumber points us directly to a clean point of failure. A missing template error, for example, is very specific. When the message doesn't tell us exactly what we need to do next, however, that's a good case for a view spec.

Is there any functionality beyond basic CRUD actions/views?
View specs provide us with an opportunity to discover APIs that we need from the controllers and models. This is not that valuable when the APIs are following the most standard conventions. The value increases, however, as we stray from them.

In general, our recommendation is to err on the side of too many view specs rather than too few. The only way to really get a feel for the benefits of them is to learn to write them well. And only once you really understand how they fit in the flow are you going to be able to make well-grounded decisions about if and when to use them.

23.5 What We've Learned

The user interface changes more often than just about anything else in an application. View specs help us specify the details that should remain stable through markup changes and help discover the requirements of other components further down the stack. In this chapter, we discussed these facts as well as the following:

• View specs use a custom example group provided by the rspec-rails library.

- View specs live in a directory tree parallel to the views themselves and follow a naming convention of spec/path/to/view.html.erb_spec.rb for app/path/to/view.html.erb.

- Use Webrat's have_xpath() and have_selector() matchers for view specs.

- Use mock_model() and stub_model() to isolate view specs from the database and underlying business logic of your models.

- Helpers have their own specs that live in the spec/helpers directory.

As we mentioned earlier, view specs help us identify the instance variables that our controllers will need to supply. In the next chapter, we'll take a look at specifying controllers in isolation from views and take a look at models.

Rails' controllers are like waiters in a restaurant. A customer orders a steak dinner from a waiter. The waiter takes the request and tells the kitchen that he needs a steak dinner. When the steak dinner is ready, the waiter delivers it to the customer for her enjoyment.

▶ Craig Demyanovich

Chapter 24

Rails Controllers

The restaurant metaphor does a great job describing the role of controllers in a Rails application. Just as a waiter doesn't need to know how to prepare a steak dinner, a controller doesn't need to know the details of building a model. Keeping these details out of the controller provides a natural separation of concerns between the controller and the model, which makes the models easier to change, extend, and reuse.

This chapter will show you how to develop controllers outside in using controller specs as the driving force.

24.1 Controller Specs

A controller spec is a collection of examples of the expected behavior of actions on a single controller. Whereas views are inherently state-based, controllers are naturally interaction-based. They wait at the edges of a Rails app to mediate interaction between models and views, given an incoming request. We therefore set expectations about interactions, process the action, and look at assigned instance variables and flash messages made available for the view.

By default, controller specs don't render views.[1] Combine that fact with judicious use of mocks and stubs for interaction with the model, and now we can specify controller interactions in complete isolation from the other components. This pushes us to build skinny controllers and helps us discover objects with well-named methods to encapsulate the real work.

---

1. See the sidebar on page 356 for more about isolation from views.

A simple guideline for a controller is that it should know *what* to do but not *how* to do it. Controllers that know too much about the *how* become responsible for too many things and as a result become bloated, messy, and hard to understand. This will become clear as we work through an example.

MessagesController

In the previous chapter, we built up the view that contained the form to create a message. Now we're going to develop a controller action responsible for processing that form submission and creating the message.

If you haven't been through Chapter 23, *Rails Views*, on page 327 yet, that's OK. Just bootstrap a new Rails app as described in Section 23.1, *Getting Started*, on page 328. Once you've done that, generate a MessagesController and its spec:

```
script/rails generate controller Messages --no-helper
  create  app/controllers/messages_controller.rb
  invoke  erb
  create    app/views/messages
  invoke  rspec
  create    spec/controllers/messages_controller_spec.rb
```

With Rails 3, RSpec is able to register itself as the test framework, so specs get generated instead of test/unit tests. By default, the controller generator generates a helper and its spec as well, so we disabled that with the --no-helper flag. Now update messages_controller_spec.rb so it reads like this:

rails_controllers/messages/01/spec/controllers/messages_controller_spec.rb

```ruby
require 'spec_helper'

describe MessagesController do
  describe "POST create" do
    it "creates a new message"
    it "saves the message"
  end
end
```

Run rake spec:controllers, and you'll see that we have two pending examples:

```
2 examples, 0 failures, 2 pending
```

You read about several approaches to generating pending examples in Section 12.2, *Pending Examples*, on page 142. These examples are *pending* because they have no blocks. The first example specifies that the create() action builds a new message, so let's add a block that sets that expectation.

rails_controllers/messages/02/spec/controllers/messages_controller_spec.rb

```
it "creates a new message" do
  Message.should_receive(:new).with("text" => "a quick brown fox")
  post :create, :message => { "text" => "a quick brown fox" }
end
```

This fails with uninitialized constant Message. Remember that we didn't have to create the Message when we were writing view specs, so there has been no need until now.

Time to Introduce the Model

Now that we need to interact with a model class in a spec, generate it and its spec using the Rails generator:

```
script/rails generate model Message
    invoke  active_record
    create    db/migrate/20100723170657_create_messages.rb
    create    app/models/message.rb
    invoke  rspec
    create      spec/models/message_spec.rb
rake db:migrate
```

Run rake spec:controllers again, and you'll see one of two failures. If you created a new Messages app at the beginning of this chapter, you'll see this:

```
No route matches {:message=>{"text"=>"a quick brown fox"},
  :controller=>"messages", :action=>"create"}
```

In this case, we're missing the route, so add it to config/routes.rb to resolve this error:

rails_controllers/messages/04/config/routes.rb

```
Messages::Application.routes.draw do
  resources :messages
end
```

If you're using the same Messages app we created in Chapter 23, *Rails Views*, on page 327, then you probably already added these routes. Whether you added them in the previous chapter or just added them now, run rake spec:controllers again, and now you'll see that the example fails with No action responded to create, so add the create action

> ### ⚡ Joe Asks...
>
> #### Doesn't Message.should_receive(:new) Specify Implementation?
>
> At some level, yes it does, but it's not the same as specifying internal implementation details that occur only within the object being spec'd. We're specifying the interaction with other objects in order to isolate this example from anything that might go wrong or that does not yet exist in the other objects. That way, when a controller spec fails, you know that it's because the controller is not behaving correctly and can quickly diagnose the problem.
>
> One of the motivations for this approach in Rails controller specs is that we don't have to worry about changes to model validation rules causing failures in controller specs. Rails fixtures can also help solve that problem if you use them judiciously. Test data builders like Fixjour, Factory Girl, Object Daddy, and Machinist can also help. But fixtures and test data builders all use a database, which slows down the specs, even if they maintain rapid fault isolation.

now, implementing just enough code to change the error message we're getting:

```
rails_controllers/messages/05/app/controllers/messages_controller.rb
def create
end
```

Now we get a new error: Missing template messages/create. We don't, however, want to add a template for this. The conventional approach is to redirect to a resource's index after a successful create. Let's shift gears for a second and get that in place.

Temporarily Pending

While we work on introducing the redirect, let's make the example we've been working on pending. Once we get the redirect working, we'll remove the pending declaration. Until then, we can work without having to worry about this example failing.

Update spec/controllers/messages_controller_spec.rb as follows:

> rails_controllers/messages/06/spec/controllers/messages_controller_spec.rb

```ruby
require 'spec_helper'

describe MessagesController do
  describe "POST create" do
    it "creates a new message" do
      pending("drive out redirect")
      Message.should_receive(:new).with("text" => "a quick brown fox")
      post :create, :message => { "text" => "a quick brown fox" }
    end

    it "saves the message"

    it "redirects to the Messages index" do
      post :create
      response.should redirect_to(:action => "index")
    end
  end
end
```

Run rake spec:controllers, and you'll see the same message about missing a template for messages/create. To get it to pass, modify app/controllers/messages_controller.rb as follows:

> rails_controllers/messages/07/app/controllers/messages_controller.rb

```ruby
def create
  redirect_to :action => "index"
end
```

That's enough to get that example to pass. Run rake spec:controllers, and you should see 3 examples, 0 failures, 2 pending. Now let's remove the pending declaration from the first example:

> rails_controllers/messages/08/spec/controllers/messages_controller_spec.rb

```ruby
it "creates a new message" do
  Message.should_receive(:new).with("text" => "a quick brown fox")
  post :create, :message => { "text" => "a quick brown fox" }
end
```

Run rake spec:controllers, and you should see this:

```
Failure/Error: Message.should_receive(:new).with("text" => "a quick brown fox")
(<Message(id: integer, created_at: datetime, updated_at: datetime) (class)>).
                                  new({"text"=>"a quick brown fox"})
    expected: 1 time
    received: 0 times
```

This is the logical failure we've been aiming for, and we are now in a position to get this example to pass. Add the following to app/controllers/messages_controller.rb:

rails_controllers/messages/09/app/controllers/messages_controller.rb

```
def create
▶   Message.new(params[:message])
    redirect_to :action => "index"
  end
```

Success! We now have two passing examples, leaving only one remaining pending example. This one specifies that the controller saves the message. Again, add a block to express the expectation:

rails_controllers/messages/10/spec/controllers/messages_controller_spec.rb

```
it "saves the message" do
  message = mock_model(Message)
  Message.stub(:new).and_return(message)
  message.should_receive(:save)
  post :create
end
```

The example should fail with the following message:

```
Failure/Error: message.should_receive(:save)
(Mock "Message_1001").save(any args)
    expected: 1 time
    received: 0 times
```

To get this to pass, all we need to do is call save() on the message:

rails_controllers/messages/11/app/controllers/messages_controller.rb

```
def create
▶   message = Message.new(params[:message])
▶   message.save
    redirect_to :action => "index"
  end
```

Run the spec again, and you'll see the second example is now passing, but we broke the first example in the process: 3 examples, 1 failure. There is no message object in the first example, and there needs to be one for the code in the action to run.

We can get the first example to pass without impacting the second example by introducing a mock message:

rails_controllers/messages/12/spec/controllers/messages_controller_spec.rb

```
it "creates a new message" do
▶   message = mock_model(Message)
    Message.should_receive(:new).
```

```
      with("text" => "a quick brown fox").
▶       and_return(message)
      post :create, :message => { "text" => "a quick brown fox" }
    end
```

Here we create a mock message and then tell the Message class to return it in response to new(). Run the examples, and...the example is *still* failing, but this time for a different reason. The create action calls message.save, but the mock_model is not expecting it. We can use as_null_object, which we discussed in Section 23.2, *Mock Example*, on page 330, to tell the mock message to ignore any unexpected messages:

rails_controllers/messages/13/spec/controllers/messages_controller_spec.rb

```
    it "creates a new message" do
▶     message = mock_model(Message).as_null_object
      Message.should_receive(:new).
        with("text" => "a quick brown fox").
        and_return(message)
      post :create, :message => { "text" => "a quick brown fox" }
    end
```

Run rake spec:controllers again, and you'll see 3 examples, 0 failures. No failures, no more pending.

Tidy Up

We've made progress, but we've also introduced some duplication between the two examples. We can clean that up by extracting the common bits to a let() and a before(:each) hook:

rails_controllers/messages/14/spec/controllers/messages_controller_spec.rb

```
require 'spec_helper'

describe MessagesController do
  describe "POST create" do
    let(:message) { mock_model(Message).as_null_object }

    before do
      Message.stub(:new).and_return(message)
    end

    it "creates a new message" do
      Message.should_receive(:new).
        with("text" => "a quick brown fox").
        and_return(message)
      post :create, :message => { "text" => "a quick brown fox" }
    end
```

```ruby
    it "saves the message" do
      message.should_receive(:save)
      post :create
    end

    it "redirects to the Messages index" do
      post :create
      response.should redirect_to(:action => "index")
    end
  end
end
```

The let(), which we introduced in Section 5.4, *let(:method) {}*, on page 55, defines a message() that returns and caches the value of the block the first time it is called in any one example and then returns the cached value on subsequent calls. The before() hook then instructs the Message class to return the message object.

Looks cleaner, yes? And it looks like we're done, yes? No! We've only specified how the create action should behave when it successfully saves a message. But what about when the save fails?

24.2 Context-Specific Examples

Controllers typically do different things depending on whether the work they delegate succeeds or fails. We started with the *happy path*, in which a save succeeds. But what happens when it fails? Before we address that, let's wrap the success path examples in a context:

When save() Succeeds

rails_controllers/messages/15/spec/controllers/messages_controller_spec.rb

```ruby
require 'spec_helper'

describe MessagesController do
  describe "POST create" do
    let(:message) { mock_model(Message).as_null_object }

    before do
      Message.stub(:new).and_return(message)
    end

    it "creates a new message" do
      Message.should_receive(:new).
        with("text" => "a quick brown fox").
        and_return(message)
      post :create, :message => { "text" => "a quick brown fox" }
    end
```

```
    it "saves the message" do
      message.should_receive(:save)
      post :create
    end

►   context "when the message saves successfully" do
►     it "sets a flash[:notice] message"
►
►     it "redirects to the Messages index" do
►       post :create
►       response.should redirect_to(:action => "index")
►     end
►   end
  end
end
```

The only example that we already have that is specific to the happy path
is the one that specifies the redirect to index, so that's the only one we
move to the next context. We'll also want a flash notice, so that's added
as a pending example. Now let's fill that one in.

rails_controllers/messages/16/spec/controllers/messages_controller_spec.rb

```
it "sets a flash[:notice] message" do
  post :create
  flash[:notice].should eq("The message was saved successfully.")
end
```

Run that, and watch it fail:

```
Failure/Error: flash[:notice].should eq("The message was saved successfully.")
expected "The message was saved successfully."
     got nil
```

It fails because the flash[:notice] is nil, so update the create action to add
a flash message when the save succeeds:

rails_controllers/messages/17/app/controllers/messages_controller.rb

```
    def create
      message = Message.new(params[:message])
►     if message.save
►       flash[:notice] = "The message was saved successfully."
►     end
      redirect_to :action => "index"
    end
```

Run that, and you'll see that it passes. Now we have two passing examples that specify the happy path, so let's move on to examples of what
should happen when the save fails.

When save() Fails

Instead of redirecting to the index, we'll want to rerender the new template, which will need an @message instance variable assigned. Add a new context with pending examples for these requirements:

`rails_controllers/messages/18/spec/controllers/messages_controller_spec.rb`

```
context "when the message fails to save" do
  it "assigns @message"
  it "renders the new template"
end
```

Now fill in the first example:

`rails_controllers/messages/19/spec/controllers/messages_controller_spec.rb`

```
it "assigns @message" do
  message.stub(:save).and_return(false)
  post :create
  assigns[:message].should eq(message)
end
```

The assigns() method returns a hash representing instance variables that were assigned to the view by the controller. Run rake spec:controllers, and the new example fails with this:

```
expected #<Message:0x81b0b900 @name="Message_1005">
    got nil
```

Now convert the local message variables to instance variables to make it pass:

`rails_controllers/messages/20/app/controllers/messages_controller.rb`

```
  def create
▶   @message = Message.new(params[:message])
▶   if @message.save
      flash[:notice] = "The message was saved successfully."
    end
    redirect_to :action => "index"
  end
```

Run rake spec:controllers, and you'll see no failures and one pending example remaining. Fill that one in as follows:

`rails_controllers/messages/21/spec/controllers/messages_controller_spec.rb`

```
it "renders the new template" do
  message.stub(:save).and_return(false)
  post :create
  response.should render_template("new")
end
```

Run rake spec:controllers again, and you'll see this fail with the following:

```
Failure/Error: response.should render_template("new")
expecting <"new"> but rendering with <"">
```

Update the controller action as follows to get that to pass:

rails_controllers/messages/22/app/controllers/messages_controller.rb

```
    def create
      @message = Message.new(params[:message])
      if @message.save
        flash[:notice] = "The message was saved successfully."
►       redirect_to :action => "index"
►     else
►       render :action => "new"
►     end
    end
```

Run rake spec:controllers one more time, and you should see that all the examples are passing:[2]

```
MessagesController
  POST create
    creates a new message
    saves the message
    when the message saves successfully
      sets a flash[:notice] message
      redirects to the Messages index
    when the message fails to save
      assigns @message
      renders the new template

Finished in 0.03591 seconds
6 examples, 0 failures
```

Learn from the Output

Reviewing this output, it's easy to spot that we have a bit of redundancy in the examples. We have an example that specifies that the controller action tries to save the message, but we also have two contexts that describe what happens when we try to save the message.

There's really no need for the "saves the message" example anymore, so go ahead and delete it.

---

2. If you started with a fresh Rails app in this chapter, instead of continuing with the app from the previous chapter, you'll probably get a missing template error on messages/new at this point. If that happens, just create an empty app/views/messages/new.html.erb file, and everything should pass.

Tidy Up

Now let's look for any opportunities to clean up the spec:

`rails_controllers/messages/23/spec/controllers/messages_controller_spec.rb`

```ruby
require 'spec_helper'

describe MessagesController do
  describe "POST create" do
    let(:message) { mock_model(Message).as_null_object }

    before do
      Message.stub(:new).and_return(message)
    end

    it "creates a new message" do
      Message.should_receive(:new).
        with("text" => "a quick brown fox").
        and_return(message)
      post :create, :message => { "text" => "a quick brown fox" }
    end

    context "when the message saves successfully" do
      it "sets a flash[:notice] message" do
        post :create
        flash[:notice].should eq("The message was saved successfully.")
      end

      it "redirects to the Messages index" do
        post :create
        response.should redirect_to(:action => "index")
      end
    end

    context "when the message fails to save" do
      it "assigns @message" do
        message.stub(:save).and_return(false)
        post :create
        assigns[:message].should eq(message)
      end

      it "renders the new template" do
        message.stub(:save).and_return(false)
        post :create
        response.should render_template("new")
      end
    end
  end
end
```

The most obvious bit is the duplication in the past two examples, so let's extract that to a before hook inside the failure context:

```ruby
context "when the message fails to save" do
  before do
    message.stub(:save).and_return(false)
  end

  it "assigns @message" do
    post :create
    assigns[:message].should eq(message)
  end

  it "renders the new template" do
    post :create
    response.should render_template("new")
  end
```

Once that's in place, there is an imbalance between the success and failure contexts. The success context has no code in it that explicitly shows the successful save. It doesn't *need* it to run, because as_null_object() causes the message to return a *truthy* value in response to save().[3] Even so, we can make the spec clearer by adding a before hook to the success context, and then if we remove as_null_object() later, those examples should still pass. Go ahead and update as follows:

```ruby
context "when the message saves successfully" do
  before do
    message.stub(:save).and_return(true)
  end

  it "sets a flash[:notice] message" do
    post :create
    flash[:notice].should eq("The message was saved successfully.")
  end

  it "redirects to the Messages index" do
    post :create
    response.should redirect_to(:action => "index")
  end
end
```

---

3. Rubyists use the term *truthy* to indicate any value other than false or nil.

Now everything is balanced and clear. The "creates a message" example is outside of either the contexts because that should happen in any case. The before hooks in the two contexts are balanced and make perfectly clear what the contexts mean in code.

What We Just Did

The create() action we just implemented is typical in Rails apps. The controller passes the params it receives to the model, delegating the real work. By specifying the interactions with the model instead of the result of the model's work, we are able to keep the spec and the implementation simple and readable.

This is what it means to have a controller know *what* to do without knowing the details of *how* to do it. Any complexity related to building a message will be specified and implemented in the Message model.

The spec we used to drive this action into existence can be used to illustrate some basic conventions we like to follow for controller specs:

Directory organization The directory structure for controller specs parallels the directory structure found in app/controllers/.

File naming Each controller spec is named after the controller it provides examples for, with _spec.rb appended to the filename. For example, sessions_controller_spec.rb contains the specs for sessions_controller.rb.

Always require spec_helper.rb Each controller spec should require the spec_helper.rb file, which sets up the environment with all the right example group classes and utility methods.

Example group names The docstring passed to the outermost describe() block in a controller spec typically includes the type of request and the action the examples are for.

While driving out the create() action, we focused on one example at a time. Once each example passed, we looked for and extracted any duplication to a before block, allowing each example to stay focused, clear, and DRY. And when we found examples that pertained to a given context, we used context blocks with clear descriptions to organize them.

This spec also introduced a number of methods that provide a good foundation for writing controller specs. Many of these methods come directly from ActionController::TestCase, which Rails uses for functional tests. Let's look closer at each of the methods we used.

assigns()

We use assigns to access a hash, which we use to specify the instance variables that we expect to be assigned in the view.

Note that the assigns hash in controller specs is different from the one in view specs. In view specs, we use assigns to set instance variables for a view *before rendering the view*. In controller specs, we use assigns to set expectations about instance variables assigned for the view *after calling the controller action*.

flash()

We use flash to access a hash, which we use to specify messages we expect to be stored in the flash. It uses the same API to access flash in the spec as you would use in the controller, which makes it convenient and easy to remember when working with flash.

post

We use the post() method to simulate a POST request. It can take three arguments. The first argument is the name of the action to call. The second argument (optional) is a hash of key/value pairs to make up the params. The third argument (also optional) is a hash of key/value pairs that make up the session hash for the controller.

```
# no params or session data
post :create

# with params
post :create, :id => 2

# with params and session data
post :create, { :id => 2 }, { :user_id => 99 }
```

The post() method comes directly from ActionController::TestCase, which offers similar methods for get, put, delete, head, and even xml_http_request requests. All but the xml_http_request and its alias, xhr, have the same signature as the post() method.

The xml_http_request() and xhr() methods introduce one additional argument to the front: the type of request to make. Then the other arguments are just shifted over. Here's an example:

```
# no params or session data
xhr :get, :index

# with params
xhr :get, :show, :id => 2

# with params and session data
xhr :get, :show, { :id => 2 }, { :user_id => 99 }
```

<u>**Isolation from View Templates**</u>

By default, controller specs do not render view templates. When we stub out the model layer as well, we can drive out controllers in complete isolation from the code in our views and models. This keeps the controller specs lean and reduces the noise involved with managing a web of dependencies in the view or the model. It also provides quick fault isolation. You'll always know that a failing controller spec means that the controller is not behaving correctly.

The one slight rub is that the view templates *do need to exist* even though we don't render them. This was not the case with RSpec-1/Rails-2, but the way in which ActionView locates templates changed sufficiently in Rails 3 that it didn't make sense to try to support isolation from even the existence of templates.

If you're more comfortable with the views being rendered, you can tell the spec to do so with the render_views() method:*

```
describe MessagesController do
  render_views
  ...
```

In this mode, controller specs are like Rails functional tests—one set of examples for both controllers and views. The benefit of this approach is that you get wider coverage from each spec. Experienced Rails developers may find this an easier approach to begin with; however, we encourage you to explore using the isolation mode and revel in its benefits.

---

*. integrate_views() in rspec-rails-1

render_template

We use the render_template() method to specify the template we expect a controller action to render. It takes a single argument—the path to the template that we are rendering.

The path argument can be in any of three forms. The first is the path to the template minus the app/views/ portion:

```
response.should render_template("messages/new")
```

The second is a shorthand form of the first. If the template being rendered is part of the controller being spec'd, you can pass in just the template name:

```
# this will expand to "messages/new" in a MessagesController spec
response.should render_template("new")
```

The third approach is to specify the full filename of the template to be rendered including the filename extension. This lets us specify that the controller should pick a template in the same way it does when the app runs. For example, we can set an expectation that the controller will find and render the messages/new.js.erb template when making a request for JavaScript:

```
# controller action
def new
  respond_to :js, :html
end

# in the spec
get :new, :format => "js"
response.should render_template("new.js.erb")
```

redirect_to

We use the redirect_to() method to specify that the action should redirect to a predefined location. It has the same API as its Rails' counterpart, assert_redirected_to().

```
# relying on route helpers
response.should redirect_to(messages_path)

# relying on ActiveRecord conventions
response.should redirect_to(@message)

# being specific
response.should redirect_to(:controller => "messages", :action => "new")
```

24.3 Specifying ApplicationController

We typically specify controller behavior directly through controller actions, but sometimes we want behavior applied to every controller and invoked indirectly. Perhaps we want to log every incoming request or add application-wide error handling. We don't want to specify this over and over again on every action, so let's explore a technique that allows us to specify these sorts of behaviors just once.

AccessDenied!

Let's add uniform error handling for AccessDenied exceptions. We'll start by creating spec/controllers/application_controller_spec.rb with the following content:

rails_controllers/messages/25/spec/controllers/application_controller_spec.rb

```ruby
require 'spec_helper'

describe ApplicationController do
  describe "handling AccessDenied exceptions" do
    it "redirects to the /401.html (access denied) page" do
      get :index
      response.should redirect_to('/401.html')
    end
  end
end
```

This should fail with the following:

```
Failure/Error: get :index
No route matches {:controller=>"application"}
```

In most controller specs, we write examples for controllers used directly in the app. Here we specify behavior of every controller's superclass, ApplicationController, which isn't exposed to the app.

controller DSL

To help us out with this situation, RSpec provides a simple DSL for creating an anonymous subclass of ApplicationController right in a spec. We need an index action, so we'll add that to the controller, programming it to raise the AccessDenied error that we're expecting in the example.

rails_controllers/messages/26/spec/controllers/application_controller spec.rb

```ruby
require 'spec_helper'

describe ApplicationController do
  controller do
    def index
      raise AccessDenied
    end
  end

  describe "handling AccessDenied exceptions" do
    it "redirects to the /401.html (access denied) page" do
      get :index
      response.should redirect_to('/401.html')
    end
  end
end
```

The controller() method also defines implicit routes for the controller so you don't have to set those up either. Now run the specs, and you should see this:

```
uninitialized constant AccessDenied
```

We can get past this by defining an AccessDenied exception. Create a file named lib/access_denied.rb with this content:

```
rails_controllers/messages/27/lib/access_denied.rb
```

```
class AccessDenied < StandardError
end
```

Now add this line to config/application.rb:

```
rails_controllers/messages/27/config/application.rb
```

```
config.autoload_paths += %W( #{config.root}/lib )
```

This tells Rails to autoload classes defined in files in the lib directory.

Now the spec fails with AccessDenied, which is the logical failure we want. All that's left to do is to rescue from the AccessDenied error and redirect to "/401.html" in ApplicationController:

```
rails_controllers/messages/28/app/controllers/application_controller.rb
```

```
class ApplicationController < ActionController::Base

  rescue_from AccessDenied, :with => :access_denied

protected

  def access_denied
    redirect_to "/401.html"
  end

end
```

Success! We now have 1 example, 0 failures.

24.4 What We've Learned

In this chapter, we learned the following:

- Controllers coordinate the interaction between the user and the application and should know *what* to do but not *how* to do it.

- Specifying the desired interaction helps us to discover objects with well-named methods to encapsulate the real work.

- Controller specs use a custom example group provided by the rspec-rails library.

- Controller specs live in a directory tree parallel to the controllers themselves and follow a naming convention of spec/controllers/my_controller_spec.rb for app/controllers/my_controller.rb.

- Use the redirect_to() matcher to confirm redirects.

- Use the render_template() matcher to confirm the template being rendered.

- Use the assigns() method to confirm the instance variables assigned for the view.

- Use the flash() method to confirm the flash messages stored for the view.

- Use mock_model() and stub_model() to isolate controller specs from the database and underlying business logic of your models.

Until this point we've been specifying the behavior of the Rails parts of our applications and using that process to discover the needs of our model. Well, here's where the rubber hits the road. In the next and final chapter of our exploration of RSpec and Rails, we'll take a close look at specifying the behavior of Rails' models.

If Rails controllers are like waiters in a restaurant, Rails models are the kitchen staff. They know how to cook a steak to order.
▶ Zach Dennis

Chapter 25

Rails Models

Rails models reflect the problem domain for which we're providing a software solution, and they vary significantly from app to app and from model to model. Some models will be rich objects with complex behavior, while others may be simple data containers.

When we work outside in, we *discover* model interfaces in Cucumber step definitions, view specs and views, and controller specs and controllers. These are the places we write *the code we wish we had*, and letting them guide us results in model interfaces that best suit the needs of the application.

Once we've learned what models we need, we can drive them out just as we would any type of object. In this chapter, we're going to do just that, building on the messaging application we've been working on in Chapter 24, *Rails Controllers*, on page 341 and Chapter 23, *Rails Views*, on page 327, using RSpec model specs to drive out the behavior of our models.

25.1 Writing Model Specs

Rails models are a lot closer to POROs[1] than Rails controllers and views. We can create them using new(), and we can call methods on them directly. This makes specs for Rails models a lot more straightforward. As you'll see, we approach them just like we did in the Codebreaker example in Part I of this book.

---

1. Plain old Ruby objects

There are some differences between Rails models and POROs, however, so RSpec offers a specialized ExampleGroup for specifying models. Similar to the ExampleGroups for controllers and views, the ModelExampleGroup wraps the behavior defined in ActiveRecord::TestCase. This gives us access to facilities like fixtures and, by default, wraps each example in a transaction so that our database is always in a known state at the beginning of each example.

We won't be able to answer every question about specifying Rails models in a single chapter, because there is certainly enough material here for an entire book. Our goal is to demonstrate some basic principles and guidelines that you can use as you work on your own applications. And with that, let's write some code.

Making It Real

In Chapter 23, *Rails Views*, on page 327, we used mock_model() to provide views with the code we wish we had. Now it's time to take what we learned about the requirements of the model and make it real. We know from the view specs that we need text and title attributes for instances of Message. Let's imagine they also lead us to want a recipient_id to represent the user who receives the message and that all of these fields are required for a Message to be considered valid.

We left off with a Message class that does not have any attributes, so we need a new migration. Rather than building up a migration by hand, let's roll back the database:

```
$ rake db:rollback
```

Now delete the create_messages migration (db/migrate/XXXXXXXXXXXXXX_create_messages.rb) and regenerate the model, like this:

```
$ script/rails generate model message title:string text:text recipient_id:integer
      invoke  active_record
      create    db/migrate/20100725145316_create_messages.rb
   identical    app/models/message.rb
      invoke    rspec
   identical      spec/models/message_spec.rb
$ rake db:migrate
$ rake db:test:prepare
```

Specifying Validations

Since we know what fields are required, we'll create pending examples for each of them to start.

Go ahead and replace the generated code in message_spec.rb with the following:

rails_models/messages/01/spec/models/message_spec.rb

```ruby
require 'spec_helper'

describe Message do
  it "is valid with valid attributes"

  it "is not valid without a title"

  it "is not valid without text"

  it "is not valid without a recipient"
end
```

The first example will make clear what it takes to produce a valid message and provide context for the other examples. Run that spec with rake spec:models or rspec spec/models, and you should see 4 examples, 0 failures, 4 pending. All four examples are pending, so let's implement the first example as follows:

rails_models/messages/01/spec/models/message_example1_spec.rb

```ruby
it "is valid with valid attributes" do
  Message.new.should be_valid
end
```

Run the spec again, and you should see 4 examples, 0 failures, 3 pending this time. The first example is passing without making any changes, because the model, by default, does not validate the presence of any attributes. Now implement the second example as follows:

rails_models/messages/01/spec/models/message_example2_spec.rb

```ruby
it "is not valid without a title" do
  message = Message.new :title => nil
  message.should_not be_valid
end
```

Now we have 4 examples, 1 failure, 2 pending, with the example we just implemented failing. Modify the model as follows to get it to pass:

rails_models/messages/02/app/models/message.rb

```ruby
class Message < ActiveRecord::Base
  validates_presence_of :title
end
```

The new example passes with that change, but we still have 4 examples, 1 failure, 2 pending. The is valid with valid attributes example is failing because we changed what it means for a Message to be valid. We'll need to update the example so that it constructs the Message with a title:

rails_models/messages/02/spec/models/message_example1_spec.rb

```
it "is valid with valid attributes" do
  Message.new(:title => "foo").should be_valid
end
```

Now we have 4 examples, 0 failures, 2 pending. The first two examples are both passing, so we've made some progress. Of course, we still have two pending examples, so implement the next example as follows:

rails_models/messages/02/spec/models/message_example2_spec.rb

```
it "is not valid without text" do
  message = Message.new :text => nil
  message.should_not be_valid
end
```

Run the spec, and we get 4 examples, 0 failures, 1 pending. Only one example pending means that we now have three examples passing. But wait a minute. Weren't we expecting this new example to fail? We were, but we're getting a false positive. The example passes because the model is invalid, but the model is invalid because it's missing the title attribute, not the text attribute that is the subject of the example. To expose this, update the example to supply a title:

rails_models/messages/02/spec/models/message_example3_spec.rb

```
it "is not valid without text" do
  message = Message.new :text => nil, :title => "foo"
  message.should_not be_valid
end
```

With that change, the third example now fails as expected, so make it pass by validating the presence of text in the model. Of course, once you do that, the is valid with valid attributes example will fail again because we only set it up with a title and it's validating the presence of text now as well. Update that example to provide both the title and text as follows:

rails_models/messages/02/spec/models/message_example4_spec.rb

```
it "is valid with valid attributes" do
  Message.new(:title => "foo", :text => "bar").should be_valid
end
```

Now we have 4 examples, 0 failures, 1 pending.

Looking back at the is not valid without text example, it seems odd that we have to specify a title attribute in an example for the text attribute. If we don't add a text attribute to the example for the title, we can never be certain that it's passing for the right reason. The examples are leaking! Let's refactor a bit before we move on to the last pending example.

Refactoring Leaky Examples

Each example is setting up the model in the appropriate state by supplying the proper attributes. This worked fine when we had only one attribute to worry about, but as soon as we added the second attribute, we ran into issues. If we keep heading down this path, we'll end up with verbose examples that are brittle and time-consuming to maintain.

Let's take the approach of setting up a valid message once, in a before(:each) block. This allows each example to configure the message with the appropriate state without having to worry about additional criteria used to set up a valid message.

The first example, is valid with valid attributes, is already building a valid message, so we can borrow its implementation. Create a before(:each) block, which assigns a valid Message to an @message instance variable:

rails_models/messages/03/spec/models/message_example1_spec.rb

```
describe Message do
  before(:each) do
    @message = Message.new(:title => "foo", :text => "bar")
  end

  it "is valid with valid attributes" do
    Message.new(:title => "foo", :text => "bar").should be_valid
  end
```

Run the spec, and you should see 4 examples, 0 failures, 1 pending. Now update the first example to rely on the @message instance variable instead of constructing its own message:

rails_models/messages/03/spec/models/message_example2_spec.rb

```
describe Message do
  before(:each) do
    @message = Message.new(:title => "foo", :text => "bar")
  end

  it "is valid with valid attributes" do
    @message.should be_valid
  end
```

The spec should still be passing, with one pending example. Update the second example also to rely on the @message instance variable:

rails_models/messages/03/spec/models/message_example3_spec.rb

```
it "is not valid without a title" do
▶   @message.title = nil
▶   @message.should_not be_valid
end
```

The spec should still have 4 examples, 0 failures, 1 pending. As we've refactored, we've made several changes that have not changed the result. Let's do a sanity check to make sure that everything is still wired up correctly. Comment out @message.title = nil in the second example, rerun the spec, and watch it fail with expected valid? to return false, got true.

With the second example failing for the right reason, uncomment that line, update the third example to rely on the @message instance variable, and then run the spec. With a green bar and three clean examples, we can implement the pending example, is not valid without a recipient:

rails_models/messages/03/spec/models/message_example4_spec.rb

```
it "is not valid without a recipient" do
▶   @message.recipient = nil
▶   @message.should_not be_valid
end
```

The example fails with undefined method 'recipient='. Although we have a recipient_id attribute on the Message model, we want recipient to be an association pointing to the user who's receiving the message. Let's define the association in the Message model:

rails_models/messages/04/app/models/message.rb

```
class Message < ActiveRecord::Base
▶   belongs_to :recipient, :class_name => "User"

    validates_presence_of :title, :text
end
```

Run the spec again, and now it's failing with the expected message: expected valid? to return false, got true. Update the Message model to require a recipient:

rails_models/messages/05/app/models/message.rb

```
class Message < ActiveRecord::Base
    belongs_to :recipient, :class_name => "User"

▶   validates_presence_of :title, :text, :recipient
end
```

The example we just wrote is passing now, but the first example is valid
with valid attributes is failing again because it doesn't account for the
recipient. We can fix this by giving the @message instance variable a
recipient:

rails_models/messages/05/spec/models/message_example1_spec.rb

```
   before(:each) do
▶    @message = Message.new(
▶      :title => "foo",
▶      :text => "bar",
▶      :recipient => mock_model("User")
▶    )
   end
```

We use mock_model() so we don't have to worry about generating the
User yet. Now all examples are passing: 4 examples, 0 failures. Here's the
full message_spec.rb:

rails_models/messages/05/spec/models/message_example2_spec.rb

```
require 'spec_helper'

describe Message do
  before(:each) do
    @message = Message.new(
      :title => "foo",
      :text => "bar",
      :recipient => mock_model("User")
    )
  end

  it "is valid with valid attributes" do
    @message.should be_valid
  end

  it "is not valid without a title" do
    @message.title = nil
    @message.should_not be_valid
  end

  it "is not valid without text" do
    @message.text = nil
    @message.should_not be_valid
  end

  it "is not valid without a recipient" do
    @message.recipient = nil
    @message.should_not be_valid
  end

end
```

> \\// **Joe Asks...**
> ?ç
> ~ <u>**Should I Spec Associations?**</u>
>
> Generally speaking, no. Well, not directly, anyhow. Associations should not be added unless they are serving the needs of some behavior. Consider an Order that calculates its total value from the sum of the cost of its Items. We might introduce a has_many :items association to satisfy the relevant examples. Since the association is being added to support the calculation that is being specified, there is no need to spec it directly.
>
> The same applies to association options. The :foreign_key or the :class_name options are structural, not behavioral. They're just part of wiring up the association, and an association that requires them won't work correctly without them, so there is no need to spec them directly either.

What We Just Did

We started with a migration for the messages table that included attributes we learned about while specifying other parts of the application. Then we drove the validation requirements of the Message model one example at a time. When the examples started to leak, we stopped adding functionality and refactored them so we could easily add the next example. This not only kept the examples DRY, but more importantly it kept them clear and focused.

In addition to the examples we wrote, we can use the spec to illustrate some basic conventions about model specs:

Directory organization The directory structure for model specs mimics the directory structure found in app/models/. For example, specs in spec/models/ will be for models in app/models/.

File naming Model specs are named after the model they provide examples for, with an _spec.rb appended to the filename. Thus, message.rb would have a corresponding spec named message_spec.rb.

require 'spec_helper' Every model spec will need to require the spec_helper.rb file. Otherwise, you will get errors about core rspec or rspec-rails methods not existing.

Now that we have the basic behavior of the Message model specified, let's introduce some business rules into the application.

25.2 Specifying Business Rules

In his article "Skinny Controller, Fat Model,"[2] Jamis Buck recommends pushing business logic down to the model, keeping views and controller actions lean. This guideline helps us to follow the Single Responsibility Principle by keeping controllers and views focused on application logic and keeping the models focused on business logic.

Express Business Rules in Models

Our message app works well for sending unlimited messages, but our customer wants users to sign up for subscriptions that limit the number of messages they can send in a month. We'll imagine that we've already expressed these new requirements in Cucumber scenarios, and we're ready to start driving out code that will satisfy them.

If you've been following along since Chapter 24, *Rails Controllers*, on page 341, the app has a MessagesController with a create() action that looks like this:

```
def create
  @message = Message.new(params[:message])
  if @message.save
    flash[:notice] = "The message was saved successfully."
    redirect_to :action => "index"
  else
    render :action => "new"
  end
end
```

In this design, the MessagesController is responsible for building and then saving a message. Because we are about to add some complexity to this functionality, now would be a good time to push that responsibility down to the model. We can do that by modifying the create() action so that it tells the current_user to send a message, rather than creating it directly in the action.

---

2. http://weblog.jamisbuck.org/2006/10/18/skinny-controller-fat-model

We're not going to make that change now, because we'd need to divert our focus to the controller and its specs, but here's an example of how it might look if we did make the change now:

```
# For discussion purposes only
def create
►   @message = current_user.send_message(params[:message])
►   if @message.new_record?
      flash[:notice] = "The message was saved successfully."
      redirect_to :action => "index"
    else
      render :action => "new"
    end
end
```

The line that sends the message not only helps push the logic to the model but is also a much better expression of what's really going on in the action. We're not just creating a message; we're sending one from the current user. This clarity is a small win, but as the code base grows, these little wins make an application much easier to understand and evolve.

Before we press forward, create a User model using the Rails' model generator:

```
script/rails generate model User login:string
rake db:migrate
rake db:test:prepare
```

User models usually need more than just a login attribute, like passwords, but we're not concerned with those aspects of a user right now. Now we're ready to drive out these new business rules.

Focus on Behavior

When thinking about models, it's tempting to jump ahead and think of all of the relationships and functionality we *just know* they're going to need. Developing models this way can lead to inconsistent APIs with far too many public methods and relationships, which then become hard to maintain.

Focusing on the behavior first leads to clean, cohesive models, so that's what we're going to do. Create a spec for the User model, which describes the behavior of send_message.

```ruby
require 'spec_helper'

describe User do

  describe "#send_message" do
    it "sends a message to another user"
  end

end
```

The happy path for send_message is that the user has not gone over the monthly limit and will be able to send a message to another user. Let's move this pending example into a new context() to better express this:

```ruby
require 'spec_helper'

describe User do

  describe "#send_message" do

    context "when the user is under their subscription limit" do
      it "sends a message to another user"
    end

  end

end
```

Now fill in the example with what we expect to happen when one user sends a message to another:

```ruby
describe "#send_message" do

  context "when the user is under their subscription limit" do

    it "sends a message to another user" do
      msg = zach.send_message(
        :recipient => david
      )
      david.received_messages.should == [msg]
    end

  end

end
```

Now that we've defined a clean interface for sending messages, we've run the spec, and it fails with undefined local variable or method 'zach'. With the expectation clear, let's supply the necessary setup for the example to run, starting with zach and david as local variables:

`rails_models/rules/01/spec/models/user_example4_spec.rb`

```
describe "#send_message" do

  context "when the user is under their subscription limit" do

    it "sends a message to another user" do
▶     zach = User.create!
▶     david = User.create!
      msg = zach.send_message(
        :recipient => david
      )
      david.received_messages.should == [msg]
    end

  end

end
```

Run the spec again, and the example fails with undefined method 'send_message'. Add an empty send_message() method to the User model:

`rails_models/rules/02/app/models/user.rb`

```
class User < ActiveRecord::Base

▶   def send_message(message_attrs)
▶   end

end
```

The example still fails, but now it's because of undefined method 'received_messages' on User. We need a received_messages association, so add that and run the spec:

`rails_models/rules/03/app/models/user.rb`

```
class User < ActiveRecord::Base
▶   has_many :received_messages, :class_name => Message.name,
▶     :foreign_key => "recipient_id"

  def send_message(message_attrs)
  end

end
```

Now the example fails because it expects david.received_messages() to return [msg] but got [] instead. To get this to pass, modify send_message() such that it creates a message using the message_attrs parameter. This is :recipient => david in our example.

`rails_models/rules/04/app/models/user.rb`

```ruby
class User < ActiveRecord::Base
  has_many :received_messages, :class_name => Message.name,
    :foreign_key => "recipient_id"

  def send_message(message_attrs)
    Message.create! message_attrs
  end

end
```

Run the spec, and it fails with Validation failed: Text can't be blank, Title can't be blank. This is happening because the Message validates the presence of the title and text attributes. Because send_message() is just passing the attributes hash to the Message constructor, we can include those attributes directly in the example:

`rails_models/rules/04/spec/models/user_example1_spec.rb`

```ruby
it "sends a message to another user" do
  zach = User.create!
  david = User.create!
  msg = zach.send_message(
    :title => "Book Update",
    :text => "Beta 11 includes great stuff!",
    :recipient => david
  )
  david.received_messages.should == [msg]
end
```

Voila! The spec is now passing with 1 example, 0 failures. We've added the title and text attributes to get the sends a message to another user example to pass, but what should happen to those attributes? Let's add an example that specifies that those values make their way to the Message:

`rails_models/rules/04/spec/models/user_example2_spec.rb`

```ruby
it "creates a new message with the submitted attributes" do
  zach = User.create!
  david = User.create!
  msg = zach.send_message(
    :title => "Book Update",
    :text => "Beta 11 includes great stuff!",
    :recipient => david
  )
  msg.title.should == "Book Update"
  msg.text.should == "Beta 11 includes great stuff!"
end
```

This passes right away, but that's OK in this case, because the example communicates a requirement of this method.

Additional Outcomes

At this point, a user can send a message to a recipient, but the sender has no way to review the messages he or she sent. We need to add an expectation that the sender is associated with the message as well as the recipient. Add an example to express that expectation:

rails_models/rules/04/spec/models/user_example3_spec.rb

```
context "when the user is under their subscription limit" do
▶   it "adds the message to the sender's sent messages"
  end
```

This example is similar to the example we just got passing, so let's copy its example body into the new example and change the expectation to look at the sender's sent_messages:

rails_models/rules/04/spec/models/user_example4_spec.rb

```
    it "adds the message to the sender's sent messages" do
      zach = User.create!
      david = User.create!
      msg = zach.send_message(
        :title => "Book Update",
        :text => "Beta 11 includes great stuff!",
        :recipient => david
      )
▶     zach.sent_messages.should == [msg]
    end
```

Running the spec results in the example failing with an undefined method 'sent_messages'. We'll need to add an association to make this pass. Also, the messages table doesn't have a sender_id field, so be sure to make a migration that adds it. Here's what the model should end up looking like:

rails_models/rules/05/app/models/user.rb

```
class User < ActiveRecord::Base
  has_many :received_messages, :class_name => Message.name,
    :foreign_key => "recipient_id"
▶ has_many :sent_messages, :class_name => Message.name,
▶   :foreign_key => "sender_id"

  def send_message(message_attrs)
    Message.create! message_attrs
  end

end
```

Execute the spec, and the example is still failing because it expects an array with one message but found an empty array. Now let's update the send_message() method implementation to use the sent_messages association to create the message:

`rails_models/rules/06/app/models/user.rb`

```
class User < ActiveRecord::Base
  has_many :received_messages, :class_name => Message.name,
    :foreign_key => "recipient_id"
  has_many :sent_messages, :class_name => Message.name,
    :foreign_key => "sender_id"

  def send_message(message_attrs)
►   sent_messages.create! message_attrs
  end

end
```

And we're back to green with 3 examples, 0 failures.

Tidy Up

Now we can safely clean up the duplication between the examples. To start, let's consolidate the creation of zach and david in one spot. Pull up the assignments of zach and david into a before(:each) block as instance variables:

`rails_models/rules/06/spec/models/user_example1_spec.rb`

```
describe "#send_message" do
►   before(:each) do
►     @zach = User.create!
►     @david = User.create!
►   end

    it "creates a new message with the submitted attributes" do
```

The spec should still be green, although we're not using the new instance variables. Update the first example, creates a new message with the submitted attributes, to rely on the instance variables:

`rails_models/rules/06/spec/models/user_example2_spec.rb`

```
it "creates a new message with the submitted attributes" do
►   msg = @zach.send_message(
      :title => "Book Update",
      :text => "Beta 11 includes great stuff!",
►     :recipient => @david
    )
    msg.title.should == "Book Update"
    msg.text.should == "Beta 11 includes great stuff!"
  end
```

Run the spec, make sure it's still green, and then update the other two examples to use the instance variables. When you're done, the spec should still be at a green bar, 3 examples, 0 failures.

With specs for the happy path passing with the supporting code implemented, now it's time to start exploring the edge cases. We'll begin with what happens when the user exceeds their subscription's monthly limit.

Edge Cases

When we tell a User to send a message, a record is created in the messages table. We can use that knowledge to specify what happens when a message is not sent: it should not create a record in the messages table. Let's express that in a new example in user_spec.rb:

```
rails_models/rules/06/spec/models/user_example3_spec.rb
context "when the user is over their subscription limit" do
  it "does not create a message" do
    lambda {
      @zach.send_message(
        :title => "Book Update",
        :text => "Beta 11 includes great stuff!",
        :recipient => @david
      )
    }.should_not change(Message, :count)
  end
end
```

Run the spec, and watch that new example fail with count should not have changed, but did. We need to set up the example so the user has already reached their subscription limit. Writing the code we wish we had, we might end up with something like this in send_message():

```
def send_message(message_attrs)
  if subscription.can_send_message?
    sent_messages.create message_attrs
  end
end
```

This lets the subscription dictate whether a message can be sent on a user-by-user basis. Run that, and you'll see four failures with undefined local variable or method `subscription`. We have a few different things to do to get this to pass, so let's back that change out and run the examples again to make sure they're all passing.

Introduce a before(:each) block inside the context that utilizes a *stub* to ensure a user can't send a message:

```
rails_models/rules/06/spec/models/user_example4_spec.rb
```

```
context "when the user is over their subscription limit" do
▶   before(:each) do
▶     @zach.subscription = Subscription.new
▶     @zach.subscription.stub(:can_send_message?).and_return false
▶   end

    it "does not create a message" do
      lambda {
        @zach.send_message(
          :title => "Book Update",
          :text => "Beta 11 includes great stuff!",
          :recipient => @david
        )
      }.should_not change(Message, :count)
    end
end
```

Now the latest example fails with uninitialized constant Subscription. We need a Subscription model and a migration that generates the subscriptions table and a subscription_id on the users table. Go ahead and add all that, run rake db:migrate && rake db:test:prepare, and then the example should fail with an undefined method 'subscription=' . Now let's add a Subscription association to the User model:

```
rails_models/rules/08/app/models/user.rb
```

```
▶ belongs_to :subscription
```

The spec should be back to the original failure, count should not have changed, but did. Update send_message to rely on the stubbed can_send_message?() method:

```
rails_models/rules/09/app/models/user.rb
```

```
▶ def send_message(message_attrs)
▶   if subscription.can_send_message?
▶     sent_messages.create! message_attrs
▶   end
▶ end
```

The does not create a message example should now be passing, but the other three are failing. We're relying on the subscription to determine when messages can be sent, so we'll need to update @zach to be able to send messages for the failing examples.

Add the following before block to the context for the failing examples:

rails_models/rules/10/spec/models/user_spec.rb

```
context "when the user is under their subscription limit" do
▶   before(:each) do
▶     @zach.subscription = Subscription.new
▶     @zach.subscription.stub(:can_send_message?).and_return true
▶   end
```

Run the spec; you should have 4 examples, 0 failures. Right now the two inner before blocks give @zach a Subscription. Let's remove the duplication by pulling up the subscription assignment to the outer before block:

rails_models/rules/10/spec/models/user_example1_spec.rb

```
describe "#send_message" do
  before(:each) do
▶     @zach = User.create! :subscription => Subscription.new
    @david = User.create!
  end

  context "when the user is under their subscription limit" do
    before(:each) do
      @zach.subscription.stub(:can_send_message?).and_return true
    end
```

Run the spec again; it should still be green with 4 examples, 0 failures. This wraps up the User model, given our current needs. Next up: specify the can_send_message?() method on the Subscription model.

25.3 Exercise

As you can see from the work we've done so far, model specs are not all that different from the kind of specs we would write for any PORO. We have a little bit of work left to satisfy the requirement of limiting the number of messages sent in a month, and we're going to leave this work as an exercise for you.

All that remains to satisfy the requirement is to implement the can_send_message?() method on Subscription. To control how many messages can be sent in a month, the subscription will need to know how many messages have already been sent. We can build two different sets of examples from this information:

- When a user has not exceeded the limit for the month

- When a user has exceeded the limit for the month

Assume, for now, that Subscription.has_one(:user). Create a Subscription spec with these contexts for the can_send_message?() method.

```
rails_models/rules/11/spec/models/subscription_example2_spec.rb
```

```ruby
describe "#can_send_message?" do
  context "when a user has not reached the subscription limit for the month" do
▶    it "returns true"
  end

  context "when a user has reached the subscription limit for the month" do
▶    it "returns false"
  end
end
```

Now go forth and write failing examples, get them to pass, and refactor your code! Be sure to keep the cycles small and keep the example and implementation code clean and readable. Don't worry too much about whether you get the perfect examples or code. The important thing is that you use the opportunity to get more comfortable with the red/green/refactor cycle of TDD.

25.4 Useful Tidbits

In addition to what we've just gone through, here are a few more pieces of useful information you can employ when writing model specs.

DB or Not DB

The model specs we've written have all relied on interaction with a database. This is one way to write model specs, but it's not the only way. We can also disconnect model specs from a database. You may be wondering why would you want to do that. Well, speed!

Hitting a database for each example takes time. Connections need to be made, queries need to be sent/parsed/optimized/executed, and results need to be returned. Over time, a project accumulates more models and more behavior, and models specs can easily go from taking a few seconds to several minutes. And the longer they take, the *less we tend to run them*. This works against our effort to produce quality code quickly.

There are many cases in which we write examples for business logic that happens to belong in a model but doesn't require a database. Removing the database bottleneck when we don't need it can speed things up considerably.

The rspec-rails library doesn't provide a way to do this natively, but we can look to libraries such as Dan Manges' UnitRecord[3] and Avdi Grimm's NullDb[4] for help. They both disconnect specs from the database by using the schema.rb to supply information about the tables and attributes that models rely on.

There are times, however, when we want to interact with the database to expose behavior or to boost confidence that an example is actually exercising something. UnitRecord and NullDb both provide ways for examples to interact with a database for these cases. This gives us the best of both worlds. Speed takes priority by default, but we can access a database when we need it.

Test Data Builders

Test data builders give us a centralized mechanism we can use to construct objects in code examples. They allow for variability in the test data being created, which in Rails typically means accepting overriding values via a hash.

The Test Data Builder pattern separates the construction of an object from its representation so the construction process can be reused. This can turn an overly verbose and obfuscated example into a clear, easy-to-read example.

Here's an overly verbose example that obfuscates the important part of the example. It's hard to tell that the :text attribute is important:

```
it "is not valid ..." do
  message = Message.create!(
    :title => "some title",
    :text => "some text",
    :recipient => User.create!(
      :login => "bob",
      :password => "password",
      :password_confirmation => "password"
    )
  )
  ...
end
```

Here's what the construction of the message in this example would look like using test data builder libraries designed specifically to work with

---

3. http://github.com/dan-manges/unit-record/tree/master
4. http://nulldb.rubyforge.org

ActiveRecord. They all remove unnecessary verbosity, increase readability, and make it immediately apparent that the :text attribute is important to the example:

```
# Fixjour and FixtureReplacement
message = create_message(:text => "some text")

# FactoryGirl
message = Factory(:message, :text => "some text")

# ObjectDaddy
message = Message.generate(:text => "some text")

# Machinist
message = Message.make(:text => "some text")
```

Fixjour, FixtureReplacement, FactoryGirl, Machinist, and ObjectDaddy are all battle-tested and offer mature APIs, relying on convention and offering namespaces, declarative methods, sequences, association support, and DSL-like definitions.

Custom Macros

We can write custom macros for model specs using the same techniques we employed in Chapter 24, *Rails Controllers*, on page 341.

- Identify an example or group of examples to pull into a macro

- Extract the example(s) into a method on a module

- Update spec/spec_helper.rb to include the module

- Update the spec to use the macro

Matchers

rspec-rails provides some additional matchers that can be useful in model specs.

be_valid

The be_valid() matcher is used to set the expectation that your model is or is not valid:

```
model.should be_valid
model.should_not be_valid
```

error_on and errors_on

The error_on() and errors_on() methods extend RSpec's have() matcher for use with ActiveRecord models in order to set an expectation that a particular attribute has an error or not. It will call valid?() on the model in order to prepare the errors.

```
model.should have(:no).errors_on(:title)
model.should have(1).error_on(:body)
model.should have(2).errors_on(:caption)
```

record and records

The record() and records() methods also extend the have() matcher for use with ActiveRecord models. These let us set an expectation of the number of records. It calls find(:all) on the model in order to determine the count.

```
ModelClass.should have(:no).records
ModelClass.should have(1).record
```

Writing Your Own

You can always write your own matchers when you find yourself duplicating the same expectation in multiple examples or in a more verbose way than you'd like. The techniques to write custom matchers for ActiveRecord models are the same that you learned in Section 16.7, *Custom Matchers*, on page 229.

25.5 What We've Learned

Throughout this chapter we focused on the behavior of models by setting clear expectations through examples. By combining the outside-in approach with our knowledge of Rails, we were able to write good clean specs while still taking advantage of ActiveRecord benefits in our implementation.

- Models reflect the problem domain for which you're providing a software solution, and they vary significantly from model to model and from app to app.

- Models house the domain logic for an application.

- Models in Rails usually refer to ActiveRecord models, although you may find you create models that are straight-up POROs.

- Model specs use a custom example group provided by the rspec-rails library.

- Model specs live in a directory tree parallel to the models themselves and follow a naming convention of spec/model/my_model_spec.rb for app/model/my_model.rb.

- Focusing on model behavior while taking advantage of ActiveRecord-provided features can save time and effort.

- Use mock_model() and stub_model() to isolate controller specs from the database and underlying business logic of your models.

- Test data builder libraries can be used to reduce unneeded verbosity and improve clarity, maintainability of specs, and even step definitions for Cucumber scenarios.

- You can extract duplication and common patterns in your model specs into custom macros and matchers using the same techniques you'd use for view specs and controller specs.

- rspec-rails provides a few helpful ActiveRecord matchers to make writing model examples more expressive: be_valid(), errors_on(), and records().

RubySpec

by Brian Ford

Ruby is a fabulous language. The first time I encountered it was around 1997 in response to a friend who was singing the praises of Python. I missed the part about blocks in the README and read the part about the Perl-ish globals. I had recently tried to learn Perl and I hated it, so I closed the file and went back to Python. Fortunately, when I found *Programming Ruby* on the Web, I gave it another try and was smitten after the first couple chapters. Maybe it was all the Python.

As great as Ruby is, there were two things that bothered me. It wasn't that fast, a fact that others never tire of pointing out. And the implementation was not very sophisticated. Early on, I had signed up to the YARV English-language developer mailing list but never got past just checking out the source and building.

Then I heard about Rubinius, a project attempting to write a Ruby implementation from scratch and to write as much of it as possible in Ruby. Further, this guy Evan Phoenix talked about test-driving the development. I was intrigued.

On another front, I had been eagerly following RSpec since Dave Astels' blog post, "A New Look at Test-Driven Development," and Steven Baker's first implementation. I was convinced it was an excellent way to test Ruby code, and I was using it almost exclusively for all the Rails projects I was working on.

These two threads came together in the question, How do you write a completely new implementation of Ruby and ensure that it performs exactly as the existing one? In my mind, there was only one answer.

I asked Evan in the #rubinius IRC channel if it was acceptable to write RSpec specs for Rubinius. Ever adventurous, he replied, "Sure, go ahead."

RubySpec was born.

A.1 The Project

The goal of RubySpec is to write a complete, executable specification for the Ruby programming language. RubySpec attempts to capture the behavior of the reference implementation of Ruby, generally referred to as MRI for Matz's Ruby Implementation. RubySpec intends to support compatibility, development, and experimentation among the alternative Ruby implementations.

Compatibility among the Ruby implementations is essential to prevent fragmentation in the community. There will inevitably be some incompatibilities, but they will be small. There is no reason that the vast majority of Ruby language features, and hence the vast majority of programs, cannot perform the same on different implementations.

There are sure to be pros and cons for each implementation, but those will not have the same importance during the life of a Ruby application. Consider developing an application and then determining that a particular client would benefit from integrating a .NET library. You simply install IronRuby and launch the application on it. How do you know it will work? Because IronRuby passes the RubySpecs. Granted, this is somewhat idealized right now, but that is the intent of the project.

RubySpec aids development immensely. How else would you know what works and what does not? The tens of thousands of expectations in the RubySpecs indicate exactly what to do. And when there are regressions, you know about it immediately.

Finally, the RubySpecs encourage experimentation. To experiment, you need code examples that are sufficiently decoupled from the implementation. Since RubySpec is run by every major implementation, there is continual pressure, assuring that the examples truly spec the interface of the Ruby language features.

A.2 Syntax

One of the most important goals of a test suite is communication. This is also one of the greatest challenges. Indeed, communication is always a challenge. Anything that helps the process is welcome. For RubySpec, we have the four C's to describe the quality of the specs: correct, clear, consistent, and concise. These are ordered by priority. The specs must be correct above all. The next most important characteristic is clarity. Consistency is an invaluable aid to communication, but consistency will be trumped by clarity. Conciseness is also an aid to communication, but a slightly more verbose spec will be preferred if it is more consistent with similar specs.

The RSpec syntax provides an essential tool for communication through the specs. The describe block avoids the pressure of choosing a descriptive test subclass name while the string for the block provides essential documentation about the purpose of the grouping. The it block string reads naturally in English with normal punctuation. Even the simplest code examples may have semantic nuances that can be explained only with natural language. The combination of example block strings and the code they contain provide the optimum information from two perspectives to communicate the meaning and purpose of the spec.

Not only is the syntax of RSpec better for communicating, but the implementation of a very simplistic harness for running specs is quite straightforward. It requires defining methods on classes and calling those methods. There is no need for the reflective methods that a Test:: Unit-like harness requires.

The following is the actual code for the first minispec runner that we used in Rubinius:

```ruby
# minispec
#
# Very minimal set of features to support specs like this:
#
# context "Array" do
#   specify "should respond to new" do
#     Array.new.should == []
#   end
# end

class PositiveSpec
  def initialize(obj)
    @obj = obj
  end

  def ==(other)
    if @obj != other
      raise Exception.new("equality expected")
    end
  end
end
```

```ruby
class NegativeSpec
  def initialize(obj)
    @obj = obj
  end

  def ==(other)
    if @obj == other
      raise Exception.new("inequality expected")
    end
  end
end

class Object
  def should
    PositiveSpec.new(self)
  end

  def should_not
    NegativeSpec.new(self)
  end
end

def specify(msg)
  print '.'
  begin
    yield
  rescue Exception => e
    print msg
    print " FAILED\n"
    print e.message
    print "\n"
  end
end

def context(msg)
  yield
end
```

This simple code uses no advanced Ruby language features and requires almost no support from the Ruby core library. It relies only on the ability to create classes and define methods, instantiate objects, call methods with arguments, yield to blocks, and raise exceptions. It is also quite limited, providing only for checking equality or inequality. However, this tiny set of features enabled us to write a very large number of specs.

A.3 Guards

In an ideal world, there would be a single version of Ruby that runs identically on any hardware platform and operating system and, of course, has no bugs. For better or worse, we don't inhabit an ideal world. And neither does RubySpec. Consequently, there must exist some method for dealing with different byte orderings, word sizes, operating system services, versions, bugs, and implementations.

For this purpose, RubySpec provides block-based helpers called *guards*. There are four basic categories of guard. These are document platform, version, implementation differences, and bugs in MRI.

The guards function by yielding to the block based on the environment in which the specs are executing. The guards also provide visually consistent documentation as an essential part of the code examples that comprise the specs. Since the guards function by yielding or not, they work fine with RSpec without it knowing anything about them.

The following spec illustrates using the ruby_bug guard. Since bugs in MRI are discovered after a particular version of MRI has been released, RubySpec needs a way to prevent those specs from running on MRI as well as ensuring that the correct behavior is implemented both in later versions of MRI and in all alternative implementations. The ruby_bug guard requires a ticket number and a version string. The guard will yield on all alternative implementations and on any version of MRI greater than the versions listed.

```
describe "Array#==" do
  ruby_bug "#11585", "1.8" do
    it "calls to_ary on its argument" do
      obj = mock('to_ary') obj.should_receive(:to_ary).and_return([1, 2, 3])
      [1, 2, 3].should == obj
    end
  end
end
```

There are a variety of other guards for platform differences and for features that alternative implementations comply with, deviate from, or extend. The guards essentially permit multiple, mutually exclusive versions of RubySpec to be combined in one place. This aids in understanding all the variations of behavior of a particular Ruby feature.

A.4 Extensibility

As useful and as simple as the describe/it syntax is, there are situations where a more suitable syntax is possible. The subtle simplicity of the block-based structure of the RSpec syntax was illustrated in the RubySpec guards. The Rubinius compiler specs are another example.

Basically, a compiler is a formal transformation from one data form to another that preserves meaning. An ideal syntax allows for juxtaposing the various forms while verification occurs behind the scenes. This maintains the declarative nature of the specs and minimizes visual noise.

Currently, the Rubinius compiler specs contain three forms: the Ruby source code, the parsed s-expression, and a representation of the stack-based instruction set. The additional syntax correlates or groups these forms. The word chosen for the grouping block is relates.

The following examples show the Ruby code in both double-quoted string format and as a heredoc. The describe block groups as normal, while the relates block introduces the Ruby code and groups the various representations.

```ruby
describe "A Call node" do
  relates "self.method" do
    parse do
      [:call, [:self], :method, [:arglist]]
    end


    compile do |g|
      g.push :self g.send :method, 0, false
    end
  end
end

describe "A Class node" do
  relates <<-ruby do
    class X < Array
    end
  ruby

    parse do
      [:class, :X, [:const, :Array], [:scope]]
    end

    compile do |g|
      g.push_const :Array
      g.open_class :X
    end
  end
end
```

The parse and compile helpers are creating examples programmatically. This is apparent when running the specs with specdoc output.

```
A Class node
- is parsed from
    class X < Object
    end
- is compiled from
    class X < Object
    end
```

In the future, we will likely extend these examples with, for example, helpers such as ast, llvm, or asm that represent the abstract syntax tree (AST) nodes, LLVM IR, or machine code from the JIT compiler. The format provides for visually comparing the various forms as well as easily writing them.

A.5 MSpec

MSpec is a simple, modular, event-driven, and purpose-built framework that supports the RSpec syntax for code examples, commonly known as *specs*.

RSpec, like Ruby itself, is both an implementation and a standard. RSpec presents a particular syntax for writing specs. MSpec replaces the implementation while conforming to the syntax.

MSpec is purpose built. It has to be because it must be able to run in a hostile proto-environment where many beloved Ruby language features don't yet exist. MSpec makes assumptions that are reasonable for its use but not reasonable for general Ruby applications. MSpec is not intended to, nor does it aspire to, serve as an alternative to RSpec— unless you're running the RubySpecs.

MSpec provides a number of command-line scripts for working with RubySpec. The mspec script runs the specs and provides options for choosing which implementation to run the specs, selecting which specs to run, and selecting how to format the output. There is also the mspec-ci script that excludes from running the specs tagged as failing, and the mspec-tag script that aids in adding and removing tag metadata.

A.6 Tags

Implementing Ruby is a long and arduous road. Along the way, it would be nice to know precisely which specs are expected to pass. However, that information is metadata, and it has nothing to do with the correctness of a spec. One implementation may fail a spec that other implementations pass. Constantly editing the specs to add and remove this sort of metadata would severely limit the utility of RubySpec by introducing too much churn and confusion in the specs.

The need to associate metadata with the specs prompted the idea of tags. The tags are contained in files in a different directory where each tag file corresponds to a particular spec file. By locating the tag files in a different directory tree, the various Ruby implementations can share the specs but maintain their own set of tags.

Tags have three components: name, comment, and description. The comment is the part inside (and including) the parentheses. The comment is optional. The comment is any arbitrary textual data to associate with the tag. It could be a bug number, platform note, or benchmark time. The name is the part preceding the comment. It is essentially a category, and certain names have special meaning for the runner scripts. For example, fails and critical are tags that will cause mspec-ci to exclude specs tagged by these names from running. The description is a string that is concatenated from the strings for the describe block and the it block. For example, the following is a failing spec tag:

```
fails(#538):Array#at returns the item at an index
```

The one limitation of this approach to adding metadata to the specs is that if the spec strings are changed, existing tags are no longer related to the spec whose string changed. In practice, this has not been a significant issue. The mspec-tag script has an option to purge tags that no longer refer to specs.

A.7 Community

We have been using RubySpec in Rubinius for nearly four years. During that time, the development of Rubinius has progressed at a high velocity. The stability provided by RubySpec has unequivocally contributed to that velocity. RubySpec has also provided an easy path for many people to begin contributing to Rubinius.

The Ruby community in general benefits from the availability of numerous alternative implementations. In almost every environment niche today, there is a working Ruby implementation, whether it is Java or .NET, Windows or Linux, or traditional desktop/laptop computers or mobile phones. Ruby developers benefit from each of these implementations behaving the same. Users of software written in Ruby benefit from software that performs correctly, and such software is easier to write when there are not arbitrary implementation differences. Despite that some competition exists between implementations, RubySpec reminds us that we are all working toward a higher goal, bringing the beauty of the Ruby language to as many developers as want to use it.

That being said, there is still a significant amount of work to do. Ruby is still evolving, and there are still many rather arbitrary platform differences that unnecessarily complicate developers' lives. For example, the differences between Ruby on Windows and Ruby on other platforms can be painful. Also, there are pressures on some platforms to prize special features over compatibility with MRI, the Ruby standard implementation. These pressures can lead to fragmentation of the Ruby community. RubySpec provides a means to keep these forces in check but only if the Ruby community widely prizes a consistent definition of Ruby and is vocal about requiring that Ruby implementers faithfully adhere to the standard specification.

Everyone has a role to play in making Ruby an even better language. RubySpec has a part to play in that endeavor. Those of us working on RubySpec hope you will join us in improving both RubySpec and Ruby.

RSpec's Built-in Expectations

Here is a summary of all the expectations that are supported directly by RSpec.

Equality

Expression	Passes If...
actual.should equal(expected)	actual.equal?(expected)
actual.should eql(expected)	actual.eql?(expected)
actual.should == expected	actual == expected

Expression	Passes Unless...
actual.should_not equal(expected)	actual.equal?(expected)
actual.should_not eql(expected)	actual.eql?(expected)
actual.should_not == expected	actual == expected

Arbitrary Predicates

Expression	Passes If...
actual.should be_[predicate]	actual.predicate?
actual.should be_a_[predicate]	actual.predicate?
actual.should be_an_[predicate]	actual.predicate?

Expression	Passes If...
actual.should be_[predicate](*args)	actual.predicate?(*args)
actual.should be_a_[predicate](*args)	actual.predicate?(*args)
actual.should be_an_[predicate](*args)	actual.predicate?(*args)

Arbitrary Predicates (continued)

Expression	Passes Unless...
actual.should_not be_[predicate]	actual.predicate?
actual.should_not be_a_[predicate]	actual.predicate?
actual.should_not be_an_[predicate]	actual.predicate?

Expression	Passes Unless...
actual.should_not be_[predicate](*args)	actual.predicate?(*args)
actual.should_not be_a_[predicate](*args)	actual.predicate?(*args)
actual.should_not be_an_[predicate](*args)	actual.predicate?(*args)

Regular Expressions

Expression	Passes If...
actual.should match(expected)	actual.match?(expected)
actual.should =~ expected	actual =~ expected

Expression	Passes Unless...
actual.should_not match(expected)	actual.match?(expected)
actual.should_not =~ expected	actual =~ expected

Comparisons

Expression	Passes If...
actual.should be < expected	actual < expected
actual.should be <= expected	actual <= expected
actual.should be >= expected	actual >= expected
actual.should be > expected	actual > expected

Collections

Expression	Passes If...
actual.should include(expected)	actual.include?(expected)
actual.should have(n).items	actual.items.length == n or actual.items.size == n
actual.should have_exactly(n).items	actual.items.length == n or actual.items.size == n
actual.should have_at_least(n).items	actual.items.length >= n or actual.items.size >= n
actual.should have_at_most(n).items	actual.items.length <= n or actual.items.size <= n

Collections (continued)

Expression	Passes Unless...
actual.should_not include(expected)	actual.include?(expected)
actual.should_not have(n).items	actual.items.length == n or actual.items.size == n
actual.should_not have_exactly(n).items	actual.items.length == n or actual.items.size == n

Errors

Expression	Passes If...
proc.should raise_error	proc raises any error
proc.should raise_error(type)	raises specified type of error
proc.should raise_error(message)	raises error with specified message
proc.should raise_error(type, message)	raises specified type of error with specified message

Expression	Passes Unless...
proc.should_not raise_error	proc raises any error
proc.should_not raise_error(type)	raises specified type of error
proc.should_not raise_error(message)	raises error with specified message
proc.should_not raise_error(type, message)	raises specified type of error with specified message

Symbols

Expression	Passes If...
proc.should throw_symbol	proc throws any symbol
proc.should throw_symbol(type)	proc throws specified symbol

Expression	Passes Unless...
proc.should_not throw_symbol	proc throws any symbol
proc.should_not throw_symbol(type)	proc throws specified symbol

Floating-Point Comparisons

Expression	Passes If...
actual.should be_close(expected, delta)	actual > (expected - delta) and < (expected + delta)

Expression	Passes Unless...
actual.should_not be_close(expected, delta)	actual < (expected + delta) and > (expected - delta)

Contracts

Expression
actual.should respond_to(*messages)

Passes If...
messages.each { |m| actual.respond_to?(m) }

Expression
actual.should_not respond_to(*messages)

Passes Unless...
messages.each { |m| actual.respond_to?(m) }

When All Else Fails...

Expression
actual.should satisfy { |actual| block }

Passes If...
the block returns true

Expression
actual.should_not satisfy { |actual| block }

Passes Unless...
the block returns true

Appendix C

Bibliography

[Bec02]   Kent Beck. *Test Driven Development: By Example.* Addison-Wesley, Reading, MA, 2002.

[Coh04]   Mike Cohn. *User Stories Applied: For Agile Software Development.* Boston, MA, Addison-Wesley Professional, 2004.

[Eva03]   Eric Evans. *Domain-Driven Design: Tackling Complexity in the Heart of Software.* Addison-Wesley Professional, Reading, MA, first edition, 2003.

[FBB⁺99]   Martin Fowler, Kent Beck, John Brant, William Opdyke, and Don Roberts. *Refactoring: Improving the Design of Existing Code.* Addison Wesley Longman, Reading, MA, 1999.

[HT00]   Andrew Hunt and David Thomas. *The Pragmatic Programmer: From Journeyman to Master.* Addison-Wesley, Reading, MA, 2000.

[JAH02]   Ron Jeffries, Ann Anderson, and Chet Hendrickson. *Extreme Programming Installed.* Addison-Wesley, Reading, MA, 2002.

[Mes07]   Gerard Meszaros. *xUnit Test Patterns: Refactoring Test Code.* Addison-Wesley, Reading, MA, 2007.

[MRB97]   Robert C. Martin, Dirk Riehle, and Frank Buschmann. *Pattern Languages of Program Design 3.* Addison-Wesley Professional, Boston, MA, 1997.

[Rai04]   J. B. Rainsberger. *JUnit Recipes : Practical Methods for Programmer Testing.* Manning Publications Co., Greenwich, CT, 2004.

[TFH05]   David Thomas, Chad Fowler, and Andrew Hunt. *Programming Ruby: The Pragmatic Programmers' Guide.* The Pragmatic Programmers, LLC, Raleigh, NC, and Dallas, TX, second edition, 2005.

[TFH08]   David Thomas, Chad Fowler, and Andrew Hunt. *Programming Ruby: The Pragmatic Programmers' Guide.* The Pragmatic Programmers, LLC, Raleigh, NC, and Dallas, TX, third edition, 2008.

Index

D

F

The Pragmatic Bookshelf

Available in paperback and DRM-free eBooks, our titles are here to help you stay on top of your game. The following are in print as of October 2010; be sure to check our website at pragprog.com for newer titles.

Title	Year	ISBN	Pages
Advanced Rails Recipes: 84 New Ways to Build Stunning Rails Apps	2008	9780978739225	464
Agile Coaching	2009	9781934356432	248
Agile Retrospectives: Making Good Teams Great	2006	9780977616640	200
Agile Web Development with Rails	2009	9781934356166	792
Beginning Mac Programming: Develop with Objective-C and Cocoa	2010	9781934356517	300
Behind Closed Doors: Secrets of Great Management	2005	9780976694021	192
Best of Ruby Quiz	2006	9780976694076	304
Cocoa Programming: A Quick-Start Guide for Developers	2010	9781934356302	450
Core Animation for Mac OS X and the iPhone: Creating Compelling Dynamic User Interfaces	2008	9781934356104	200
Core Data: Apple's API for Persisting Data on Mac OS X	2009	9781934356326	256
Data Crunching: Solve Everyday Problems using Java, Python, and More	2005	9780974514079	208
Debug It! Find, Repair, and Prevent Bugs in Your Code	2009	9781934356289	232
Deploying Rails Applications: A Step-by-Step Guide	2008	9780978739201	280
Design Accessible Web Sites: 36 Keys to Creating Content for All Audiences and Platforms	2007	9781934356029	336
Desktop GIS: Mapping the Planet with Open Source Tools	2008	9781934356067	368
Domain-Driven Design Using Naked Objects	2009	9781934356449	375
Enterprise Integration with Ruby	2006	9780976694069	360
Enterprise Recipes with Ruby and Rails	2008	9781934356234	416
Everyday Scripting with Ruby: for Teams, Testers, and You	2007	9780977616619	320
ExpressionEngine 2: A Quick-Start Guide	2010	9781934356524	250
From Java To Ruby: Things Every Manager Should Know	2006	9780976694090	160
FXRuby: Create Lean and Mean GUIs with Ruby	2008	9781934356074	240

Continued on next page

Title	Year	ISBN	Pages
GIS for Web Developers: Adding Where to Your Web Applications	2007	9780974514093	275
Google Maps API: Adding Where to Your Applications	2006	PDF-Only	83
Grails: A Quick-Start Guide	2009	9781934356463	200
Groovy Recipes: Greasing the Wheels of Java	2008	9780978739294	264
Hello, Android: Introducing Google's Mobile Development Platform	2010	9781934356562	320
Interface Oriented Design	2006	9780976694052	240
iPad Programming: A Quick-Start Guide for iPhone Developers	2010	9781934356579	248
iPhone SDK Development	2009	9781934356258	576
Land the Tech Job You Love	2009	9781934356265	280
Language Implementation Patterns: Create Your Own Domain-Specific and General Programming Languages	2009	9781934356456	350
Learn to Program	2009	9781934356364	240
Manage It! Your Guide to Modern Pragmatic Project Management	2007	9780978739249	360
Manage Your Project Portfolio: Increase Your Capacity and Finish More Projects	2009	9781934356296	200
Mastering Dojo: JavaScript and Ajax Tools for Great Web Experiences	2008	9781934356111	568
Metaprogramming Ruby: Program Like the Ruby Pros	2010	9781934356470	240
Modular Java: Creating Flexible Applications with OSGi and Spring	2009	9781934356401	260
No Fluff Just Stuff 2006 Anthology	2006	9780977616664	240
No Fluff Just Stuff 2007 Anthology	2007	9780978739287	320
Pomodoro Technique Illustrated: The Easy Way to Do More in Less Time	2009	9781934356500	144
Practical Programming: An Introduction to Computer Science Using Python	2009	9781934356272	350
Practices of an Agile Developer	2006	9780974514086	208
Pragmatic Guide to Git	2010	9781934356722	168
Pragmatic Project Automation: How to Build, Deploy, and Monitor Java Applications	2004	9780974514031	176
Pragmatic Thinking and Learning: Refactor Your Wetware	2008	9781934356050	288
Pragmatic Unit Testing in C# with NUnit	2007	9780977616671	176
Pragmatic Unit Testing in Java with JUnit	2003	9780974514017	160
Pragmatic Version Control using CVS	2003	9780974514000	176
Pragmatic Version Control Using Git	2008	9781934356159	200
Pragmatic Version Control using Subversion	2006	9780977616657	248

Continued on next page

Title	Year	ISBN	Pages
Programming Clojure	2009	9781934356333	304
Programming Cocoa with Ruby: Create Compelling Mac Apps Using RubyCocoa	2009	9781934356197	300
Programming Erlang: Software for a Concurrent World	2007	9781934356005	536
Programming Groovy: Dynamic Productivity for the Java Developer	2008	9781934356098	320
Programming Ruby: The Pragmatic Programmers' Guide	2004	9780974514055	864
Programming Ruby 1.9: The Pragmatic Programmers' Guide	2009	9781934356081	960
Programming Scala: Tackle Multi-Core Complexity on the Java Virtual Machine	2009	9781934356319	250
Prototype and script.aculo.us: You Never Knew JavaScript Could Do This!	2007	9781934356012	448
Rails for .NET Developers	2008	9781934356203	300
Rails for Java Developers	2007	9780977616695	336
Rails for PHP Developers	2008	9781934356043	432
Rails Recipes	2006	9780977616602	350
Rapid GUI Development with QtRuby	2005	PDF-Only	83
Release It! Design and Deploy Production-Ready Software	2007	9780978739218	368
Scripted GUI Testing with Ruby	2008	9781934356180	192
Seven Languages in Seven Weeks: A Pragmatic Guide to Learning Programming Languages	2010	9781934356593	300
Ship It! A Practical Guide to Successful Software Projects	2005	9780974514048	224
SQL Antipatterns: Avoiding the Pitfalls of Database Programming	2010	9781934356555	352
Stripes ...and Java Web Development Is Fun Again	2008	9781934356210	375
Test-Drive ASP.NET MVC	2010	9781934356531	296
TextMate: Power Editing for the Mac	2007	9780978739232	208
The Agile Samurai: How Agile Masters Deliver Great Software	2010	9781934356586	280
The Definitive ANTLR Reference: Building Domain-Specific Languages	2007	9780978739256	384
The Passionate Programmer: Creating a Remarkable Career in Software Development	2009	9781934356340	200
ThoughtWorks Anthology	2008	9781934356142	240
Ubuntu Kung Fu: Tips, Tricks, Hints, and Hacks	2008	9781934356227	400
Web Design for Developers: A Programmer's Guide to Design Tools and Techniques	2009	9781934356135	300

The Pragmatic Bookshelf

The Pragmatic Bookshelf features books written by developers for developers. The titles continue the well-known Pragmatic Programmer style and continue to garner awards and rave reviews. As development gets more and more difficult, the Pragmatic Programmers will be there with more titles and products to help you stay on top of your game.

Visit Us Online

The RSpec Book's Home Page
http://pragprog.com/titles/achbd
Source code from this book, errata, and other resources. Come give us feedback, too!

Register for Updates
http://pragprog.com/updates
Be notified when updates and new books become available.

Join the Community
http://pragprog.com/community
Read our weblogs, join our online discussions, participate in our mailing list, interact with our wiki, and benefit from the experience of other Pragmatic Programmers.

New and Noteworthy
http://pragprog.com/news
Check out the latest pragmatic developments, new titles and other offerings.

Save on the eBook

Save on the eBook versions of this title. Owning the paper version of this book entitles you to purchase the electronic versions at a terrific discount.

PDFs are great for carrying around on your laptop—they are hyperlinked, have color, and are fully searchable. Most titles are also available for the iPhone and iPod touch, Amazon Kindle, and other popular e-book readers.

Buy now at pragprog.com/coupon.

Contact Us

Online Orders: www.pragprog.com/catalog
Customer Service: support@pragprog.com
Non-English Versions: translations@pragprog.com
Pragmatic Teaching: academic@pragprog.com
Author Proposals: proposals@pragprog.com
Contact us: 1-800-699-PROG (+1 919 847 3884)